14.50

THE CRISES OF FRANCE'S
EAST CENTRAL EUROPEAN DIPLOMACY
1933-1938

ANTHONY TIHAMER KOMJATHY

EAST EUROPEAN QUARTERLY, BOULDER
DISTRIBUTED BY COLUMBIA UNIVERSITY PRESS
NEW YORK

1976

EAST EUROPEAN MONOGRAPHS, NO. XXI

To My Mother

ACKNOWLEDGMENTS

The dearest, and at the same time the hardest, duty of any author is, I suppose, the writing of acknowledgments. It is the dearest because one has a chance to express his thanks and gratitude to those persons who helped in the creation of the study, and it is the hardest because it is an almost impossible task to list the names of all those persons who contributed something to the quality of that work. Even after an author has made up the list of his most helpful friends and advisors, he has to face one more problem: in which order should he mention these many people so as not to unwillingly violate some protocol or sensitivity. I hopefully shall solve this second problem by using a list assembled according to chronology.

First, I am very glad to mention the names of those persons who inspired me to write this study. My dear friend, former Major General Béla K. Király—presently Professor of History at Brooklyn College of the New York City University—encouraged me to pursue an academic career, as well as to utilize my energy in researching and writing about the history of Central Europe. Furthermore, he willingly discussed my problems and gave me precious suggestions whenever I sought his advice.

Professor Walter Gray at the Loyola University of Chicago directed the research and writing of my dissertation, which is incorporated in this book.

I would like to express my special thanks to the following gentlemen who were kind enough to grant me personal interviews and made it possible for me to learn of and use not very widely known details about important events: Dr. Pál Auer (Attorney of the French Embassy in Budapest, 1926-1930; President of the Committee to Promote Economic Cooperation of the Danubian states, 1932-1933), General Julien Flipo (Chief of Staff of the French Military Mission in Prague, 1931-1938), General Gustave Hennyey (Hungarian Military Attache in Athens and Belgrade, 1933-1934; Chief of the Intelligence Department of the Hungarian General Staff, 1934-1935), Dr. Theodore Hornbostel (Political Secretary-General of the Austrian Ministry of Foreign Affairs, 1933-1938), Baron Anton Radvánszky (First Secretary of the Hungarian Minister of Foreign Affairs, 1933-1934), and Prince Dr. Francis Schwarzenberg (Official in the Czech Diplomatic Service, 1936-1939; Professor at the Loyola University of Chicago). My dear friends Elizabeth de Gelsey and Ernest Rigóni made my job easier by arranging these interviews for me. Many thanks for their help.

During my research trips in Europe, my work could not have been successful without the precious help of Professor C. A. Macartney, All Souls College, Oxford. He helped me during my research by directing my attention to valuable source materials. He also read my manuscript, suggesting important changes to make the narrative easy-flowing and more complete. Professor Stephen Kertész, University of Notre Dame, Indiana, discussed the manuscript with me in detail, and his precious suggestions contributed greatly to the elimination of the shortcomings of my study. His advice was priceless concerning the preparation of the final form of this book.

Professor Stephen Fischer-Galati, Editor of the *East European Quarterly*, University of Colorado, gave of his precious time and offered the most benevolent and useful editorial advice, thereby helping me greatly in the final preparation of the manuscript for the printers.

Finally, I would like to mention—though I honestly feel that hers is the first place—my wife, Edith. She gave me encouragement and comfort and throughout the years accepted without complaint the lonely evenings while I was working on my study. She then listened patiently to my reading of the paragraphs and, with her remarks, helped me to write a study that is hopefully enjoyable for the general public also.

Looking back on this list of names, one may wonder what was my share in this study? I wonder myself! One thing, however, I can say for sure: if there are any faults or mistakes in my study, they are mine and have nothing to do with the above-mentioned persons to whom I shall feel indebted for the rest of my life.

TABLE OF CONTENTS

TABLE OF CONTENTS

INTRODUCTION

On January 30, 1933, Hitler became the chancellor of Germany, and with him the reign of the National Socialist regime began. Very few people suspected at the time that this date would mark the beginning of a new era, not only for Germany but for all mankind. Only the pessimists stressed such disturbing omens as the renewal of the 1926 Treaty of Berlin between Germany and the Soviet Union, the revival of German nationalism and revisionism, rumors of German economic designs concerning Central Europe,[1] secret negotiations between Germany and Poland,[2] and Japan's withdrawal from the League of Nations. The optimists pointed out that France was still the most powerful continental power, the Little Entente was strong, Mussolini was in a cooperative mood, Germany was militarily weak, and the new regime was not in a position to challenge the status quo drafted by the Versailles Peace Treaty.

Three years later, however, the situation was different. Hitler's moves were so spectacular and unexpected that very few Western statesmen paid attention to anything but the German problem. Central Europe came to the fore again during the Czech crisis and at the time of the Münich Agreement, but this was too late. Developments soon led to World War II.

It is necessary to point out here that the terms "Central Europe," "Eastern Europe," and "South-Eastern Europe" are used arbitrarily by statesmen, politicians, and historians. It is not an easy task to define the territory of Central Europe. The definition has changed several times throughout history, even during the twentieth century.[3]

In the 1930's, Western statesmen referred to Poland and the Danube basin countries as Eastern Europe or Central Europe. Their usage of the expression depended on their purposes. If they wanted to include these territories in their own spheres of interest, they referred to Central Europe; if they wanted to exclude them, they referred to Eastern Europe. Nicolae Titulescu always considered Rumania a Central European state.[4] German Nazi terminology, on the other hand, used the expression "South-Eastern Europe," although Hungary vigorously objected to this definition.[5] Following World War II, the Soviet statesmen and press began to describe this territory as Eastern Europe. expressing their conviction that the W had no jurisdiction over it. Then, whether consciously or unconsciously, the Western press, statesmen, and historians accepted the Iron Curtain as a dividing line between East and West. Central Europe, as such, was erased from our dictionary.

The Central European states may be seen as a bridge between Western and Eastern Europe. Here, Western religions mix with the Eastern Orthodox; Western political ideas are freely accepted and accomodated; history and tradition connect the peoples to the West as well as the East; culture and civilization of the West are amalgamated with the local taste and custom. Perhaps most important, however, *the people living in this territory regard themselves as Central Europeans.* Accepting their definition, Central Europe is comprised then of Austria, Czechoslovakia, Hungary, Poland, Rumania, and Yugoslavia.

Keeping this in mind, we should ask some questions from the historian's point of view. Did the events of Central Europe develop separately, without influencing Western European affairs? Had the Western European states no reason to pay more attention to Central Europe before 1938? Did contemporary Western statesmen make a great mistake when they neglected the history of Central Europe? Is it not possible that in 1933-1936 the German annexation of Austria, the destruction of the unity of the Little Entente, the dissolution of Czechoslovakia, and even the outbreak of World War II could have been prevented?

All these questions, if asked at all, have been asked from the point of view of tne Great Powers. Only a few writers have attempted to interpret the policy of the small Central European states from their respective nationalist view points, and even these interpretations have been dismissed by Western academic authorities as biased, chauvinistic, and narrow-minded. But can we really pass judgment on the Central European statesmen according to our own standards, praising them if they were useful for the Western powers and condemning them if they were not? Should we not try to understand them as they were—representatives of small nations? Should we blame the Austrian, Hungarian, or Yugoslavian leaders who, after experiencing the unconcern of the Western democracies, tried to serve the interests of their respective peoples by accepting an anti-Entente and pro-Nazi foreign political line or a strict neutral position?

Furthermore, the basic question of whether the small states ever had a chance to make independent foreign policy decisions or were always pressured to fall in line with the foreign policy of their respective Great Power patrons has not been decided.

Based on their past histories, one might expect that Poland would strengthen her ties with the Little Entente states, especially Czechoslovakia, and would never come to an understanding with revisionist Germany— yet, just the opposite happened. One might expect that Austria would work for a unification with Germany, and yet the opposite happened. One might expect that Czechoslovakia, having former members of the Czech Legion in influential administrative positions, would become an enemy of the Soviet Union, but just the opposite happened. One might expect that Hungary would be the firmest enemy of Germany, and yet the opposite happened. Also, one might expect that Yugoslavia would follow Pan-Slavic political plans, and again just the opposite happened. Poland was the best ally of France against the revival of German imperialism, and in case of war she represented a possible second front against Germany. Naturally, one might expect that France would cherish Poland's friendship. Instead, Hitler was the one who understood the national interests of Poland, and with the non-aggression pact, he eliminated the threat of a two front war. Austria was created by the victors of World War I, and one might expect that the victors would defend her most vigorously. Instead, her traditional foe, Italy, became her best patron. Hungary and Yugoslavia became friends in the camp of their greatest enemy, Germany, and signed a treaty of "eternal friendship." Czechoslovakia, the champion of democracy and a stronghold of the status quo, was the first country deserted by the democratic states and the other pro-status quo powers. There are as many puzzles as there are countries. The oversimplified answers of historians writing from the Great Powers' view point are partly misleading and partly unsatisfactory.

There are many reasons for analyzing the relationship of these countries with France. Up to 1933, France, with the help of the League of Nations, seemed to be the unchallenged leader of the European continent. All of Central Europe, except Austria and Hungary, was firmly allied with her; even within these two countries, there were influential political groups who would have welcomed stronger ties with her. Ironically, while the general diplomatic conceptions of France were brilliant, attempts made for their realization were less than fortunate. She displayed almost complete unconcern toward Hungary, was hesitant toward Austria, and was agressive toward Poland and the Little Entente. This French indecisiveness and aggressiveness influenced the political decisions of these smaller states. It was France, not Germany, who created the opportunities for the German penetration of Central Europe. It was an incomprehension of the interests of these small states on the part of France (and in 1938, England) that started the chain reaction ending with the complete dissolution of the French security system.

Therefore, this study shall analyze and interpret the actions and passivity of the selected states from their own particular points of view. The basis for judging these states will not be their usefulness or uselessness to the Great Powers, rather, judgment will be based on how the Austrian, Czechoslovakian, Hungarian, Polish, Rumanian, and Yugoslavian statesmen served the interests of their respective countries.

CHAPTER I
EFFECTS OF THE PEACE SETTLEMENTS IN CENTRAL EUROPE

After signing the Versailles and connected peace treaties,[1] the Western democracies looked at their newly created Central Europe with satisfaction. It was perhaps imperfect in small details, but they thought they had found the best solution under the existing circumstances. The Austro-Hungarian Empire, "the last citadel of authoritarianism, of aristocratic control, of Catholic Church influence, of minority oppression" had disappeared.[2] The old empire was divided among the different nationality groups which formed new nation-states. The principle of national self-determination had seemingly triumphed, and the idealistic dreams of President Wilson were realized.

Minority Problems

Reality denied the peacemakers' claim that they had realized the principle of national self-determination, for the newly created states rejected this principle and accepted instead the aims and methods of aggressive nationalism. Rather than organizing homogeneous national units *in lieu* of the Habsburg Empire, the peacemakers, for various reasons,[3] had created so-called "nation-states" where the state-supporting nationality was often actually in the minority. The loss of nationality groups for the benefit of other countries created resentment in those who lost the war and promoted revisionist ideas, thus making the restoration of peace of mind even a harder task.

Minorities in the Successor States

Austria. Austria lost about one-third of the German-speaking population of old Austria.[4] According to the March 1923 census, the new Austrian republic included 6,272,892 Germans and 225,571 non-Germans. With only a negligible number of other nationalities, Austria had no minority problems, but Austrian nationalists were bitter over the loss of so many of their compatriots to neighboring states. Czechoslovakia incorporated about 3 million Sudeten Germans and 20,000 Germans from the northern part of Lower Austria.[5] Italy received the territory of South Tyrol with an overwhelming majority of German-speaking people (218,250 out of a total population of 225,000), while Yugoslavia was awarded 65,000 Austrians.[6] The loss of so many Austrians made the demand for revision of the St. Germain Treaty very popular in Austria and strengthened the Pan-German sentiments of a great part of Austria's population.

Czechoslovakia. During the peace treaty negotiations[7] the Czechs successfully combined the concept of historical rights with the principle of nationalism, and the demand for economic viability with strategic interests. Occasionally they applied the racist Pan-Slav argument with no less success. As a result, the newly created Czechoslovakia resembled more the multinational Habsburg Empire in miniature than a real nation-state. According to the census of February 1921, Czechoslovakia comprised the following nationality groups:[8]

Czechoslovaks[9]	8,760,937	65.5%	Germans	3,123,568	23.4%
Ruthenes	461,879	3.5%	Magyars	745,431	5.6%
Poles	75,853	0.5%	Jews[10]	180,855	1.3%
Rumanians	13,974	0.1%	Others	11,897	0.1%

Total: 13,374.394

If we divide the number of Czechoslovaks into Czechs (5,873,590) and Slovaks (2,653,564),[11] the picture changes. The Czechs, the state-creating nationality group, numbered 5,873,590 while the other slavic groups (Slovaks, Poles, Ruthenes) equaled 3,191,296 and the non-slavic groups (Germans, Magyars, Rumanians, Jews and others) numbered 4,075,725. The state-supporting nationality group thus represented a minority— 43.9 percent—compared with the other nationalities.

The true picture needs one more mathematical operation. Since the Germans, Magyars, Poles and Rumanians inhabited territories next to their respective mother countries and, therefore, were receptive to revisionist propaganda, about 29-30 percent of the population was outspokenly hostile. Without the cooperation of the other Slavic groups, who comprised 23.8 percent of the population, the successful governing of the state was an almost impossible task. The Czech government found the solution to this problem in a strong Czech nationalist policy, concentrating first of all on language. Thus, the Czechs, who always bitterly opposed the use of a state language in the Habsburg Monarchy, ironically enough discovered the need for one in their own nation-state and with that antagonized even the Slavic minority groups.

Hungary. The Treaty of Trianon shocked the Magyar population of Hungary. Out of 325,000 square kilometers, only 93,000 were left for them, and the former population of 21 million was reduced to 8 million.[12] It is true that in the territories incorporated in Czechoslovakia, Rumania, and Yugoslavia, the Hungarians were in the minority; yet, their number was considerable (745,431 in Czechoslovakia, 1,463,311 in Rumania; and 467,652 in Yugoslavia).[13] The great number of Hungarians living in the successor states of Central Europe provided a chance for friction both within and between the states. "The number of pure Magyars placed by the treaty under Czech, Rumanian, and Yugoslavian rule was so large as to cause legitimate bitterness to any Hungarian."[14] This "legitimate bitterness" demanded that every Hungarian government keep revisionism in its program in order to command the loyalty of the masses.[15] Thus, revisionism became the first important axiom of Hungarian policy and determined Hungary's role on the stage of international politics.

Perhaps a greater problem for the Hungarian government was caused by those people who were not willing to accept life in the territories annexed by Czechoslovakia, Rumania, and Yugoslavia and migrated in great numbers to the territory of Trianon-Hungary. The majority of these refugees were of middle-class origin, educated mostly for administrative and bureaucratic positions. Though the Hungarian government tried to absorb a great number of them—a gesture which created an unhealthy, oversized bureaucracy for such a small country[16]—most did not find positions comparable to their former ones. As a result, these refugees felt that the Trianon Treaty was responsible for their misfortune and the deterioration of their living standards. These disappointed, frustrated middle-class elements found hope for their future in nationalist socialist ideas. Their number forced the conservative governments to listen to their demands, which the leadership tried to satisfy, at least politically, by advocating strong nationalism and revisionism.

Poland. For Poland, the acquisition of Silesian territories and the Danzig Corridor created a German minority situation. The Treaty of Riga, awarding great parts of Ukraine to Poland, also produced minority questions; while the territory of Wilno, with its Lithuanian population, poisoned Polish-Lithuanian relations. Yet, since the Poles made up a great majority (69.2 percent) of the whole population,[17] there was no significant minority problem until Hitler came to power in Germany.

According to the census of December 1931, there were 741,000 Germans living in Poland, only 2.3 percent of the total population.[18] The German minority problem grew out of proportion, however, for two reasons: historical background and Polish nationalism. During the nineteenth century, the Germans of Silesia and Pomerania ruled with an iron fist over the poor, uneducated Polish peasants. The Versailles Treaty reversed this authority, converting the Germans "from masters into second-class citizens."[19] Of course, the Germans resented it, especially when the Polish government began to appropriate some of the large German-owned estates. The German landlords fought against these measures, eventually bringing the issue to the Permanent Court of International Justice in The Hague,[20] and thus transforming domestic concerns into an international affair. However, since the rights of minorities were guaranteed in the Minority Treaties of 1919, and since the faithful execution of these treaties was entrusted to the League of Nations, the Germans' action in turning to the International Court was correct.

On the other hand, the government of Poland was strongly nationalistic and saw in the Minority Treaties an excuse for the Great Powers to meddle in Polish domestic affairs. The Poles viewed these treaties as limitations on their authority and resented them as "a destructive factor in our internal affairs."[21] There was no chance for conciliation between the Polish majority and the German minority as long as the Germans demanded the return of their *historical rights*, and the Poles were not even willing to grant them *equality*. The Germans became strongly revisionist, the Poles even more nationalist.

Rumania. Within "Great Rumania," the Rumanian population held an impressive 71.9 percent majority.[22] However, in the newly annexed territories of Transylvania and Banat, there was only a 58 percent majority of Rumanians. With 26.7 percent of the population, the Hungarians represented the largest minority and they were a hostile group since in the new state they had lost their long enjoyed predominance. The Ukranians of Bukovina and Bessarabia represented an even greater national minority problem for the Rumanian government. These territories were taken from the Soviet Union, and the Soviets did not recognize Rumania's right to them.[23] Rumanian politics was dominated then by the fear of Soviet, as well as Hungarian, revisionist demands.

Yugoslavia. When World War I ended, the little kingdom of Serbia found herself on the side of the victors. Due to this fact, and to the Wilsonian principles of self-determination, she was awarded territories that formerly belonged to Austria, Hungary, and Bulgaria. The dream of the Serbian patriots was the creation of a nation-state. However, statistics denied that the realization of this dream had any realistic basis. According to the census taken in January 1921, the Yugoslavians represented 82.8 percent of the population.[24] Time proved, however, that these statistics were misleading for the 9,931,416 people who were called "Yugoslavians" were incorrectly identified. There was no such national group. The census of March 1931 broke down Yugoslavians into their original nationality groupings: 5,953,000 Seribans; 3,221,000 Croatians; 1,134,000 Slovenes; and 2,593,000 other non-Slavic minorities.[25] Yet, these numbers did not reflect the real situation either, because the Macedonian minority, representing the most militant opposition to Serbian nationalism, was included in the number of Serbians. All of these minority groups were in opposition to the government. Their numbers were overwhelming—some 7 million people against the 5,900,000 Serbians (disregarding the Macedonians).[26] Even the most skillful party politician could not rule successfully amidst such conditions without grave compromises.

Political Refugees

The disregard for national self-determination and the territorial clauses of the peace treaties produced a great flow of refugees in Europe. From the territories of the dissolved Habsburg Empire, great numbers of Germans, Poles, Hungarians, and Bulgarians migrated, usually to their respective mother countries. These refugees did not represent any significant political force, with the exception of the Hungarians and Bulgarians who were able to convince their governments to adopt a strong revisionist policy.

A much greater problem was the case of ethnic groups with no independent mother country and thus no place to migrate. At the same time, these groups were large enough to demand at least a certain degree of autonomy from the states in which they lived. In Yugoslavia, there were three such ethnic groups: the Macedonians, the Slovenes and the Croats. Their political leaders openly advocated either federalism or separatism, both of which would have meant an end to the unified Yugoslavian nation-state. Under these circumstances, King Alexander saw no other alternative than to assume the role of a royal dictator[27] on February 6, 1929. The separatist leaders of the Macedonian and Croatian minority groups had to face the alternatives of imprisonment or "voluntary" political exile.

The bulk of Macedonians took refuge in Bulgaria,[28] a country which also held part of the former Macedonia but had not pursued a strong nationalistic policy against the Macedonians. The most militant Macedonian group was the Internal Macedonian Revolutionary Organization (IMRO), formed in 1896 as a secret political organization with the purpose of liberating Macedonia from Turkish rule. Up to 1912, the IMRO "was a spontaneous expression of the people's irrepressible will for freedom."[29] After 1920, however, the IMRO directed its main activities against Yugoslavia, and under the leadership of Ivan Michailoff, chief of the IMRO from September 12, 1924, it piled up a long record of underground activities. Beginning in 1931, the Bulgarian government became more and more dissatisfied with the IMRO involvement in domestic political questions and in the de facto existence of an IMRO state within Bulgaria.[30]

The Croatian refugees, being more Western-oriented, looked for and found asylum in almost every country of Europe, especially France and Switzerland.[31] They, too, organized an aggressive, militant organization, the USTASHE, whose members enjoyed the hospitality of Italy and Hungary—both governments hoping to use them for the promotion of their own designs concerning Yugoslavia.

Economic Problems

The geographic features of Central Europe indicate that the Danube Basin is a unique, natural economic unit. The Danube represents a lifeline for the whole basin, providing easy transportation facilities for the region. The other navigable rivers connect the mountainous regions with the plains and again promote commercial exchange between the peoples of the mountains and those on the plains. With the help of the waterways, timber, coal, iron, and precious metals were exchanged for grain, meat, industrial products and foodstuffs. During the Habsburg Monarchy other transportation routes, such as railroads and highways, also were built to serve the economic needs of the Danube Basin.

The accusation that the Habsburg lands were bastions of feudal landlords and miserable peasants is an exaggeration. The problem of these territories was not mainly the agricultural situation, but the lack of industry. It is true that land reforms performed in the successor states awarded a certain amount of land to the landless peasants, yet these land distributions did not alter the basically agricultural character of these states. "Even in 1930, after a decade of frantic industrialization, 76 percent of the Yugoslavs, 72 percent of the Rumanians, 60 percent of the Poles and 51 percent of the Hungarians were still dependent on agriculture. Only in Czechoslovakia (33 percent) and Austria (26 percent) did less than half the population till the soil."[32]

During the last decade preceding World War I, the economic growth of the Habsburg Empire was faster than that of Britain or Germany; in Austria (Czech lands included) real income increased by 71 percent, while in Hungary the increase reached 75 percent. After World War I, however, the newly drawn national frontiers, artificial custom barriers, trade restrictions, and the world economic crisis all contributed to the economic decline of this area. Economic nationalism worsened the situation. Instead of trading with each other as natural partners, the Central European states tried to establish economic relations with other countries, and after 1933, Germany became the chief trading partner of every Central European country.[33]

The consequences of the peace treaties and economic nationalism were greater and more depressing than the politicians of the victorious powers ever expected. These economic consequences also raised difficult problems for the statesmen of Central Europe by creating contradictions between the economic and foreign political interests of their respective countries.

Domestic Political Problems

President Wilson and many of his aides dreamed about a new Central Europe where every state would organize its life under a republican form of government and according to the rules of democracy. To make the establishment of these new democratic governments easier, they prohibited the Habsburgs from living in any of these states. In this way, they tried to prevent a restoration attempt. However, these democratic designs proved to be failures in the long run, since the promoters of democracy had disregarded the basic fact that none of the Central European peoples had ever lived under a democratic form of government. Their ideal remained the strong, heroic and paternal leader instead of a democratically elected president.[34] The job of the new democratic statesmen was very hard. None had former practical experience in government; none had a nationally known name; and they naively believed that their compatriots were happy with the new democratic rights, despite the fact that the people did not know how to use them. Repercussions of the Bolshevik victory in Russia proved to these leaders that their peoples were not yet ready for democracy. During the 1920's, one country after another turned to strong leaders and became more or less authoritarian states. The realistic British and French statesmen, because of their fear of communism, did not object.

Austria. At the end of World War I, while the supporters of the Habsburg Monarchy hoped for a reorganization of the state on a federative basis, the different nationality group leaders, with the sanction of the victorious powers, declared their secession. With this act, they actually ended the monarchy. By November 1918, it was clear that German-speaking Austria was alone and had to organize her own nation-state. The real irony of the situation was that very few Austrians wanted this independence. A great number of Austrians wanted to join their German brothers and hoped for an *Anschluss*; others nostalgically yearned for a Habsburg restoration. However, such solutions to the problem were forbidden by the peacemakers.

The decade following the peace treaties was marked in Austria by progressively sharper differences between the two major political parties: the Marxist Social Democrats and the conservative Christian Socialists. The fundamental questions dealt with were social welfare, church-state relations, and, later, the returning *Anschluss* problem. Competition was so uncompromising that each party organized its own private army: the Socialist formed the *Schutzbund*, while the Conservatives commanded the *Heimwehr*.

The great depression pushed Austria to the edge of revolution. By May 1932, any possibility of cooperation between the three major parties (Social Democrat, Christian Socialist, Pan-German) came to an end. Chancellor Engelbert Dollfuss turned to the Fascist *Heimwehr* for support, allowed the Parliament to "dissolve itself," and by assuming emergency powers, actually became the dictator of Austria. After fourteen years of bitter political struggle, democracy ended in Austria. To tell the truth, not too many Austrians shed tears over its grave.

Czechoslovakia. Politically, the Czech-Slovak Republic[35] had a democratic form of government supported by a variety of different political parties. The Agrarian Party was the strongest, participating in every coalition government. Its composition, however, was much more complex than the name suggests, since the Agrarians attracted many people who were not peasants. The party defended farmers possessing middle-size holdings and paid attention to the interests of city bourgeoisie but neglected, more and more as time passed, the needs of the smallholders.

The National Socialist Party, next in importance, was not a Hitlerian Nazi party but "was firmly attached to democratic institutions and violently nationalistic."[36] Its membership, which included Edouard Benes, came mostly from the middle class. The Social Democrats competed for membership with the Communist Party; their hold on the working classes alternated. But while the Communists had a united party throughout Czechoslovakia, the Social Democrats had three parties divided along nationality lines: Czech, German, and Hungarian.

The National Democrat Party was comprised of militant Czech nationalists. Being both antiminority and anticlerical, the party gradually lost membership. Nationalist ideas were strong also among the Slovaks, who were utterly disappointed when they saw that the Czech government was not willing to give them political autonomy. As a result, the National Party, with a program of moderate decentralization of the state, advocated cooperation with the Czechs, while the Slovak People's Party demanded the realization of the promised autonomy. The Ruthenes, though they did not have different political parties, were also divided on the question of autonomy.

The political picture of Czechoslovakia, then, was not too promising. The strong centralization and Czech nationalistic measures of the government alienated the non-Slavic minority groups as well as a significant number of Slovaks and Ruthenes.

Hungary. On November 16, 1918, Hungary declared herself an independent "peoples republic." However, the inexperienced government, under the leadership of the highly idealistic Count Michel Károlyi, could not withstand the attack of the Communists, who advocated armed defense of the country against the resolution of the Supreme Council of the Entente Powers.[37] The short period of Béla Kun's Communist, proletarian dictatorship ended with the Rumanian occupation of a great part of Hungary in order to liberate the country from communism. The fear of communism, especially in France, and the French reaction to the Hungarian Communist takeover helped the former ruling classes of Hungary to regain power. Hungary was declared a constitutional kingdom—according to the resolution of the peacemakers—with an unoccupied throne; and Admiral Nicholas Horthy was elected Regent of Hungary.[38] The conservative government in the 1920's, under the premiership of Count Stephen Bethlen, retained this power by continuing the usage of the 1922 election laws, which limited suffrage and introduced open ballots in rural areas. This election law *ab ovo* secured the elections for the government party, which "was not a real political party, but a collection of individuals of proved loyalty and usefulness to the regime.[39]

The opposition was made up of three parties: the Independent Smallholder Party, which represented the medium peasants' interests; the Liberal Party, whose membership came from the ranks of democratic intellectuals; and the Social Democratic Party, which limited its activities to industrial workers. Thus, the landless peasants and agricultural workers had no real representatives in parliament. At the same time, 55-60 percent of Hungary's population was employed in agriculture.[40]

With the help of the League of Nations and other foreign loans, the Bethlen government was able to lead the country toward prosperity in the second half of the 1920's, although the economic crisis of 1929 wiped out these results. The orthodox financial policy prescribed for Hungary by the League of Nations[41] indebted the peasantry and caused high unemployment for industrial workers.

In August 1931, Count Bethlen resigned. His successor, Gyula Károlyi, was another conservative aristocrat. During his premiership, the economic crisis grew to such proportion that the country came to the edge of a social revolution. The most influential group of dissatisfied elements was represented now by the rightists. Károlyi, unable to solve the crisis, resigned in September 1932.

Regent Horthy, instead of following the easiest way out of such a crisis (such as declaring a dictatorship), appointed Captain Gyula Gömbös, the leader of the radical Right, to the position of prime minister. Horthy, though his powers were very limited according to the constitution, was able to command the respect of all of Hungary. He kept his constitutional authority until the early 1940's, making Hungary the only Central European state which was able to preserve its form of government and a certain degree of independence even in the first years of World War II.

Poland. Politically, the newborn Poland started out as a parliamentary democracy with several active political parties after Josef Pilsudski's *coup d'état*, however, differences centered more around his person than around political issues. Pilsudski simplified the political picture by dividing the Poles into two camps: his supporters and his opponents. Political parties continued to exist, but they lost significance. In the November 1927 elections, the government block won 135 seats and the Socialists 64 seats, while once strong parties such as the Peasant, Christian Democratic, Nationalist, and Labor Parties together won only 150 seats. However, this number indicated that the opposition to Pilsudski remained strong. In 1930, several opposing party leaders were arrested. The following new elections produced an absolute majority 247 seats for the government block. With this victory, Pilsudski and his followers secured a free hand to deal with domestic problems in the way they considered right.[42]

Rumania. The land reforms executed in 1918 by Rumania reduced the number of large landowners. A small "gentry, together with the small urban business and professional" class formed the "dominant class in political and social life."[43] The agricultural population, however, held an overwhelming majority against this small ruling class. Consequently, the peasant parties played a much more important role in Rumania than in other East-Central European countries. After World War I, the Rumanian peasantry had two parties: the Peasant Party, representing the peasants of the Old Rumanian kingdom, and the National Party of the Transylvanian peasantry. The Communist Party never gained mass support in Rumania, partly because after the land reforms the peasants were satisfied and partly because the Communists denounced the acquisition of Bessarabia, thus making themselves despised by every Rumanian nationalist.

The Liberal Party, representing the ruling class, advocated an industrialization program directed and financially supported by the government as well as a strong centralization of power to solve minority problems by the Rumanization of minority groups. The Liberals controlled Rumania's political life until King Ferdinand's death in 1927. Since Crown Prince Carol had renounced his rights to the crown, a regency was formed for his young son Michael. The elections of December 1928 gave the government to the National Peasant Party. They opened the country to foreign investments and thus lightened the tax burden on the peasantry who, under Liberal rule, had been forced to pay the price of industrialization.

The depression and crop failures undermined the popularity of the Peasant rule, however, and gave impetus to the growth of radical rightist parties. Finally, the National Peasants considered the return of King Carol to Rumania as a way out of their dilemma. But they were greatly disappointed with the King. He soon assumed dictatorial powers and Rumania's experience with democracy came to an end in 1930.

Yugoslavia. The experiment of a parliamentary kingdom in Yugoslavia failed primarily because of minority problems. The completely alien minority groups (Germans, Hungarians, and Rumanians) proved to be more easily reconcilable than the Slavic groups (Croats, Macedonians, Slovenes). All these groups hoped for complete autonomy according to the Wilsonian principles. What they got instead was a strong centralization attempt on the part of the ruling Serbs. Though the name of the

Serbian kingdom was changed to Yugoslavia, the so-called Yugoslavian spirit and patriotism could hardly camouflage the goal of the Belgrade government, that is, to unite the Slavic nationality groups according to Serbian interests and under Serbian leadership. When events threatened to run out of hand, King Alexander dissolved parliament and in 1929 began to rule with dictatorial methods. Having solved domestic political issues with the police, he turned his attention more and more to foreign policy, hoping that a rapprochement with Yogoslavia's neighbors would ease tensions within his own country.

Foreign Policy of the
Central European States

Austria. Hard-pressed by economic and domestic political problems, Austria tried to manage her foreign relations within the League of Nations. Her main political goal was to secure the goodwill of the League. In May 1932, when Dollfuss became chancellor, he initiated a policy of closer cooperation with Italy and Hungary at the expense of loosening ties with the League of Nations. Dollfuss made this move partly for economic reasons and partly because of ideological and political considerations. He was seeking security and trustworthy allies against the German menace of *Anschluss.*

Czechoslovakia. After acquiring territories not by the will of the inhabitants[44] but by the goodwill of the peacemakers, Czechoslovakia naturally considered her right place in international politics to be on the side of France. The withdrawal of the United States from European politics and Britain's declining interest in the continent left France the strongest power to guard the status quo. Thus friendship with France was one of the basic axioms of Czechoslovak foreign policy. Other considerations did not contradict this axiom, but recommended the extension of diplomatic relations to countries having similar problems and, therefore, common interests with Czechoslovakia. The new Czech state had to consider as dangerous the demand for revision of the peace treaties, a demand sounded very early by Hungary. The plausible solution against this Hungarian revisionism was the creation of an alliance system with Rumania and Yugoslavia.[45] The revisionism of Germany seemed to be successfully checked by France and by the weak condition of Germany herself.

Geography also influenced Czech foreign policy. Czechoslovakia incorporated geographically separated territories with different economic interests into one political unit. These geographic and economic factors suggested at least friendly economic relations with her neighbors, especially Austria and Hungary. The clash of political and economic interests concerning friends and allies created the first permanent problem for Czechoslovak foreign policy. The geographic features of the country also created problems for the Czech military leadership. The organization of defenses was an impossible task unless the Czech frontiers were fortified and her neighbors kept in a state of military inferiority.

Finally, the greatest obstacle to the creation of political unity was the older generation, people who had grown up in the Austro-Hungarian Empire nurtured a certain nostalgia for the past. Especially after the great depression struck, they yearned for the restoration of the old monarchy, which would have meant an end to Czechoslovakia. Thus, the maintenance of the status quo was the goal of Czechoslovakian foreign policy. Yet, a pro-status quo foreign policy meant passivity; initiative rested with the other side. No really dangerous initiatives appeared in the 1920's, however. The French alliance, the League of Nations, and the Little Entente seemed to satisfy the Czech requirements for national security.

Hungary.   Hungary was completely isolated. The aim of Hungarian foreign policy was stated by Prime Minister Bethlen in a speech on April 22, 1926.[46] "We Hungarians do not want to become a vassal of the Russians, and want to maintain our independence of the Germans. . . . We want to remain Hungarians and live our independent national life." Hungary wanted not only independence, she wanted the revision of the Trianon Treaty as well.

Since a peaceful revision could be attained only by the unanimous vote of the League of Nations, logic dictated creating friendly relations with all nations. It was especially important to gain the goodwill of France, but France remained the uncompromising ally of the Little Entente. In 1925 overzealous Hungarians, without the knowledge of the regent or the government, printed large amounts of counterfeit French francs, hoping to create a monetary crisis for France. They did not succeed. The following investigation and trial proved that the Hungarian government was not involved, and the affair was closed without international consequences.[47] The event was successfully used for anti-Hungarian propaganda, though and thus helped to prolong Hungary's isolation. While commercial and trade treaties were concluded with neighboring states, diplomatic negotiations failed, even though Horthy stated optimistically in August 1926 that he hoped the "old friendship and understanding of Serbs and Hungarians can return soon."[48] The only diplomatic success that Hungary achieved during this period was the 1927 signing of a Friendship Treaty with Italy,[49] which proved to be the first step out of isolation for Hungary and the first step in seeking greater influence in the Danube Basin for Italy.

Poland. Poland was recognized unanimously as an independent state by the Treaty of Versailles. However, Britain and France had individual designs in mind for the future of Poland and these ideas did not always coincide with the dreams of Polish patriots. During the peace negotiations, these three different plans for the future of Poland caused serious friction.[50]

Britain envisaged Poland as a potential obstacle to the spread of communism. While supporting Polish ambitions for the Eastern frontiers, British statesmen resented Polish claims for the "historical frontiers," which on the West included a large number of Germans.[51] A great Poland restored to its historical frontiers was, in British eyes, a potential trouble spot in Central Europe. Therefore, the inflexible, nationalistic Polish demands and the support given to these plans by French military leaders created great anxiety in the minds of many British statesmen.

France, in contrast to Britain, saw Poland as a bastion of high strategic value against the possible revival of German imperialism. France bound Poland to French interests with a Mutual Assistance Treaty and a Secret Military Convention as early as February 1921.[52] According to these documents, the two countries agreed to act in cooperation against a renewal of any kind of German menace. The treaties also satisfied the minimum Polish demand concerning a possible Soviet-Polish war. These agreements gave sufficient security to Poland against her two main enemies in 1921. However, the documents were not adjusted in later years to the changed political, economic, and military interests of the two countries; and so by the 1930.s, they became mere paper documents without real practical value.

The first change in the international scene occurred on April 17, 1922, with the signing of the Rapallo Treaty, which "introduced a period of political and military cooperation" between Germany and the Soviet Union and "was aimed primarily against Poland."[53] A more important change was produced by the Locarno Pact, signed on December 1, 1925, by Belgium, Britain, Czechoslovakia, France, Germany, Italy, and— without real enthusiasm—Poland. In this treaty, "the German-Polish frontiers, unlike the Franco-German ones, were not guaranteed."[54] At the same time, the new French-Polish Guarantee Treaty, which was signed one day before the Locarno Pact, omitted the French guarantees given to Poland in 1921 against a possible Soviet invasion.[55] Poland's growing insecurity was magnified when France fell behind schedule in the shipment of promised arms and ammunition.[56]

On April 24, 1926, the Soviet Union and Germany signed a neutrality pact. It marked the beginning of their secret military cooperation and was interpreted by both countries as a framework for possible "concerted frontier claims against Poland."[57] Then in 1927, the French General Staff attempted to revise the Military Convention of 1921 by omitting entirely the French guarantees given to Poland against a possible Soviet attack.[58] These negotiations ended in a deadlock because of firm Polish opposition; the original treaty was not changed, but Polish confidence in French guarantees was undermined even more.

During the First Hague Conference in August 1929, the Polish delegation made several attempts to restore mutual understanding and strengthen Franco-Polish cooperation; but their actions were fruitless, mostly because France made future actions against Germany dependent on British cooperation and approval.[59] France was willing to help Poland financially but listed so many difficulties standing in the way of possible military cooperation that they hardly covered the real truth, which was that France did not want to get involved in any German-Polish or Soviet-Polish controversy.

Rumania. The peace negotiations found Rumania on the side of the victors who fulfilled the dreams of Rumanian nationalists by awarding the territories of Transylvania and Bessarabia to the Rumanian kingdom, making her a really important country. The desire to keep these territories under their control defined foreign policy requirements for Rumanian diplomats. They were on the side of the pro-status quo powers, opposed revisionism in any form and, having the Soviet Union on their frontier, considered communism one of their main enemies. The national minority groups, also representing a danger, were supposedly taken care of by the strong centralization measures introduced by the new 1923 constitution. Hungarian revisionism was to be fought with the help of Czechoslovakia and Yugoslavia. The danger of Habsburg restoration received the same consideration as in Czechoslovakia.

Though Rumania's frontiers were geographically natural frontiers *vis à vis* Hungary, no such thing existed against the Soviet Union, unless one considers the Prut river as such. This made it necessary to find allies against the Soviet Union. Though Rumanian politicians tried to find a solution to this problem, only the Balkan Entente negotiations of 1930-1933 provided relative security for Rumania against an outside attack.

It is a hotly discussed question even today whether Rumania belongs to the Balkans or to East-Central Europe. Looking at the activities of Rumanian diplomats, one may get the impression that Rumania was interested only in Western European politics. The reason for that may be found in the distance which separated Rumania from France, the greatest defender of the status quo. Rumanian statesmen, realizing that in case of war they could hardly expect direct help from France, considered the best defense for their country to be rigid observation of the status quo everywhere in Europe. This same conviction made them also extraordinarily active in the League of Nations.

Yugoslavia. Yugoslavia's foreign policy also aimed to keep the status quo. The former Serbian kingdom acquired territories from Austria, Hungary, Albania, and Bulgaria. Relations with Bulgaria were not good because the Bulgarian government gave asylum to Macedonian terrorists. The territories acquired from Austria and Hungary also caused problems: the population included Croats and Slovenes who historically had enjoyed a privileged status within the Habsburg Empire. While the Serbs wanted to make a strongly centralized Serbian kingdom,[60] the Croats, Slovenes and Muslims of Bosnia-Herzegovina resented the idea and wanted a federative kingdom.[61] These nationalities did not hesitate to accept help for the realization of their goals from powers outside of Yugoslavia, so that Austria and Hungary automatically became the enemies of the Serbian Kingdom.

Greater problems were created by the secret Treaty of London, signed on April 26, 1915, which promised rich rewards to Italy (Fiume, Triese and the Dalmatian coast) for entering World War I on the side of the Entente powers. President Wilson, not knowing about the secret treaty, promised Fiume, part of Albania, and the islands along the Dalmation coast to Serbia.[62] The tension between Italy and Serbia continued during the postwar period. King Alexander's attempt to ease the situation failed on the stubborn refusal of Mussolini who, by the 1927 signing of a Friendship Treaty with Hungary, felt he had gained the upper hand. Thus, Yugoslavia remained a trustworthy member of the Little Entente and a good ally of France against Hungary and Italy.

French Designs for Central Europe

After World War I, the main concern of France's foreign policy was the security of France. She hoped to serve her own security by alliances with Poland and Czechoslovakia. Poland, however, being wedged in between Germany and a Soviet Union cooperating with Germany, was almost defenseless and more a liability for France than a guarantor of French security. Czechoslovakia, having acquired territories from Austria, Hungary, and Poland, was much more interested in her own security vis à vis these revisionist states than in France's security versus Germany.[63] Rumania and Yugoslavia, not having common frontiers with Germany, could not play a significant role in the French security system. Thus, the Versailles Treaty did not provide the anticipated security for France. Perhaps more important, the dissolved Austro-Hungarian Empire left a power vacuum in the Danube valley.

If France wanted to have a real counterweight in the rear of Germany, then she had the following alternatives: organize a "Cordon Sanitaire" on the Eastern frontiers of Germany by including Poland, Czechoslovakia, and Austria in a solid, anti-German alliance; select France's enemies and allies according to ideological considerations, i.e., regard the states with democratic forms of government as allies and those with non-democratic forms of government as enemies; or select allies on the basis or World War I, with those who were enemies in 1918 still regarded as enemies.

The Treaties of St. Germain, Trianon, and Riga were undoubtedly generous to Czechoslovakia, Rumania, Yugoslavia, and Poland. Since the generosity of these treaties was mostly the product of French patronage, skillful diplomacy could have directed these states toward conditions meeting the demands of French security. Also, a defeated Austria and Hungary, because of their great domestic political and economic problems, most certainly would have been willing to give concessions to France and take their prescribed places in the French security system.

The time to realize any kind of cooperation of Central European states was the period immediately following World War I. The Central European states looked for leadership and were expecting France to assume this role. However, France had no positive plans and seemed unwilling to take the responsibilities of a leader.[64] Her weak attempts failed, and for a decade French foreign policy in Central Europe was directed more according to the interests of the Little Entente states than according to the interests of France. As a result, Austria and Hungary were continuously looked upon as enemies, and their exclusion from French interests still left a vacuum in Central Europe. Only a few French statesmen recognized the importance of the Central European states and their cooperation. Their attempts to create a *Danubian Union,* a *Pan-European Union,* or *Danubian Pact* were unsuccessful. Between the two wars, French foreign policy in Central Europe was based not on realistic considerations, but on the misconception that the alliances with the Little Entente alone satisfactorily served the security of France.

France's Situation Up to 1934

By the end of the 1920's, France was anxiously pursuing British-French cooperation and beginning to neglect her Central European allies. Then, in 1930, the economic crisis struck Europe. Curiously enough, among French statesmen, only André Tardieu understood the world-wide scope of the economic situation, and he alone tried to warn his country of the possibility of a crisis in France. The Chamber of Deputies, though, disregarded his warnings and "continued in their customarily irresponsible attitude toward economics and finance."[1]

It is, however, too harsh of a judgment to call the deputies irresponsible. Since 1929 there had been an oversupply of raw materials, especially wheat, and the financial crisis had effected, first of all, the producers of agricultural products. Albrecht-Carrié described the possible consequences of such a situation as: "agricultural interests will clamor for subsidiaries and tariffs, which least appeal especially to industrial interest, while industrial workers will equally resist a diminuation of their wages and, if wholly deprived of employment, will turn to the state for assistance."[2] The government, as well as the deputies, was equally pressured and caught in the middle in this situation. It was not the political principles of the different parties that caused the fall of so many French governments in rapid succession between the years 1930-1934, but their ability or inability to deal with the crisis. This frequent change of leadership undoubtedly weakened France's international authority, hindered cooperation with other nations, and very decisively influenced and promoted the decline of French preeminence in Central Europe. However, it was perhaps more significant that France lost her importance *economically* in the trade transactions of these states, and with her declining role in economics, she also lost political influence.

France took great interest in the economic well-being of Poland during the peace negotiations. She secured for Poland the rich coal deposits of Silesia and the Corridor to the Baltic Sea. However, economic relations and trade between the two countries were always insignificant. Poland's import-export business with France, though slowly growing year by year, did not in the early 1930's exceed 1 percent of the French trade.[3] France, meanwhile, held only 6.7 percent of Polish import and 5.5 percent of Polish export trade in 1933, which made France the fourth business partner of Poland.[4]

The French economic relationship with Austria showed a steady decline from 1929 to 1932. The amount of French export to Austria fell from 94 million schillings to an all-time low of 31 million schillings while the import from Austria declined from 79 million schillings to 29 million schillings.[5] Although in the following two years French exports reached 36.9 million schillings and imports climbed back to 33.9 million schillings, France still ranked only tenth among the most important business partners of Austria.[6]

Nor did France do much better in Rumania. She imported the greatest amount of goods in 1931, buying 565.6 million francs worth of Rumanian products and, at the same time, selling 115.1 million francs of merchandise, however, by 1934, Rumanian imports fell to 246.7 million francs while France increased her exports to 167.1 million francs.[7] With these amounts, Rumania ranked fifteenth as a client in French trade and twenty-third as a supplier among the forty most important business partners of France.[8] Rumania was especially hit by the decline of Rumanian oil exports to France, which was due to the Soviet-French and Iraqi-French commercial treaties signed in 1934.[9]

Czechoslovakia. Czechoslovakia imported close to 220 million francs of French merchandise in 1931, while France bought more than 330 million francs of Czechoslovakian products. In 1934, the export to Czechoslovakia had risen to 225 million frances worth of goods, though the imports declined to 190 million francs.[10]

Yugoslavia. Yugoslavia exported to France 74.3 million dinars worth of merchandise in 1933 but only 51.4 million dinars in 1934, while France sold to Yugoslavia 120.6 million dinars worth of merchandise in 1933 and 177.6 million dinars in 1934.[11] By 1934, France had slid to sixth as a supplier and eleventh as a customer of Yugoslavia.[12] During the 1930-1934 period, on the other hand, France's share in the import business of Hungary grew with France remaining the fifth most important business partner of Hungary, although holding only 3.2 percent of the Hungarian foreign trade.[13]

The general picture that can be drawn from these statistics shows a steady decline of the dominant French role in the economic life of the Central European states. The successor states searched desperately for new markets to sell their wheat, oil, and timber (to mention only the most important items) and found ready buyers in Germany and Italy. The decline of French trade with Central Europe accelerated during the first half of 1935 and drastically changed the French position by allowing German economic penetration of this area.

The roots of this disastrous French foreign trade policy can be found in the even more disastrous domestic economic policy of the consecutive French governments and the methods they applied to fight the economic crisis. Instead of cooperating with England and the United States in their efforts to stabilize the world financial situation, France remained stubbornly faithful to the gold standard. She alone of the Great Powers refused to devalue her currency and in this way priced herself out of the foreign markets.[14] At home France followed a deflation policy, and as a result, prices sank at least 15 percent during the year 1934.[15] The closing of the gap between agricultural and industrial prices was intended to regain the competitive capacity of French products on foreign markets. However, this deflation policy created great hardship in France: salaries were cut back, wages declined, and production lowered. The conditions of French workers in offices, factories, and on the farms deteriorated.[16]

It is small wonder that dissatisfaction with the economic situation took the form of political protest. It is also natural that this political protest was directed not only against the government but also against political parties, groups, and ideologies. The president of the Chamber of Deputies was correct when he said, "[All] peoples are alienated from parliamentarianism without anyone knowing what one can use to replace it."[17] The irony of this situation was that the Communists, as well as the moderate Marxist-Socialists, frequently joined forces with the Right in an effort to undermine and defeat existing bourgeois-radical governments. Clubs, leagues, and organizations which looked with admiration at the economic and political successes of Nazi Germany sprang up in France. By the beginning of 1934, these groups were demanding the overthrow of not just the French government, but of the whole parliamentary republican system.

Domestic Situation in 1934

The history of the Third Republic is rich in scandals. The most important and the best known in the 1930's was the Stavisky affair because it triggered political events of great consequences. Born in Kiev, Serge A. Stavisky migrated with his parents to Paris where as early as 1912, he was tried for fraud. In 1926 he was arrested again, but his trial was postponed, and in 1927 he was released due to the intervention of mysterious patrons. Stavisky also became involved in Central European affairs. When the Little Entente states confiscated the estates of landlords of Hungarian origin, these landlords sued for compensation at the International Court of Justice. Great numbers of them won their cases but were unable to collect any money. Stavisky bought these court decisions at prices well below their actual value.[18] Meanwhile, he continued his fraudulent activities by floating worthless bonds. In January 1934, the French newspapers discovered these new frauds and demanded the punishment of Stavisky and his patrons among whom were high government officials. Although Stavisky committed suicide, the papers (especially *L'Action Française*) kept the issue alive, demanding the resignation of the government.[19]

The political Right found a common cause in the Stavisky affair. They united not only to discredit government circles, but also to force the direction of French politics toward the Right. A concerted effort of the rightist groups produced a mass demonstration on February 6, 1934, which led to street fights between the rightists, ironically joined by many Communists,[20] and the police. Though the police gained the upper hand, and the Chamber of Deputies voted confidence in his government, Prime Minister Edouard Daladier resigned. On February 9, 1934, Gaston Doumergue, who was thought to be above parties, formed a new coalition government which was dominated by the conservatives, although all political parties held positions, with the exception of the Socialists and Communists, who refused to participate.

The danger of a rightist revolution was over for the time being, but the self-confidence of the Republican leaders was badly shaken. One month after the riots, the president of the Senate told the visiting Austrian ambassador: "In every country, energetic authoritarian government chiefs should take over the leadership, as was the case in France during the time of Clemenceau, in order to surmount the general political difficulties all over Europe."[21]

Doumergue aroused high hopes in the country concerning the possibility of curtailing inflation and creating, with the use of constitutional reforms, a more stable government. Political party interests, however, proved to be stronger than the partriotic appeals of Doumergue,[22] and he was forced to resign in November 1934.

Military Situation

Since the end of World War I, France's main concern had been the possible revival of German power and the possible turn of German foreign policy toward revisionist lines. To be ready to deal successfully with such a situation in the 1920's France created a network of alliances with the Little Entente states.[23] Although these treaties looked impressive on paper, their application depended on the military capacity of France and on the will of the French government to use that military might. However, the French military and political leaders made two basic mistakes. The first was their evaluation of the events of World War I and its conclusion. They stressed the superiority of defensive tactics and strategy over the offensive and as a result, spent millions of francs on building the Maginot line while neglecting the development of mobile units.[24] Their second mistake was unilateral disarmament following the peace treaties. They gradually reduced the size of the army between 1921 and 1933 from 857,000 men to 560,000 with almost 40 percent not serving on the continent, which left only 224,000 men for the defense of France proper; and the 52 infantry divisions were reduced to 20 divisions.[25]

According to the plans of the French General Staff for the modernization of equipment, retraining of personnel, and completion of the Maginot line, the army needed 5,040 million francs in eight annual amounts of 630 million francs, however, from 1927 until the end of 1934, the French government appropriated only 2,097 million francs for the military budget, less than half of the amount requested.[26] The army leaders were alarmed when they learned at the end of 1933 that the military budget proposed for 1934 would force them to further reduce the size of the army to less than 100,000 men.[27] This reduction sounded terrifying in light of reports from the Deuxième Bureau estimating the strength of the German army at 21 combat divisions, backed by 30 to 50 reserve divisions.[28] Yet the new, lower army budget bill was not altered;

it was passed by the deputies over the protest of the Army Council. Why did the deputies close their eyes to the threatening signals produced by Germany when Hitler withdrew from the Disarmament Conference on October 14, 1933, and then, five days later, left the League of Nations?

The reasons for this behavior are numerous. The first and most widely accepted refers to the effects of World War I. In 1917, the French army already displayed signs of war wearinesss: "The thirty-two months of hardship that many soldiers had experienced, the repeated promises of swift victories that seemed forever to go unfilled, the lack of confidence in their leaders and a growing feeling of the pointlessness of so much carnage had led to a number of mutinies."[29] The memories of this hardship and frustration were not erased from the minds of the former soldiers by the victorious end of the war.

The loss of human life also influenced the thinking of the civilian population. France had lost a million and a half soldiers.[30] This was slightly less than the German loss, but Germany had a population of 65 million while France's population was only 41 million. The psychological effects of these conditions prevailed in the sinking popularity of the army, in the spreading of pacifist convictions (especially among the Socialists), and in the mood of the consecutive governments and deputies, who hesitated to vote for army appropriations.

This reasoning is only part of the picture since the losses suffered in World War I "left no permanent scar."[31] It has also been argued that the French army, after the victorious end of World War I, found no new mission for herself, since "Alsace Lorraine was French once again and the deepest source of inspiration for patriotism. . .no longer existed.[32] Further, the economic consequences of the war, such as the devastation of northern France, the termination of the German indemnity payments, and the great depression, forced the French political leaders to be more concerned with immediate social and economic problems than with the question of national security. The declining army budget and unsatisfactory pay forced more and more army officers "to look for an opportunity to leave the service."[33]

Nationalism was not dead in France, however, as seen in the growing membership of patriotic rightwing organizations, "In 1936 the *Croix de Feu*, for example, boasted two million members."[34] Even the Socialists agreed on the importance of the defense of France. Their opposition to the army was rooted in Socialist dogma, which put political consciousness of a soldier ahead of military skill, equipment, and training. Finally, Maurice Baumont has expressed the conviction that the overriding issues in the eyes of the respective governments and in the minds of the deputies were centered more on party strifes and struggles than on questions of national security.[35] Although the recognition of this short-sighted policy led to the formation of the Government of National Unity under Doumergue in February 1934, the idea of national unity was not yet dominant in the last months of 1933.

On December 18, 1933, while the new budget was being discussed in the Army Council and the Chamber of Deputies, Hitler sent an official proposal for a disarmament agreement in which the strength of the German army was fixed at half that of the French.[36] Germany was ready to renounce the use of offensive weapons (heavy tanks, airplanes), and a reciprocal control system was suggested. Hitler also asked for the return of the Saar Valley to Germany without a plebiscite and recommended the conclusion of a non-aggression pact.[37] French domestic problems delayed an answer to this proposal until April 1934 when it was rejected.[38] In other words, after the further reduction of the size of her army, France closed the doors to diplomatic negotiations.

After the February riots, Marshall Philippe Pétain, the hero of Verdun, took over the defense ministry. The condition of the army continued to deteriorate. The military leadership now had to fight even their own minister, since Pétain felt that the Maginot line provided satisfactory defense and opposed the modernization of the army.[39] They sent desperate appeals to the government: "In its present state, the French Army will be in no situation to face a threat without grave risks."[40] The government, however, was not moved.

The political consequences of this weakening of the army were initially far more important than the military consequences. A weakened French army alarmed her allies and created doubts as to whether or not France could fulfill her obligations. Although the alliances with Poland and the Little Entente were designed as mutual assistance treaties, the secret military clauses provided actual assistance only for the small states, not for France.[41]

Poland was to be helped with war material and technical personnel. France's duty was to secure communication lines and maritime transportation routes to Poland in case of war; control of the "Sound" between Denmark and Sweden was the key to the success of that plan. However, the French navy was far too weak to accomplish such a task, although among the branches of the armed forces, the navy was in the best condition.[42] The army had not even prepared plans to fulfill this obligation through a speedy occupation of Denmark. The treaty, therefore, was a military absurdity.

The treaty with Rumania envisaged military cooperation "in case of necessity," but no exchange of views ever took place between the two General Staffs.[43] The Czech treaty projected the creation of a coordinated military operation against a "common enemy," but no such plan was ever worked out.[44] The security treaty with Yugoslavia did not even include any military conventions. When the Yugoslavian General Staff proposed a "conversation" between the two staffs in 1928, the French government found the time to be "inopportune," and the subject was dropped forever.[45]

Naturally, for France the most important question was her own defense against Germany. Mutual assistance treaties, especially with Belgium, Poland, and Czechoslovakia, were of utmost importance to her. Yet, the building of the Maginot line, the openly accepted principle concerning the superiority of defense, and the drastic reduction of her army brought home the point even to her most faithful allies that *France was concerned only with her own security.* This mistaken French attitude was rightly evaluated by her allies: Poland started negotiations for a non-aggression pact with Germany; Benes began to look for security in the Soviet Union; and Yugoslavia sought an understanding with Italy. In the arena of Great Power politics, Britain continued negotiations with Germany for an agreement on the proportion of German rearmament, and the United States refused to participate in European politics.[46]

The security system designed for France by Clememceau was near total collapse. French domestic conditions remained fluid under the influence of the economic crisis. Her allies became the business partners of Germany and Italy. Their economic interests demanded rapprochement with these two states, even at the expense of possible French rancour. The French army was only a weak shadow of its former strong past. It was necessary for the French diplomacy either to rebuild France's Security system or to provide a new one, negotiating from a position of weakness and not of strength. It was quite a task.

CHAPTER III
THE FIRST CRISIS:
POLAND'S INDEPENDENT FOREIGN POLICY

Since Polish foreign policy of the interwar period was interwoven with the decisions and actions of Josef Pilsudski, it is necessary to know a little about this strong leader. Pilsudski received his basic education in Wilno, where the school's Russification program evoked Polish resentment and turned the young Pilsudski into a strong Polish patriot. In 1887 he was involved in a plot against Czar Alexander III and was sentenced to five years of exile in Siberia. Here he became acquainted with and impressed by socialism with the result that, after his return in 1893, he joined the Polish Socialist Party "because it combined revolt against social injustice with the struggle for national integrity."[1] By 1908 however, he was disappointed with international socialism although he retained his nationalist convictions.

After the Russian revolution in February 1917, Pilsudski was invited to join the revolutionary camp and fight for an independent Poland. Though not joining, he did not flatly reject the invitation. For this and his refusal to take an oath of allegiance to the German-sponsored Polish state,[2] the Germans imprisoned him. He was released on November 10, 1918, one day before the armistice was signed. Pilsudski returned to Warsaw as the head of the new Polish state and commander-in-chief of the Polish army.

Since the beginning of statehood, the Polish parliament hindered by political party rifts, struggled hopelessly with the enormous problems caused by the long and devastating war. By 1926, the domestic situation seemed to be near an explosion. Pilsudski felt it necessary to interfere with politics in order to prevent a possible outbreak of violence, so he staged a *coup d' état*. Limiting the powers of parliament, he tried to correct the existing bad domestic situation by using authoritarian measures.

Meanwhile, Poland felt secure and in control of the foreign political scene as long as Germany was weak and divided, the Franco-Polish Mutual Assistance Treaty was in effect, and Soviet-German cooperation was restricted to commerce and trade. However, by 1932, conditions had deteriorated from the Polish point of view. The Franco-Polish alliance was at the edge of complete dissolution. Germany, whose violations of the armament limitation clauses of the Versailles Treaty were open secrets, gained more and more rights at the Disarmament Conference. Extending cooperation to the military field, Germany and the Soviet Union renewed their treaty concerning the exchange of information received in military espionage matters, and a Soviet military mission attended German field exercises held near the Polish frontier.[3]

Thus, the main problem of Polish foreign policy in the 1930's was still the threat of a possible concentrated action by her two great neighbors—the Soviet Union and Germany. France's skillful diplomatic evasion of the guarantees demanded by Poland made it urgent for Pilsudski to try and find another way to secure his country's frontiers. The strong nationalist and anti-Communist feelings of Pilsudski were not the only decisive factors in Polish foreign policy after he assumed virtually dictatorial powers. Pilsudski and his advisors did not disregard the foreign political principles and practices which Poland had pursued since the 1920's. Their independent foreign political decisions, which surprised France like electric shocks, were not sudden decisions at all but culminations of a long evolutionary process.

FOREIGN POLICY BEFORE 1933

Relations with Neighboring States

Germany.   Polish-German relations were strained from the very beginning because of the Versailles Treaty. During the treaty negotiations, Polish claims were strongly supported by France, since "the more Germany was weakened in the East, the less menace she offered on the West," while Britain considered French attempts to extend Polish territory as a French desire to dominate Central Europe through her client states.[4] As a result of this Great Power rivalry, Poland received considerably less territory than that of "historic" Poland. In Silesia, for instance, she received only part of the Great Coal Basin. The Polish-German frontier attempted to follow general ethnic lines, but many Germans lived in territories awarded to Poland and many Poles remained under German authority.

The Versailles Treaty restored eastern Pomerania to Poland, creating an outlet to the Baltic Sea for the otherwise landlocked country and, at the same time, separating East Prussia from mainland Germany. Poland secured access to the Baltic through the Corridor, but she did not gain control over the port of Danzig (Gdansk) which, because a majority of its population was German,[5] was made a free city under the protection of the League of Nations.

It was natural that the Germans of Danzig looked upon Germany as their patron and tried to promote German revisionist policy. According to the Versailles settlement, Poland had the authority to conduct Danzig's foreign policy, use its railways and waterways unrestrictedly, and control its customs. This had never worked satisfactorily, however, and the Poles finally built their own seaport, Gdynia, to avoid the constant arguments with the port authorities of Danzig. With the help of this new port, they secured the unhindered flow of trade to and from Poland.

The crux of the Danzig situation was not the economic, custom, and commercial problem, but the clash of German and Polish political and strategic interests. The Polish government rightly evaluated the military importance of the Corridor. It provided Poland with the only direct and dependable connection with France, her great patron. Also, an East Prussia, linked directly with Germany, could serve as an excellent base for a German invasion of Poland.[6] A separated East Prussia, completely encircled by Poland, could not offer such an opportunity.

Looking at the Corridor from Germany's side, the fact that it separated East Prussia from Germany was a great loss only from the nationalist view point, since free communication between the two parts was guaranteed by the Versailles Treaty. Anyway, the Baltic Sea provided unrestricted, inexpensive transportation lines. Also, the Corridor put a break on the military prerequisites for the possible renewal of a practical *Drang nach Osten* imperialistic policy. Furthermore, having a large number of German inhabitants, the Corridor provided Germany nationalists with the most convenient example of peace treaty injustices. Thus, the existence and preservation of the Corridor was a question of survival for Poland, whereas it was a question of minimum importance for Germany.

In 1930, while certain members of the German government expressed unrestricted revisionist feelings concerning Danzig and Silesia, Germany and Poland were involved in a bitter debate over the rights of Germans in Poland; the argument, though lasting nine months in the forum of the League of Nations, did not produce reconciliation.[7] Then, Polish complaints concerning the rights of Poles residing in Danzig triggered a long trial (March 31-December 15, 1931) at the International Tribunal in The Hague, again without satisfying results.[8] Anti-Polish sentiments grew in Germany and the Polish ambassador to Berlin reported with certain uneasiness that "There is an increasing number of foreign politicians and journalists who are of the opinion that Poland will inevitably have to give in under the pressure of public opinion."[9]

The problem of the Corridor came to the forefront of interest even in the United States where a fall 1933 article in *Foreign Affairs*[10] suggested a solution which had been promoted by East Prussian circles the previous year.[11] This plan, while eliminating the Danzig Corridor and thus reuniting East Prussia with Germany, proposed a new corridor between East Prussia and Lithuania. The new corridor would still include a great number of Germans. It would create new problems and invite the opposition of not only the Lithuanians, but most probably also the Soviet government. The location of this new corridor could serve only German interests for it connected East Prussia with Germany, awarded Germany territory for a possible continuation of the *Drang nach Osten*, and gave Germany the seaports of Danzig and Gdynia. For Poland, on the other hand, the new corridor could not equal the value of the existing one since the proposed corridor was located hundreds of miles away from the Polish coal district. Using the new corridor would force production expenses for this important export item to grow so high that it would outprice Polish coal from the international market. No wonder Poland flatly rejected the idea of this new corridor and rigidly stuck to the status quo.

Thus, the decisions of the peacemakers made both Germany and Poland dissatisfied. Poland cried out for the old historical frontiers and demanded control over Danzig. German propaganda exploited the artificial Corridor which separated East Prussia from Germany and used the German minorities in Poland to promote subversive activities against the new Polish state. The normalization of Polish-German relations seemed to be an impossible task. During the 1920's, Poland experienced a loss of sympathy, and world public opinion turned in favor of Germany. It was imperative for Pilsudski to find a solution which would stop the deterioration of world support and restore the weakened security of Poland to a more satisfactory level.

Lithuania and the Soviet Union

The borders between Lithuania and Poland were marked out in the Treaty of Riga (March 18, 1921) following the Soviet-Polish war. Poland received Wilno and its surrounding territory with a majority Lithuanian population, which created friction between Lithuania and Poland.[12] Both sides took a rigid position, though eventually Poland initiated negotiations to normalize their relationship. These attempts proved futile, however. Yet, the Lithuanian controversy was not considered important from the Polish point of view, for Lithuania was too small and weak to represent a threat. Danger could develop only if Lithuania became an ally or a client state of one of Poland's great enemies—Germany or the Soviet Union. The aim of Polish diplomacy then was to keep Lithuania independent and isolated.

After the Treaty of Riga, the Soviet Union turned her attention to domestic problems. Though friction existed between Poland and the Soviet Union, the situation remained relatively calm. The cause of this friction was represented by Eastern Galicia which, although with a majority Ukranian population, was awarded to Poland. Eastern Galicia not only had precious oil, but also was an important connecting territory between Poland and Rumania. Both states being anti-Communist, their common defense against possible Soviet expansion was more promising with the help of a common frontier. The loss of Eastern Galicia put the Soviet Union in opposition to the status quo, however, and Polish statesmen watched carefully for signs of possible Soviet revisionism concerning Eastern Galicia. Pilsudski did not consider the Soviet Union, acting alone, as a potentially dangerous enemy. However, a German-Soviet combination would represent a mortal threat, and the beginning of such a combination seemed to materialize in the late 1920's. The Polish government, in light of deteriorating French relations, had to find a new formula to prevent further German-Soviet rapprochement and thus strengthen Polish security.

Austria.   Being a small country without significant Polish trade relations, Austria was not of primary economic importance to Poland. Politically, however, Austria represented a problem. A hope for the annexation of Austria could lure Germany's attention away from the Corridor and so could lessen the German threat. Thus, if the German menace to Polish territory grew, it would be in Poland's interest to raise the question of and possibly agree to the annexation of Austria. This required a flexible foreign policy toward Austria, with Poland trying to keep neutral in the annexation matter for as long as possible.

Hungary. Poland had had good relations with Hungary for many centuries. During the Soviet-Polish War, Hungary offered her help to Pilsudski.[13] The relations between the two countries, based on the firm anti-Communist convictions of both, remained cordial during the interwar period. On the other hand, Hungary was the most devoted enemy of the status quo, continuously demanding border revisions. This put Hungary in the opposing camp. However, since Hungary had no territorial claims against Poland, Hungarian revisionism did not represent any particular danger. Some kind of cooperation between Poland and Hungary might occur if Czechoslovakia drifted into the German or Soviet camp, since it would be in the interest of both countries to counter-act such a move. For the time being, Poland's interest was to keep relations with Hungary unchanged.

Czechoslovakia. Since Czechoslovakia, like Poland, was created by the peace treaties, one might have expected the two states, both having great interest in maintenance of the status quo, to be good friends, yet just the contrary was true. Czechoslovakia was looked upon by the Poles as a treacherous foe, while the Czechs regarded Poland as an enemy of democracy. The origins of this dislike can be found partly in the peace treaties and partly in the circumstances preceding the Treaty of Riga.

The territory of Teschen, before it was divided between Czechoslovakia and Poland, was the scene of war, angry disputes, treachery, and Great Power rivalry; and it remained a sore point in Czech-Polish relations. Teschen had belonged to Poland before the three partitions, never to Czechoslovakia or to the old Czech kingdom and Polish patriots were steadfast in their desire to repossess the Teschen territory.

The Soviet-Polish war (1919-1920) produced the greatest friction between Poland and Czechoslovakia. Benes, in order to secure the territory of Teschen and obtain a common frontier with "big brother" Russia (a dream of the Pan-Slavs since the 19th century), hindered the Polish war effort against the Soviet Union.[14] He closed the

Czechoslovak-Hungarian border to block the military aid offered by the Hungarians to Pilsudski.[15] On the other hand, Benes supported Polish claims for Silesia. The common enemy, Germany, should have united the two countries in an anti-German alliance; however, this did not happen. The Polish-Czech Political Agreement, signed in Prague on November 6, 1921, demanded only a "benevolent neutrality in case one of the contracting powers would be attacked by one of their neighbors."[16]

Polish-Czech relations worsened after 1926 when Czechoslovakia gave political asylum to Pilsudski's opponents and tolerated their anti-Pilsudski propaganda. Benes' pro-Soviet attitude caused great resentment in Poland, and the hostility of Czech leaders was manifested in their attempts to "undermine the Polish-French and Polish-Rumanian friendship."[17] Benes' flat refusal to participate in an anti-German alliance[18] convinced Pilsudski that there was no chance for a rapprochement with Czechoslovakia. Yet, he had to take into consideration the strategic location of Czechoslovakia. Her adherence to either the German or Soviet camp would create an unacceptable military situation for Poland. Thus, Czech-Polish relations needed to be corrected.

Rumania. From the Polish point of view, Rumania represented an important neighbor only because of her strong anti-Communist regime. Poland had to take into consideration also the fact that Rumania had other enemies besides the Soviet Union, namely Hungary and Bulgaria. It was not in the interest of Poland to get involved in international arguments concerning countries located far away from her own territory, just as Rumania did not want to get involved in the German-Polish revisionist dispute.[19] Therefore, Rumanian relations, while binding Poland to Rumania against the Soviet Union, did not demand and did not produce closer cooperation in the foreign policy of the two countries. The existing relationship seemed to satisfy Poland's national interests.

Foreign Policy Principles

It is apparent, then, that Poland's international relations were varied. She was an anti-revisionist and a defender of the status quo concerning Silesia, Pomerania, and Wilno. She was a revisionist and in favor of changing the status quo in the case of Danzig and the territory of Teschen.

She held common interests with France concerning Germany, common interests with Germany concerning Czechoslovakia, common interests with Rumania concerning the Soviet Union, and common interests with the Soviets in case of German penetration into Lithuania. These contradictory conditions prescribed for Poland the basic principle of her foreign policy until the early 1930's. This principle was: while attempting to restore good relations with France, Poland should pursue a flexible foreign policy according to the temporary needs of Poland and according to the attitude of the nations described.

Domestic Conditions and International Trade

In 1931, Poland had 31,915,800 inhabitants, with more than 60 percent of the population dependent on agriculture.[20] The size of the average land holding was small as can be seen in the following figures:[21]

Category of Holdings	Percent of Total Number of Owners	Percent of Total Land
0-5 hectares	64.7	15.3
5-100 hectares	34.3	31.8
100 or more hectares	1.0	52.9

Land productivity depends on the use of sufficient fertilizer. Experts feel the ideal amount is 60 kilograms per hectare, yet in 1934, the use of artificial fertilizers in Poland amounted to only seven kilograms per hectare.[22] These statistics are misleading, however, since the peasantry also used natural manure, with the result that wheat production, especially in Posnania and Pomerania, equaled, if not surpassed, Western European standards.[23] Although agricultural production was good, the size of properties and the backward methods used did not secure a high standard of living for the Polish peasantry. Therefore, social problems were created for the Polish leadership, especially since foreign trade, or rather the lack of it, closed the market for exports.

The index of Poland's industrial production (1958=100 percent) reached the level of 16 percent in 1938, but only 3.29 percent of the whole population was employed in industry and mining.[24] The low industrial output and the lack of capital hindered Poland's modernization and forced her to seek the aid of richer, more industrialized nations. Because of these industrially underdeveloped conditions, Poland, had always been greatly dependent on the economic cooperation of other countries. During the peace negotiations, France and England were already competing for the possession of the coal basins of Silesia and Teschen.[25] When Germany renounced her economic treaty with Poland in 1925, the Polish coal industry faced a severe crisis, and only the British coal miner strike solved the problem as Poland was able to capture a great part of the British market.[26]

Since "control of trade with any country could bear political fruits,"[27] it is important to see the foreign trade balance of Poland in the early 1930's from this perspective. It was vital for Poland, as well as her allies, to know which country or countries could dominate Poland economically, and which country or countries could become economically dependent on Polish products.

In 1933, Poland's best trading partner in terms of imports was Germany, followed by the United States, England, and France; while in exports, England led the list, followed by Germany, the Soviet Union, and Austria.[28] Totaling export and import figures, the most important Polish trade partner was Germany, then England, the United States, France, and Austria. Germany alone commanded 17.6 percent of Poland's imports and 17.5 percent of Poland's exports. Britain, not an enthusiastic supporter of Poland, shared 10 percent of Poland's imports and 19.2 percent of her exports. France, Poland's strongest ally, participated in only 6.7 percent of her imports and 5.5 percent of the exports. These conditions, even if the political side of German-Polish relations is completely disregarded, strongly influenced the Polish leaders in seeking at least a *détente* with Germany in order not to jeopardize the economic interests of their country. The economic statistics also shed light on the importance of Danzig and the Corridor: 60.5 percent of Polish import trade and 55.1 percent of her export trade passed through the Corridor, making it the most important lifeline of Poland's economy.

In light of these trade conditions, Poland had only two courses to follow: reorganize her international trade to prevent Germany from obtaining a commanding role; or harmonize her foreign policy with her economic interests, securing the free flow of commerce and trade through the Corridor and enlarging connections with those powers who were her best buyers and suppliers. France was not in a position to effectively help the Polish economy, as a buyer or as a supplier. Since her best trading partner was Germany, Polish economic interests demanded that she find a *modus vivendi* with Germany.

Polish-Soviet Non-Agression Pact

Because of declining French support against the Soviet Union, Polish diplomacy attempted to restore the security of Poland with a bilateral agreement. The conditions for such a possibility were prepared during the late 1920's when both Poland and the Soviet Union joined the Briand-Kellogg Pact[29] and applied its principles to their local conditions in form of the Litvinov Protocol.[30] However, the realization of a non-aggression pact had to wait for several reasons. First of all, the Soviet Union was anxious not to endanger the growing German-Soviet trade cooperation. From 1930 to 1932, German imports grew from 24 percent of the Soviet Union's import trade to a very considerable 46 percent.[31] Secondly, Poland's smaller neighbors, the Baltic states, had to be included in any non-aggression negotiations with the Soviet Union in order to remove their suspicion that a Polish-Soviet pact might be directed against them.

The time for discussions grew ripe in the second half of 1931 when "internal difficulties in the Soviet Union, the threat of Japanese expansion in the Far East and the conciliatory attitude toward Germany shown by England and France combined to induce the Soviet government to seek further rapprochement with Warsaw."[32] Poland, "in concert with Finland, Estonia, Latvia and Rumania"[33] soon started negotiations with the Russians and an agreement was signed in Moscow on July 25, 1932.[34] The Soviet-Fin, Soviet-Latvian, and Soviet-Estonian Non-Aggression Pacts quickly followed the Polish signature. The Soviet-Rumanian negotiations had not produced any agreement, however, and Rumania felt offended when Poland signed her pact without waiting for the conclusion of the Rumanian-Soviet negotiations. While the Rumanian government considered the Polish-Soviet Pact "a deviation from the spirit of the Polish-Rumanian alliance," in France, "the conservative, nationalist Paris press, which had denounced the Franco-Soviet negotiations in 1931 remained consistent and criticized the Polish-Soviet Pact."[35]

The balance sheet from Poland's point of view, however, looked favorable. At the price of a mild Rumanian apprehension and French press disapproval, the Polish leaders were able to avert at least one of the great dangers threatening Poland. With the signing of the pact, Poland secured her rear and improved her chances of, with France's help, prevailing over the German forces if war were to occur.

After Hitler came to power, German-Polish relations worsened. Pilsudski and Josef Beck, his foreign minister, agreed that Poland had to review her international situation and take the necessary steps to prevent the further deterioration of Poland's security.

The Westerplatte Incident

Both Pilsudski and Beck distrusted the political intrigues of the League of Nations and believed that only a concerted action on the part of Poland and France could eliminate the growing menace of German National Socialist foreign political aims. To this end, Pilsudski recommended the waging of a preventive war, but the French answer was negative.[36] On the basis of simple mathematics, Pilsudski was right. In 1933 the weak German army[37] was no match even for the Polish army alone, not to mention the possibility of a coordinated attack with the French army. On the basis of realistic policy, however, Pilsudski greatly misunderstood the conditions and realities of France. No French government would dare to risk an international crisis, especially a war, simply because the French population would not support such an action.

After the rejection of his preventive war idea in March 1933, Pilsudski decided to give a serious warning signal to Germany without the consent of the Great Powers. On the peninsula of Westerplatte,[38] Poland had built ammunition depots and, with the permission of the League of Nations, kept a garrison of two officers, twenty non-commissioned officers, and sixty soldiers for guard duties. On March 6, 1933, one day after the German elections in which the Nazi Party had made great gains, Pilsudski sent a detachment of 120 soldiers to reinforce the garrison. He did this without informing the Great Powers or the League of Nations, hoping that "a determined attitude by Poland would be "properly appreciated in Paris and London, rousing these countries to more energetic action in the fact of the growing threat of Hitlerism."[39] However, instead of a "more energetic action," the British and French governments protested Pilsudski's measures and referred the incident and its investigation to the League of Nations. Poland was obliged by the League to restore the situation at Westerplatte to what had existed before the incident.

The French nervousness was unjustified. Hitler did not have real force at his disposal at that time, and so the Polish action did not threaten the peace of Europe. It brought home a bitter lesson to Poland, though: "It became obvious that the French government was not inclined to collaborate more actively with Poland in view of the new situation in Germany and of the growing danger of Nazism."[40]

The Polish government hardly had time to digest the bitter pill of French and British reaction to the Westerplatte incident when they received alarming news about Mussolini's ideas concerning a Four Power Pact. According to the plan, the four powers of Britain, France, Italy, and Germany would take responsibility for solving European international problems. Since the original text of the pact accepted the principle of revision where resolutions of the peace treaties had created an unjust situation which might provoke serious confrontation, Poland understood the plan as a threat. The strict interpretation of these revisionist ideas would mean the loss of the Corridor which gave Poland access to the sea and provided the life line of Polish trade, commerce, and military supplies. Being convinced after Westerplatte about the absolute passivity of France concerning the limitation of Germany's growth, the Poles easily believed that France would not oppose Mussolini's plan "to shift German expansion eastward in the direction least threatening for Italy."[41] Having this belief, Polish statesmen were faced with several vital questions: would the continuation of the presently accepted foreign policy satisfy the needs of Polish security; should and could Poland count on old alliances; and especially, was the promised French aid still reliable in case of war with Germany?

Foreign Policy Alternatives in 1933

After studying Poland's domestic conditions and foreign political relations, the Polish government had to select the new foreign policy from among the following possible alternatives.

Continuation of the Present Policy

Continuation of the present policy meant for Poland a large degree of dependence on France and the French-dominated League of Nations, both supposedly guardians of the status quo. However, the events of the last two to three years indicated that the attitude of these powers was changing, their anti-revisionism weakening. The continuation of the present policy would mean a disaster for Poland sooner or later. To avoid that, a new policy was necessary, a new policy which would restore the security of Poland by the revitalization of old alliances or, if necessary, by the reorientation of the whole Polish foreign policy.

Reactivation of the Franco-Polish Alliance

By successfully reactivating the France-Polish alliance, Poland would have peacetime security against German revisionist aims. In case of war, she would fight in cooperation with France, which meant confronting only a fraction of the German army since the bulk of the German army most likely would be employed against France. The disadvantages of renewed cooperation with France would probably appear most in the area of economic conditions. Since World War I, French capitalists had secured great privileges in Poland. The resentment against this economic control grew with Polish nationalism to such a high degree that at the end of 1932, the French ambassador to Warsaw sent a long warning report to his government characterizing the Polish attitude as "xenophobia."[42] Yet, these French economic privileges did not seem too high a price to pay for the return of national security.

More disturbing conditions were created by the development of French public opinion and the French spirit. France's foreign policy of this period has been described as neglecting "those ties which connect her own security with the security of other states. . . pretending that peace exists until her own frontiers are invaded."[43]

Poland's security was unimportant to France, at least that is how Polish leaders interpreted such sudden changes in French foreign policy as the conciliatory tone of French diplomats toward Mussolini, the transformation of strong anti-Soviet sentiments[44] to a Franco-Soviet Non-Aggression Pact, and the opinions of a growing number of French leaders.

Among the latter was Air Minister Pierre Cot who, after visiting the Soviet Union, spent several days in Prague where he agreed wholeheartedly with Benes' welcoming sentence: "At last France has understood that the line of defense of her own security must pass through Moscow."[45]

There seemed only one chance for Poland to regain the old French support, and that was for Beck to convince France that Poland would be a more worthy ally than Mussolini, Stalin, or Benes. Keeping in mind Poland's economic dependence on France (in the form of French investments in Poland), and the fact that she was even more dependent on France for military supplies, Pilsudski had to attempt a reconciliation with France, if not entirely based on the old principle, then with the help of new ideas.

Closer Alliance with the Soviet Union

A closer alliance with the Soviet Union was feasible, for the atmosphere had been more relaxed since the signing of the Non-Aggression Pact. What advantages could Poland gain by such a closer cooperation? The Soviet Union had no common frontier with Germany. In case of war, the Soviet Union could help Poland with war materials and equipment, but the German army would be confronted with only Polish troops. The theater of war would be on Polish territory.

If the Soviet Union provided troops, too, then the advantages of a Soviet alliance would increase considerably. However, the feasibility of employing Soviet troops on Polish territory was questionable. The thought of Soviet troops on Polish soil was a very distressing idea for both the government and the people of Poland. The memories of the Polish-Soviet War were too much alive, not to mention the strong anti-Communist sentiments in the country. Thus, a closer alliance with the Soviet Union seemed completely impractical.

Alliance with Czechoslovakia

Though Polish-Czech relations had been less than friendly in the past, mostly because of Polish revisionist aims concerning Teschen and Czech hostility toward the authoritarian regime of Pilsudski, there was still a basis for reconciliation. This was provided by Mussolini's Four Power Pact since it threatened Czechoslovakia and Poland equally and offered a good opportunity for them to draw closer together in an anti-German alliance.

The advantages of a Polish-Czech cooperation became clear after a glimpse at the map. In case of war, the geographic location of the Czech-German border would make it possible for the Czech army to threaten both the right flank and the rear of a Germany army marching against Poland. The combined forces of the Czech and Polish armies in 1933 far outweighed the strength of the German army and probably would for a long time. Czechoslovakia had a Mutual Guarantee Treaty with France,[46] just as Poland did. Because of the important location of Czechoslovakia,[47] though, it could be expected that both French and League of Nations aid would materialize faster in case of a German attack on Czechoslovakia than in case of a German attack on Poland. All these expected advantages urged Poland toward a closer cooperation with the Czechs.

In return for Czech cooperation, Poland most likely would have to tone down or possibly renounce her revisionism concerning the territory of Teschen. With Silesia, however, Poland was more than fairly compensated for the lost Teschen territory. Revisionist sentiments were nourished much more by nationalist feelings than by practical interest, so that stopping this revisionism would not be too high a price to pay for greatly improved Polish security. A closer alliance with Czechoslovakia was desirable from the Polish point of view. It was also feasible, success depending only on the diplomatic skill of the negotiators.

Preventive War Against Germany

A preventive war against Germany would certainly be the most radical, but at the same time the most promising, solution. The Polish army, though it was not the best trained and equipped, seemed ready for such an assignment. The German army was undergoing reorganization; it was poorly trained, ill-equipped, and numerically inferior. On the other hand, the Polish army was dependent on France for war supplies. Thus, Pilsudski could not start a preventive war without the consent of France.

A quick Polish victory would result in the repression of the growing German danger, the strict enforcement of the Versailles Treaty, the probable fall of the Hitler regime, and the end of German revisionism. All of these were high rewards for the risks involved. The disadvantages of the preventive war solution were not too overwhelming. The League of Nations might be expected to condemn Poland for her aggressiveness. Britain could be alienated completely, but her alienation would not create a critical situation for the Polish diplomacy. The Soviet Union might file a formal protest but certainly would not help Germany if France took the right diplomatic steps. The small Central European states, which were becoming more dependent on and therefore threatened by Germany, would adjust their attitudes to the new situation.

If, on the other hand, the war produced some kind of unexpected disaster and the Polish army had to retreat, Poland could count on the opening of a second front by the French, assuming they had agreed beforehand to a preventive war. The preventive war solution was, therefore, the most promising; but its initiation without French consent was too hazardous, and so its feasibility depended more on France than on Poland.

Since the Westerplatte incident, Germany judged Poland as her most militant neighbor and gave priority to the rectification of Polish-German relations. This was not too much of a basis with which to start, but certainly a slim hope for further developments existed. Thus, a Polish-German rapprochement, though with many preconditions, was also a possible alternative.

The Course of Events in 1933-1934

The Polish leadership consciously investigated the various possibilities for the direction of Poland's foreign policy. Sometimes because of the inflexible attitude of their partners, other times because of their own rigidity, one alternative after another proved unacceptable.

Reaction to the Four Power Pact

Pilsudski made an attempt to reconcile France, but according to his convictions, the first firm step had to be a French rejection of the Four Power Pact. Instead of rejection, though, France signed the pact on June 7, 1933. Polish protest brought a letter of explanation from the French government, but that did not satisfy Poland. The signing of this pact (though it was never ratified) frightened Poland, and Pilsudski tried to create a "solidarity platform of all those threatened with that political combination."[48]

Meanwhile the idea of conciliation and rapprochement with Czechoslovakia came to the foreground. Communication did not take place between the two countries, however, for according to Pilsudski's judgment, "Prague was already bowing before the Pact of the Four Powers and as could be expected, in advance shunned any more pronounced attitude."[49] This sentence gives away Pilsudski's prejudices, and no statesman should neglect the exploration of any potentially advantageous cooperation because of personal prejudice. Furthermore, Pilsudski's judgment was completely wrong. Benes, while openly cooperating with France in the preparation of the pact, quietly worked against it, and his activities "had an undoubted effect in the watering down of the Pact."[50] Because of the lack of satisfactory communication between Poland and Czechoslovakia, as well as Poland and France, the struggle against the Four Power Pact tore them further apart instead of uniting them. After this episode, the possible reconciliation of these countries was never really worked on seriously.

Poland's main action in response to the pact was diplomatic, with the move directed against Italy and the author of the pact, Mussolini. The Polish ambassador to Rome resigned, stating that he could not retain his post in good conscience since the new Italian policy was contrary to the essential international interest of Poland.[51]

The possibly dangerous results of a completed Four Power Pact prodded Pilsudski to explore the feasibility of a *détente* with Germany. Beginning in April 1933, while Poland made preparations for a preventive war against Germany,[52] several conversations took place between Beck's personal envoy, Alfred Wisocki, and German Foreign Minister Constantin von Neurath. On May 2, Hitler personally conversed with Beck. Although Poland and Germany arrived at an understanding of each other's problems, this understanding did not substantially improve their relationship. Poland could regard as a success, however, the fact that Polish-German relations were improved to a certain degree without the violation of Poland's already existing obligations toward other nations. Still, no official treaty was signed; no German guarantee was obtained for the western frontiers of Poland. In light of Polish military strength and German military weakness, though, a guarantee treaty did not seem to be an absolute necessity at the time.

Then, on May 5, 1933, Germany and the Soviet Union renewed the 1926 Treaty of Berlin; and on July 30, a new Army Law was promulgated in Germany which abolished local armed forces and created the Reichswehr. Given these developments, any further delay in a solid guarantee for the security of Poland on the part of France or Germany seemed to portend disaster. Polish diplomacy diligently tried to prevent such a situation.

German-Polish Negotiations
in the Fall of 1933

In September, during the sessions of the League of Nations, Beck found an opportunity to have conversations with Neurath. Suggesting that German-Polish problems be solved by direct negotiations, Beck indicated to Neurath that "he had also chosen the new minister in Berlin from this viewpoint."[53] Indeed, the new Polish ambassador to Berlin, Josef Lipski, worked very hard to bring about a mutual understanding with Germany and secure some kind of treaty, possibly similar to the Polish-Soviet Non-Aggression Pact, for protection against German aggression.

On October 14, 1933, Germany withdrew from the Disarmament Conference and left the League of Nations. Pilsudski interpreted these German steps as a mortal threat to Poland. Up to now, the League's forum and guarantee provided a certain security for Poland. However, what security could and would be provided by the League of Nations if Germany no longer belonged to that international body?

On October 21, Pilsudski discussed the situation with his closest co-workers and decided to make a new effort to gain French support for his preventive war plans. The French reply was more than disappointing— they flatly rejected the idea. Further, in case of a German attack on Poland, the French government offered help only in the form of armament and ammunition, although promising "the widest possible organization of world public opinion favorable to Poland.[54] In essence, the French reply simply said that under no circumstances would France alone support Poland against German aggression. Pilsudski then saw only one way out of the dilemma: direct negotiations with Germany, negotiations which had to produce a formal treaty that would guarantee the integrity and security of Poland. What the French reaction would be to such a Polish-German agreement seemed absolutely unimportant. Pilsudski gave France more than one chance to regain her prominent patron position with Poland, but now in light of the German rearmament and French passivity, there was no more time to waste. On November 5, Pilsudski personally instructed Lipski to initiate preliminary negotiations in Berlin, and, in response, the German Foreign Ministry drew up a "Declaration" which actually amounted to a non-agression pact.[55]

With this German offer, the Polish diplomacy arrived at its greatest task since the peace negotiations after World War I. It was undoubtedly in Poland's interest to conclude such an agreement with Germany while not alienating France and not offending the Soviet Union. Pilsudski did not want to take Poland completely out of the French orbit and put her into Germany's camp. What he wanted was a neutral position for Poland which would guarantee her security while also preserving the goodwill and support of her older friends, especially France.

The best way to preserve France's goodwill seemed to be to talk to the French military attache. Pilsudski believed that soldiers better understood each other, and so he invited General d'Arbonneau to the Belvedere Palace and informed him about the problems of German-Polish relations. While the French general understood Pilsudski and the French press commented on the Polish-German negotiations with certain reservation,[56] French diplomatic circles reacted with "nervous excitement," worrying about the consequences of the pact "which may cancel out the validity of the Franco-Polish alliance."[57] French diplomatic opinion was not uniform, however. The politicians who worked for a German-French détente believed that the Polish-German Pact might also bring a better understanding between Germany and France.[58]

Pilsudski followed the French reaction with great attention. He unexpectedly delayed the final approval of the pact,[59] hoping for a signal from France which would indicate that there was no need for such a direct non-agression pact with Germany since France was ready to honor her obligations concerning the security of Poland. No such signal was sent. France was too occupied with her own internal political crisis.[60]

Both the Germans and the Poles took pains to dismiss the possible misgivings of the Soviet Union concerning the negotiations as well as the purpose of the pact.[61] The negotiations took almost another month with the final text of the German-Polish Non-Aggression Pact signed on January 26, 1934, and quickly ratified in both countries. Pilsudski and Beck considered the pact a great victory for Poland since Poland's neutrality, integrity, and security were guaranteed no matter how much the validity of the French alliance continued to depreciate.

Effects of Polish Decisions on French Policy

After the peace treaties, France expected that Poland would always behave according to French desires; for, in her interpretation, Polish independence was not the creation of Pilsudski but of French diplomacy. Furthermore, it was expected that Poland would be grateful to France, awarding economic concessions and privileges to French investors.

Poland, under Pilsudski's direction, did not want to be a French puppet. Yet, this did not mean that Pilsudski wanted to join France's enemies either. Pilsudski withheld a rapprochement policy with Germany and the Soviet Union as long as he had confidence in France. He kept the door open for a reconciliation until the last minute. However, France completely misinterpreted Pilsudski's intentions. His preventive war plans were judged as dangerous and irresponsible. His refusal to grant passage rights to Soviet troops in case of war with Germany was understood as irreconcilable anti-communism. His Soviet-Polish Non-Aggression Pact, on the other hand, was interpreted as a departure from the French political line. The German-Polish Non-Aggression Pact seemed to be the best proof for many French politicians that Pilsudski had detached Poland's future from that of France.

These misinterpretations pushed them to panic. Instead of trying to understand Poland's view point, instead of finding the common interests of the two countries and trying to work out a plan of cooperation on the basis of complete equality, the French diplomats attempted to force Poland to obey their designs. When these attempts proved unsuccessful, they completely gave up the hope of reconciliation with Poland and tried to replace Pilsudski's lost friendship with the highly questionable value of Stalin's friendship.

Louis Barthou, selected as foreign minister by Doumergue in February, was basically a conservative whose foreign political conceptions generally followed Clemenceau's "hard line" policy, including the desire to have Russia as an ally against Germany. Barthou had to start almost from the beginning to rebuild a security system for France. Although the postwar governments had changed frequently, foreign policy goals—to defend the status quo created by the Versailles settlement and thus provide security for France—had never changed. However, while Barthou's predecessors believed that the status quo could be defended by using the existing system of international treaties, Barthou realized, especially after the German-Polish Non-Aggression Pact, that the system itself was in a stage of dissolution. The main objective of France's foreign policy, that is the security of France, seemed to have vanished completely.

Barthou thus found himself in a situation in which he could more or less freely decide the formula that would serve France's interest the best. Taking into consideration the existing situation, he had the following options from which to choose: continue the old policy based on the idea of international cooperation within the framework of the League of Nations (under French domination) and revitalize French alliances with Poland and the Little Entente; start a completely new foreign policy concerning allies and methods, but leaving unchanged the aim of German containment; or give up the idea of French domination and start a rapprochement policy with Germany based on equality and reconciliation. Barthou had to decide which of these alternatives promised the greatest advantages for France.

FOREIGN POLICY ALTERNATIVES IN FEBRUARY 1934

Continuation of the Old Foreign Policy

The basis of this foreign policy was the idea of international cooperation within the framework of the League of Nations, supplemented by a system of French alliances with the pro-status quo nations, that is, Poland

and the Little Entente states. The advantages of this foreign policy seemed to be well-proven in the 1920's. The League of Nations was to a large extent under French domination and devoted its activities to the preservation of the status quo. At the same time, it represented a supranational moral authority which commanded the respect of world public opinion.

Poland and Czechoslovakia represented a second front against Germany in case of a possible armed conflict. The Little Entente states firmly controlled the Danube Basin and their alliance successfully restrained Hungarian revisionism, prevented a rapprochement between Germany and Austria, and blocked Habsburg restoration attempts. In the Balkans, Bulgarian revisionism was held in check by Rumania and Yugoslavia.

Conditions changed greatly in the first few years of the 1930's. The League of Nations lost a certain degree of international respect, due to the Japanese withdrawal from membership on February 24, 1933, as a result of the Manchurian crisis; the hopeless deadlock of the disarmament negotiations from February 2, 1932, to April 17, 1934; and the withdrawal of Germany from the League on October 14, 1933. The League of Nations could not enforce its resolution against the will of a Great Power. It was futile and senseless for France to seek solutions and resolutions within the framework of the League if the power that she wanted to check most, Germany, was no longer a member. It became clear that the League had lost importance, which suggested to France that she also seek solutions outside of the League.

Ironically enough, instead of strengthening their already existing alliances, Barthou's predecessors looked for a new ally and found one in the Soviet Union. With this step they began to destroy the already existing alliances. The signing of the French-Soviet Non-Aggression Pact on November 29, 1932, and its ratification in May of the following year; the July 1933 visit to France of Maxim Litvinov, the Soviet Union's Commissar for Foreign Affairs; and the trip of French Air Minister Cot to Moscow in September all alarmed Rumania and Poland,[1] speeding up Pilsudski's new foreign policy. Pilsudski tried to disengage his country from the French alliance and secure for Poland some kind of neutral status between France, Germany, and the Soviet Union. French politicians and diplomats denied that any reason existed for this new Polish foreign policy, yet Poland's distrust of French diplomacy appeared well-founded to the Poles. To make the traditional French policy work again, it was absolutely necessary to bring Poland back into the French camp.[2] The price that France would probably have to pay for this would be the dropping of Soviet friendship. Barthou had to decide which was of more value.

The confidence of the Little Entente in France was further weakened by French participation in the Four Power Pact negotiations. The basic idea of the pact came from Mussolini who, seeing the impotence of the League of Nations, wanted to place the preservation of the peace in the care of Britain, France, Italy, and Germany.[3] The text of the pact indicated the necessity for revision of the peace treaties, which was enough to mobilize the foreign ministers of the Little Entente against it. Their protests confronted France with the dilemma of choosing between cooperation with the Great Powers and her alliances with Poland and the Little Entente. France gave way to her allies' wishes. Due to French counter-proposals, the pact hardly resembled the original draft, and although France signed the pact, it was not ratified by the Chamber.

As a consequence of the Four Power Pact negotiations, the Little Entente and Balkan states began to look after their own security instead of relying completely on France. On February 16, 1933, Czechoslovakia, Yugoslavia, and Rumania signed a pact of organization; and on February 9, 1934, Greece, Rumania, Turkey, and Yugoslavia signed the Balkan Entente treaty. These treaties signaled to France a certain amount of distrust on the part of her allies and presented her with a new problem. Although the treaties served the idea of "collective security," they did not interpret it from the French point of view. To make the old French policy prevail, it was necessary to convince these states to incorporate their new pacts into the broader French security system. However, in light of diminishing French economic relations with these states and the weakened French military power, a policy aimed at the restoration of the old French alliance system promised very little success.

Start a New Anti-German Foreign Policy

It had to be clear to Barthou that the only way to stop the growing German threat was to create new, stronger anti-German alliances. He had prospective allies for such a design—the Soviet Union, Italy, Austria, Hungary, and Britain.

An alliance with the Soviet Union had been the goal of preceding French governments. Yet, such an alliance could promise realistic benefits in case of war *only* if the Soviet Union shared a common frontier with Germany. Not having that, it would be necessary to secure the permission of the Polish and Rumanian governments for Russian troop crossings, but neither were willing to see Bolshevik troops pass through their territories. In the absence of Polish and Rumanian cooperation, an alliance with the Soviet Union had only a theoretical value, and it did not provide any security for France. Pushing for this alliance would possibly deteriorate the French-Polish relationship without any results; therefore, the pursuit of a Soviet alliance simply meant chasing utopian dreams.

Under the leadership of Mussolini, Italy was an unwelcome ally in the eyes of the French political Left. At the same time, France and Italy had a common interest in the prevention of the *Anschluss* and in the blocking of German penetration in Central Europe. The pursuit of a rapprochement with Italy was of primary interest to France, but the question of Italian friendship had other aspects which made its realization difficult. France and Italy had their differences in colonial questions, but these were unimportant.[4] A more sensitive problem was the fact that Mussolini was the champion of revisionism. Furthermore, he advocated revision of *all* the peace treaties. His thesis, if accepted, would lead to the mutilation of Czechoslovakia for the benefit of Germany, Hungary, and Poland; Rumania for the benefit of Bulgaria, Hungary, and the Soviet Union; and Yugoslavia for the benefit of Bulgaria, Hungary, and Italy. In the final analysis, it would produce the complete collapse of the French alliance system by weakening *ad absurdum* the capacity of the Little Entente to survive. A rapprochement with Italy seemed feasible only if restricted to French-Italian cooperation for the mutual guarantee of Austrian independence. Yet, at the same time, an Italian rapprochement was an absolute necessity for France in order to prevent, in case of armed conflict with Germany, the formation of a second front at her back. So, Barthou had to find an acceptable basis for cooperation with Italy.

Austria represented a difficult problem, too. It was in France's interest to preserve Austria as an independent state, but the political Left in France and the government of Czechoslovakia were extremely unhappy with the autocratic rule of Dollfuss. After the February 1934 Socialist uprising in Vienna was crushed by Dollfuss and the following investigation proved that Czech Socialists were actively involved in the preparation of the revolt, there seemed to be no chance to secure an understanding between Czechoslovakia and Austria.[5] It was Barthou's problem to find some basis for their agreement and, if possible, an alliance between them, thus strengthening the anti-German front.

Hungary played no important role in the eyes of the French government. French foreign policy was directed toward Hungary according to the interests of the Little Entente states, and any special agreement reached without their consent would alienate them from France. On the other hand, a *modus vivendi* reached in common agreement with the Little Entente would release the pressure on Czechoslovakia, enabling her to concentrate her efforts on the containment of Germany, which was in France's interest. It was up to Barthou to find such a formula.

Cooperation with Britain in Central Europe was very unlikely because of the basic differences between the political views of Britain and France concerning Germany and concerning the question of a possible revision of the peace treaties. However, there was one agreement Barthou needed to reach with Britain: to remain *absolutely* neutral. If possible, the agreement of Anglo-French cooperation declared on July 13, 1933, also should be renewed.

Given the above, Barthou could have drawn the following conclusions concerning the feasibility of *new allies*: alliance with the Soviet Union had no practical value without the cooperation of Poland and Rumania, and negotiations toward that goal could proceed only with their complete agreement and participation; alliance with Italy was of primary interest to France; alliance with Austria was not a necessity, but Austrian independence was of basic French interest; alliance with Hungary was feasible, but relatively unimportant; alliance with Britain was desirable. As the course of events showed, however, these were not Barthou's conclusions.

Rapprochement with Germany

A step toward a rapprochement with Germany would demand a complete reversion of the French foreign policy. It could trigger a renewal of demonstrations, possibly a revolution, and most certainly a further split in the national unity. Yet, there were many reasons why this policy could win the support of the majority. The average Frenchman was "a social reactionary, tending altogether toward conservation and resistance to change, a man who fears revolution."[6] The political organizations of the Right counted some 70,000 active members, and their numbers were growing rapidly, while the Left (Communists) commanded about 30,000 members. Even when adding the Socialists with their 130,000 members,[7] the Left still represented only a small minority of the population. Because of the fear of revolution and a disappointment in the whole parliamentary system, many Frenchmen believed that "the power of the Executive will have to be increased."[8] This conviction was widely held not only among the less politically educated, but also among the most politically influential personalities of the Senate and the Chamber of Deputies.[9] It was natural that people with such convictions were more or less ready to accept rapprochement with an authoritarian Germany.

A similar conclusion was reached on the basis of practical reasons. French industrial production had declined sharply and had no hope of catching up with the aggressively expanding German economy.[10] Certain French capitalist circles worked for the creation of a German-French economic block[11] as a way out of the decline. Furthermore, French military weakness, a rapidly declining population, and an aging society[12] were good enough reasons for the discontinuation of the alienation from Germany and for the change of basic foreign political principles. Finally, there was the pacifist argument against any confrontation which could lead to war. Even the *"Ancien Combattants de Guerre"* believed that "if a vote were taken (what is called a plebiscite) the whole French working class would be against war for *any reason*."[13] (italics added).

Thus, a fear of communism and disappointment in parliamentarianism, realistic economic and military conditions, and pacifist sentiment all combined to rapprochement with Germany as a feasible foreign policy from the domestic political point of view.

France also *needed* a rapprochement with Germany because of the existing French weakness. Only a mutual understanding with Germany could stop a complete German rearmament; only a mutual understanding in the economic field could stop German penetration into Central Europe and perhaps produce a division of spheres of interest; and only a rapprochement policy with Germany could secure *time* for France. Time was needed to stabilize the domestic political scene, to reorganize the crisis-ridden economic life, to rebuild and modernize the army, and to restore the confidence of old allies. These considerations demanded a policy of rapprochement with Germany.

On the other hand, there were several disadvantages to such a policy. First of all, a German-French understanding outside of the League of Nations could cause the complete collapse of that institution. If the rapprochement policy were to be initiated by France, then Germany and all of Europe would interpret it as a sure sign of France's weakness, thus producing a complete loss of confidence in France. It could bring the complete alienation of the Soviet Union; it could cause a break with Italy; it could strengthen the revisionist movement; it could lead to a collapse of the existing alliance system; and it could produce a situation in which France would live in complete isolation, depending on the goodwill of Germany. The disadvantages and the risks involved were undoubtedly much, much greater than the advantages. However, consideration of the time factor alone suggested that France should not flatly reject any new German proposal but should start negotiations and secure the time needed to put her household in order.

A Change in Foreign Policy Direction

Barthou could have done a successful job of directing French foreign policy by, as conditions changed, flexibly selecting those options which promised the most advantages for France. An acceptable policy could have been built on the following axioms: gain time by not flatly rejecting any German proposal; secure the friendship of Italy; guarantee the independence of Austria; try to bring Poland back to the side of France; and restore the confidence of the Little Entente. The simplest and most promising solution of all these problems would have been for the states concerned to agree to sign a new pact guaranteeing and protecting the basic interests of all the signatories.

"Barthou wanted to recreate the European balance of collective security. For him, Fascist Italy and Soviet Russia represented two master cards, two trump cards against Hitler. He would have liked to organize a common front against Nazism."[14] Most historians would agree with this definition of Barthou's foreign political aims. Barthou's methods, however, sometimes caused confusion. In a speech to the Chamber of Deputies on

May 25, 1934, Barthou stated that his policy was the continuation of the foreign policy of the preceding French governments.[15] Although his *actions* seemed to be the continuation of an "unchanging" foreign policy, it does not necessarily mean that his *plans* and *methods* were. One example of this is the April 17, 1934, French rejection of Hitler's rearmament proposal, an action which was decided in the cabinet by majority vote over Barthou's vigorous objections.[16]

After taking office, Barthou had only about a week to get acquainted with the foreign political conditions facing France when events began to speed up. Germany had already meddled in Austria's domestic affairs in 1933, and though the French government protested, Hitler renewed these German-supported Nazi activities in 1934. Austria submitted her complaints to France, Britain, and Italy, and the three powers signed a communiqué on February 17, 1934, in which they expressed "their common views concerning the necessity to maintain the independence and integrity of Austria in accordance with the existing treaties."[17] There was no question in Barthou's mind that Austria's independence was of primary interest to France. Because of this, he continued the foreign policy of Joseph Paul-Boncour, who had stated that "an independent Austria is an essential element of Central Europe's stability and equilibrium."[18]

The first signs of a new French foreign policy can be traced to comments regarding the Balkan Pact, which was signed on February 9, 1934. Preceding French governments had viewed Bulgaria as a revisionist state and, therefore, an enemy. Circles near the foreign ministry of Barthou, on the other hand, expressed their conviction that "the Bulgarian claim for territorial revision has mainly a theoretical and sentimental character," and they emphasized that time should be allowed for "Bulgarian public opinion to bury the long existing revisionist illusions."[19] These statements indicated that Barthou better understood France's real situation (economic, military, and political) and changed the method of foreign policy implementation from the enforcement of the peace treaty to reconciliation.

Reaction to the Rome Protocols

On March 17, 1934, Italy, Austria, and Hungary signed the Rome Protocols,[20] an action which alarmed the members of the Little Entente. The French Left interpreted it as the alliance of Fascist and Revisionist states. Barthou, on the other hand, felt that "France has to cooperate with Italy in the rebuilding of the Danube Basin and welcomes the protocols," and he hoped that "the members of the Little Entente will find out that the Rome Protocols will be beneficial for them, as well as for Europe."[21] *Le Temps*, which had excellent connections with the French foreign ministry, had already published sympathetic articles about Austria in February 1934, giving Dollfuss' side of the story on the Social Democratic uprising in Vienna. The foreign ministry, in response to a reporter who had asked about the Leftist intellectual efforts to organize a committee for the investigation of the Austrian "massacre," expressed the opinion that "from the practical political point of view, the effect of the activity of that committee up to this time is insignificant."[22]

These articles and comments indicated that Barthou had taken the decision of the three Great Powers seriously and sought some kind of friendly understanding with Italy on a more "direct" nation-to-nation basis. However, before starting out on this scheme, realism demanded he try to salvage the French alliances with Poland and the Little Entente.

His visit to Poland was carefully monitored by the French press, which did not help create a friendly atmosphere when it referred to and even republished a February 5, 1934, *Yzvestija* article that called the German-Polish Non-Aggression Pact "a denial of the French-Polish Alliance of 1921."[23] The main reasons for Barthou's failure to reconcile Poland, however, were not the hostile French public opinion and press. The reasons already existed in 1933; but by signing the Non-Aggression Pact with Germany, Poland reached the point of no return. Barthou concluded after his trip that "France cannot count on Poland anymore, and it is, therefore, urgent and necessary to befriend Italy."[24]

Barthou's visit to Czechoslovakia was refreshing after the Warsaw experiment. The Czechs displayed their friendly feelings toward France;[25] their policy was one of strict pro-status quo. Benes was sympathetic toward the Rome Protocols and agreed with Barthou that it was a further assurance against the *Anschluss*.[26] The Czech army was the best equipped and strongest army in Central Europe; and Benes, revising his former judgment, accepted the French position that Czechoslovakia's main enemy was no longer Hungary but Hitler's Germany.[27]

The news from Rumania also appeared reassuring. Though Titulescu, the Rumanian foreign minister, still refused to consider the possibility of Russian military aid, he became more flexible toward Italy and expressed his conviction to a French news reporter that "only an entente with Italy can bring the necessary relaxation which is needed to solve the problems of Central Europe."[28]

The creation of a common front with Italy seemed the best solution. Not the French-Italian differences, but the differences between the clients of the two governments hindered the French-Italian rapprochement. Because both states considered their clients indispensable, both governments made reassuring statements to them. During his visit to Hungary, Fulvio Suvich, the assistant secretary of Italian foreign affairs, expressed his feeling that "my joy would be greater only if I could have stepped on the soil of Great Hungary instead of the present, mutilated Hungary."[29] This declaration alarmed the Little Entente, which demanded reassurance from Barthou against a revisionist attempt. The creation of a French-Italian understanding, therefore, seemed distant because of the conditions in Central Europe.

The Eastern Pact Proposal

In the absence of an immediate better solution, Barthou renewed the plans of the Paul-Boncour government concerning the creation of an Eastern Locarno. Barthou regarded the participation of the Soviet Union in the Eastern Locarno as the most important condition for the security of France. He could not create a simple French-Soviet alliance because "he could neither challenge the Locarno Pact, nor appear to turn away from the spirit of the League of Nations."[30] The idea of an Eastern Locarno seemed to solve this problem. Stalin had indicated Soviet willingness to take part in such a plan when, in January 1934, he told the XVII Congress of the Soviet Communist Party: "if the interest of the Soviet Union demands rapprochement with one or another country which does not want to disturb the peace, we shall do so without hesitation."[31]

The undisguised admiration of French military experts for the Soviet armed forces also urged rapprochement with the Soviet Union. On May 18, 1934, Barthou met with Litvinov to discuss the Eastern Pact; he was accompanied by General Maurice Gamelin as military advisor. Advocating a French-Soviet rapprochement because "Russia represented the only really great Eastern counterweight needed against Germany," Gamelin stated that the French military leaders attached great importance to a

French-Soviet military collaboration, from which they hoped to obtain *not so much actual Russian military aid* as the intensification of the French military build-up.[32] (italics added)

Litvinov responded positively to the French suggestions. Barthou, having on April 11 already secured the consent of England[33] to the Soviet Union's membership in the League of Nations, began to make the necessary preparations and, at the same time, announced his great plan for an Eastern Locarno.

The Barthou-Litvinov discussions represent a turning point in the foreign policy of Barthou. Up to that time, he had rightly evaluated the realistic political conditions. Although he failed to bring Poland back to the French alliance, he was successful in reassuring the Little Entente, especially Czechoslovakia. He tried to initiate a rapprochement with Italy and, as far as Austrian independence was concerned, succeed. Then, after so much success, he suddenly gave in to the pressure of the French Left and the French General Staff, and he began a rapprochement with the Soviet Union.[34] It was a fatal mistake, not because a Soviet alliance promised no positive security for France, and therefore was not a question of first importance, but rather because of its consequences.

It indicated to Germany that French power had declined to the point where, instead of enforcing the peace through unilateral actions based on her military might,[35] France was frightened to act alone. It proved not only to Germany, but to the whole world as well, that France's military power was in such an inferior and handicapped position that her hope no longer lay in the strength of her army, but in international agreements that would provide security for France without forcing her to rebuild her own army. In other words, France wanted to maintain her superiority in Europe by asking others to make the necessary sacrifices,[36] and the Eastern Pact did not conceal this goal. The former obligations and alliances of France became unimportant[37] in the basic idea of the Eastern Pact: to gain guarantees for the Rhine frontier *without French participation.* The Soviet Union, being the only Great Power to express her willingness to participate in the Eastern Pact, was designated by France to control Central Europe. The German accusation that the Eastern Pact would only increase the Soviet influence in Central Europe was not unfounded.

The consequences of Barthou's Eastern Pact proposal were great. Britain disliked the idea of a French-Soviet alliance; Poland, on whose cooperation Soviet help depended, stubbornly refused to grant passage rights to Soviet troops and made her joining conditional on German acceptance; and a skeptical Italy prepared counterproposals.[38]

In essence, the idea of the Eastern Pact did more damage for France than good. It *did not* increase the security of France; it *did not* restore the Polish-French alliance; it *did not* bring the English government out of isolation; it *did not* dismiss Yugoslavian suspicions concerning a French-Italian rapprochement; it *did not* gain Rumania's unconditional approval; and it *did not* oblige even the Soviet Union to subscribe to French designs. However, most important of all, it *did not* help the Central European states solve their immediate economic problems. It *did*, on the other hand, create a greater Hungarian hostility toward France, engender suspicion in Italy, leave the door wide open for the continuous German economic penetration of Central Europe, and help pave the road for a Hitler-Mussolini meeting.

The negative results were overwhelming; the positive achievement was almost nil. One may wonder what made Barthou, who was such a strong realist, follow this line. One explanation is that the whole idea of the pact was aired for tactical reasons: "Though France knows that among others, neither England, Italy, nor Poland will accept the pact, she offers it so that in case of a refusal, she may put the responsibility for the failure of the disarmament and peace on these powers."[39] Even if this "tactical" success was achieved, its value was questionable. A more acceptable reason was the French domestic situation where political scandals were neither solved nor stopped, financial reform was a flop, and work programs were ineffective.[40] "The unhappy conditions in the Chamber[41] indicated disunity among the deputies. Forming a block, the Socialists and Communists decided to strengthen their attacks against the government; foreign observers did not see much chance for the Doumergue government to survive the autumn.[42]

Following the Barthou-Litvinov meeting in Geneva, however, this situation suddenly changed. The question of survival justified, from the government's point of view, the tactical step expressed in the proposal for the Eastern Pact. If the Doumergue government would have fallen, the "anti-Fascist" block would have followed a stronger pro-Soviet policy. By making concessions, Barthou secured the government's position and kept the door open for a possible and vital French-Italian rapprochement, a plan which he advocated from the beginning.[43]

For the time being, the Italian rapprochement did not promise too much success. Barthou delayed his visit to Italy, and the government indicated that such a meeting could take place only if Mussolini should ask for it.[44] Hitler was not so proud, and he realized that this was the right moment to approach Mussolini. On June 14-15, 1934, the two dictators met in Venice, which came as a surprise to the French government. While he shared Hitler's negative views concerning the Eastern Pact, Mussolini was completely hostile to Hitler's plans for Austria.[45] From the French point of view, this meant that Mussolini proved to be a trustworthy ally for the containment of Germany, and Hitler's visit did not present an obstacle in the way of a rapprochement with Italy. However, after the Hitler-Mussolini meeting, French public opinion became suspicious and "did not value the possibility of an entente with Italy."[46] The opposing politicians explained that Italy was a Great Power with a population equal to France, and that alone was reason enough to be discontent.[47] French government circles, on the other hand, stressed the necessity of a Barthou-Mussolini meeting, but added that "it would make sense *only after all the differences* have been settled between France and Italy."[48] (italics added) This indicated an unwillingness to accept compromise, and so it meant the postponement of the Italian visit—forever.

When Barthou visited England to enlist her support for the Eastern Pact, he also tried to obtain British pressure to make Mussolini more agreeable toward the pact. France believed that because of Italy's long seashores she could not resist an English demand.[49] But, the slow-moving French diplomacy was then surprised by the Austrian Nazi Putsch and Mussolini's reaction to it.

The Nazi Putsch in Vienna

The Nazi Putsch in Vienna on July 25, 1934, created a crisis for Barthou. To act immediately with energy and decisiveness would demand some military demonstration either alone or in harmony with Italy and Czechoslovakia. But the French army was organized for defense; just a few divisions were motorized, and their provisions were sufficient for only six months.[50] No commercial or military agreement took care of further provisions, especially of motor fuels. To chance a possible prolonged armed conflict with Germany would be risky. It was necessary to secure England's consent and help, but England's attitude was characterized by the absence of her ambassadors from Berlin and Rome. They were vacationing in London and did not intend to interrupt their vacations because of the Austrian crisis.[51] The Czech army, though superior in strength to the German army, also was trained only for defensive purposes and had no strategic plans prepared for such a situation.[52]

Only Italy acted with swiftness, moving four divisions to the Brenner Pass. However, instead of relief, this caused even greater "nervousness" in French diplomatic circles, and Barthou warned Mussolini about the unforeseeable consequences of further isolated steps on the part of Italy.[53] The French nervousness was understandable. A good part of the Czech press and the whole Yugoslavian press openly raised the matter that "France has to get out from the anti-German front of the Great Powers or has to deny her political and military solidarity with Yugoslavia."[54] If France did not give up her solidarity with Yugoslavia, it would mean—as the Austrian ambassador put it—that she would be "incriminating" Austria.[55]

France tried to avoid an open stand, though she recognized that "the price she has to pay for the preservation of Austria is cheaper than what she would have to pay in case of Austria's collapse."[56] No action followed up this conclusion, though. The only step the French took was a great press campaign, in which they proved beyond a doubt Hitler's responsibility for the Austrian Nazi Putsch.[57]

Barthou suggested two alternatives to avoid the possible repetition of the crisis:[58] Austria should secure the promise of Germany, through direct negotiations, to discontinue the Nazi propaganda in Austria; or a general pact should be signed which would oblige the contracting parties to respect the principle of nonintervention, to refrain from interfering in the domestic affairs of other states, to tolerate no subversive activity on their own soil directed against a foreign state. Neither of these was satisfactory for Austria. On the other hand, Austria readily accepted Mussolini's suggestion that "the Three Great Powers who are interested in the preservation of Austria's independence should announce with the greatest firmness and clearness that they will not tolerate either an *Anschluss* or a *Gleichschaltung,*" and this declaration "should be worded so *categorically and brutely* that not only Berlin, but also her sympathizers in Austria would understand it and would give up every hope of realization of their goals."[59] (italics added) The French answer to these suggestions was negative.

In the eyes of Austria, Italy remained her only sure champion. In the eyes of the Little Entente, the insecure feeling grew stronger. It was time, especially for Austria, to review her foreign relations and, if necessary, change them according to her basic interests.

CHAPTER V
THE SECOND CRISIS:
MURDER OF CHANCELLOR DOLLFUSS

Conditions in Austria

The first half of 1934 continued to be a time of great tension and of temporary diplomatic successes and setbacks for Austria. Although the rowdy German propaganda campaign was softened to a certain degree, Hitler had not given up his plans for the *Gleichschaltung* of Austria. He kept the economic pressure on,[1] while diplomatically trying to isolate Dollfuss from the rest of Europe.[2] Austria, however, was a member of the League of Nations, and Dollfuss considered the support of this international organization to be of primary importance. He was prepared to present the Austrian grievances against Germany in the next League session.[3] At the same time, he successfully tried to secure the assistance of Britain, France, and Italy and received their support in the Three Power Declaration of February 17, 1934.

Ironically enough, this support was lost the same day as the declaration was published because of the Social Democratic revolt in Vienna. The revolt was crushed mercilessly, and the Social Democratic Party was outlawed—actions which alienated the Western democracies as well as the Little Entente states.[4] So Austrian isolation came about not through German diplomatic steps, but because of domestic events in Austria. The declaration of the Rome Protocols in March, however, seemed to compensate for the lost Western support. Even more favorable for Austria was the outcome of the June Hitler-Mussolini meeting in which Mussolini warned Hitler that Austrian independence was a main concern of Italy. Dollfuss seemed to have secured for Austria the time needed to introduce the "corporative state" system step by step.

Then, on July 25, 1934, the Austrian Nazis attempted to overthrow the government. Though the attempt was unsuccessful, Dollfuss was murdered during the attack. His successor, Kurt von Schuschnigg, was convinced that in order to save Austrian independence, he "had to embark on a course of appeasement. This meant that everything had to be avoided which would give Germany a pretext for intervention, and that everything had to be done to secure some way for Hitler's toleration of the status quo."[5] Thus, Schuschnigg apparently had made up his mind concerning the possible alternatives for Austrian foreign policy and found the solution in the good graces of Hitler. Yet, the events following the misfired Nazi coup—such as the Italian troop movements, Mussolini's declaration, and the sudden decrease of German militancy[6]—indicated that he could have chosen another course for Austria, possibly even an anti-German one.

Hitler had hoped to realize the *Gleichschaltung* of Austria without using force. Austrian economic conditions were deteriorating, and Hitler thought that by speeding up the economic decline through the application of pressures (such as the restriction of German tourist traffic), he could cause the downfall of the Austrian government and prepare the way for a Nazi takeover. To understand the political developments, then, it is necessary to know a few details of the economic conditions in Austria.

Economic Conditions

Since the end of World War I, Austria had experienced acute economic problems. These problems were caused partly by the consequences of the St. Germain Treaty ("head without an empire") and partly by the Nationalist Protectionist Economic Policy[7] which was practiced all over Europe in the late 1920's. A custom union with Germany could have helped, but it was prohibited by the peace treaty. The Tardieu Plan (custom union of the Central European states under French patronage) was blocked by England and Italy. Being alone and not having fertile plains and great material resources, Austria was hit by the depression and the economic crisis more than any other country in Central Europe.

Between the years of 1922-1934, the Austrian population decreased by 1-2 percent, which amounts to 107,680 in a country of 5,384,000 people.[8] The actual working population numbered 3,134,000 or 58.2 percent. The unemployment rate reached its peak (480,000) during the winter of 1933 and remained high (440,000) in 1934 with the industrial workers being the greatest number (44.5 percent) of unemployed.[9]

In 1933, more than half of Austria's import and export business was transacted with Germany, Czechoslovakia, Poland, and Yugoslavia.[10] However, in order to draw valid conclusions concerning the influence of the political situation on the economic conditions and vice versa, it is necessary to group Austria's trade partners into friendly, neutral, and unfriendly blocks. The friendly countries in 1933 were Germany, Hungary, and Italy and in 1934, only Hungary and Italy. Those outspokenly hostile in 1933 were Czechoslovakia, Rumania, Yugoslavia, and France; but in 1934, Germany also entered this group, while France moved into the neutral block, which consisted of Poland, Switzerland, and England in 1933, and was joined by France in 1934.

Thus, while in 1933 Austria's foreign trade was fairly distributed among the friendly (34.3 percent import and 30.2 percent export), hostile (28.7 percent import and 22 percent export), and neutral (23.3 percent import and 29.1 percent export) blocks, in 1934. Austria's foreign trade pattern altered so that 45 percent of her import and 34 percent of her export trade depended on hostile nations, 22.9 percent import and 31 percent export on neutral nations, and only 15.2 percent import and 14.2 percent export on friendly nations.

Austrian economic interests demanded a good political relationship with all of her trading partners; even the smallest economic malfunction of her import-export trade could create a grave crisis. The German tourist restrictions were intended to do just that.

Political Conditions

On March 9, 1933, Chancellor Dollfuss, using a law passed during the war, assumed "emergency power" and began to rule by decree. He was thereby freed from a possible parliamentary defeat,[11] but he still lacked mass support. The Nazi movement, due to Hitler's vigorous backing, grew stronger and attracted many Pan-Germans, who had supported the government's policy. Receiving encouragement from Mussolini, Dollfuss banned the Nazi Party in Austria on June 19, 1933. In February of the next year, again with Mussolini's encouragement, Dollfuss organized a showdown with the Social democrats, who had been secretly receiving arms from Czechoslovakia.[12] This was followed by the March 17 signing of the Rome Protocols, which were designed not only to provide new commercial agreements between Austria, Hungary and Italy, but also to give some kind of guarantee against a German attempt at Austrian annexation. Then, on May 1, Dollfuss announced a new constitution, fashioned after the Italian corporate state system. The ground work was laid for a relatively sound course of Austrian consolidation.

The murder of Dollfuss and the unsuccessful Nazi *coup* created some unrest, but the government held firm. Mussolini's reaction proved to Hitler that it was more profitable for him to stop supporting the Austrian Nazis and thereby avoid creating more disturbances.

When Schuschnigg took over the chancellorship, Austria was dependent on the economic cooperation of the Little Entente states as well as Italy, Hungary and Germany. On the other hand, the Little Entente and Germany were sharp political opponents of Austria, both fearing a possible restoration of the Habsburg Monarchy.[13] In the field of domestic policy, the two most aggressive opponents of the Austrian government, the Social democrats and the Nazis, were defeated. The murder of Dollfuss spiritually united the Austrians, with exception of the Socialists; but they did not have real power anymore. Schuschnigg was in the unique position to select and pursue a foreign policy that would best serve the interests of Austria.

Alternatives for Austrian Foreign Policy

In directing Austrian foreign policy, Schuschnigg could have chosen from the following main alternatives: *continue Dollfuss' policy* by further strengthening relationships with Hungary and Italy, maintaining friendly relations with Germany (though firmly standing up to the Nazi *Gleichschaltung* plans), and maintaining "cool" but correct economic connections with France and the Little Entente states; start *a new policy of appeasement with Germany,* placing Austrian independence more at the grace of Hitler than the Rome Protocols; or completely change the traditional line, initiating a *rapprochement with France* and the Little Entente states at the price of losing the support of Hungary and possibly Italy. It is important to understand the possible advantages and disadvantages of these alternatives.

Continuation of Dollfuss' Policy

Strengthening Relations with Hungary

Relations with Hungary had been most cordial since the signing of the new commercial treaty and the Rome Protocols. However, Hungary did not offer too much security for Austria against the German danger. On

Schuschnigg's first visit to Hungary, Horthy told him: "For poor Austria, which I love and know almost like my own fatherland, there is nothing left but to seek unification with the German Reich."[14] If a substantial number of people thought along this line (and they did), then Hungary certainly did not represent a country of special value to Austrian independence.

There were other opinions in Hungary concerning the future of Austria, however, such as the conviction of Prime Minister Gömbös who considered a great Germany to be a dangerous neighbor and, therefore, emphatically asserted his interest in Austrian independence.[15] At the same time, though, he did not believe that the *Anschluss* could be delayed forever.[16]

A constant fear of an Austrian Habsburg restoration was noticeable not only in the Little Entente states, but also in Hungary. The Habsburg restoration question was the first item that Schuschnigg had to explain during his Hungarian visit. There was a Legitimist group in Hungary, not large, but powerful and influential—the Catholic higher clergy, a good number of the aristocracy, and a few higher ranking army officers who had served in the Kaiserliche und Königliche (KUK) Army. Horthy, himself an admirer of the Monarchy, said to Schuschnigg, "If the old Empire were to be re-established, I would walk on my two feet, no matter how great the distance, to offer my services again."[17] This kind of nostalgia, however, did not influence his realistic actions. As early as 1922, Horthy had blocked the way of a Habsburg restoration in Hungary,[18] and in 1934 he believed a restoration was "no longer within the range of possibility."[19]

Gömbös and the new generation of Hungarian politicians were strongly anti-restorationists. They wanted to modernize Hungary, and they saw the Fascist and Nazi systems as models. Thus, a monarchist restoration would prevent the realization of their plans, while the German "solution" to the Austrian problem would effectively block any Habsburg restoration attempt.[20] Although Schuschnigg declared to Gömbös that "an active monarchist policy was nothing but romantic nonsense," he also remarked that, privately and personally, he was a monarchist.[21] Schuschnigg had the impression that his comments satisfied Gömbös, however, Gömbös actually worked more diligently from then on for the "German solution."[22]

Hungary, therefore, represented very weak support for Austrian independence since the Hungarian fear of a Habsburg restoration in Austria directed Hungary to Germany's side. Although not welcoming a strong Germany as a next door neighbor, Horthy and Gömbös' considered this less dangerous than restoration.

For Schuschnigg to follow Dollfuss' policy concerning Hungary would be naive and unrealistic. Although it was in Austria's interest to maintain friendly relations with Hungary in 1934, Schuschnigg had to realize that this friendship was temporary, and the most that could be expected from Hungary in case of a German-Austrian open conflict was neutrality. Even this neutrality was questionable, because Austria included the former Hungarian territory of Burgenland which was excluded only temporarily from Hungarian revisionist demands.[23] Schuschnigg had to seek security for Austria in other countries.

Strengthening Relations with Italy

Schuschnigg visited Mussolini in August 1934. Mussolini's reaction to the murder of Dollfuss and to the unsuccessful Nazi coup in Vienna seemed to be the best assurance for Austrian independence. However, Schuschnigg's "frank" answers to Mussolini's questions probably did not help to improve Austrian-Italian relations.

The first thing that Mussolini learned from Schuschnigg was the undesirability of Italian armed intervention in case of an *Anschluss* attempt. "The presence of Italian troops on our soil would have rendered the position of the Austrian government untenable," Schuschnigg explained; further, in case of Italian intervention, the Czechs and Yugoslavians would mobilize and possibly enter Austria, so that just "a demonstration of Italian military might" would be satisfactory.[24] What he particularly asked of Mussolini was to intervene with Hitler in order to curtail Nazi propaganda in Austria. However, Schuschnigg's restriction of the Italian military aid most probably forced Mussolini to think twice before taking any step against the *Anschluss*, especially since the French and British reactions to the July putsch had been far weaker than the Italian.

On the other hand, Mussolini expressed his belief that the strengthening of the Austrian and Hungarian armies, along with the expansion of commercial preference treaties between Italy, Austria and Hungary (forming almost a custom union), would create a united block of 60-70 million people, which undoubtedly would have great political weight in Europe.

The question of Habsburg restoration also arose. Mussolini declared that he was a monarchist, because "monarchy, as a stabilizing factor, was of the greatest value." Schuschnigg explained his personal convictions and then went on to say that a restoration would endanger Austria's existence. Mussolini understood the problem, but declared that Italy "would certainly not object" to a restoration.[25]

In the remainder of the conversation, Schuschnigg stressed the importance of peace for Austria and rejected Mussolini's idea that in case of a German attack on Czechoslovakia, Austria might incorporate southern Moravia. Mussolini, meanwhile, urged the speedy build-up of the Austrian armed forces and offered his help in it.[26]

Having had this conversation after his Budapest visit, Schuschnigg needed to clearly see the following: Mussolini wholeheartedly supported the idea of the Rome Protocols and wanted to go even further by creating a de facto custom union between Italy, Austria, and Hungary; Mussolini and Gömbös were far apart in their judgments concerning the Habsburg restoration and the necessity of an *Anschluss;* Mussolini had doubts, which Schuschnigg reinforced, about the feasibility of using Italian troops within Austria's borders; and Mussolini's support of Austrian independence was firm, but depended on possible future changes in Italian-German relations.

Logically, the conclusion that Schuschnigg ought to have drawn from these negotiations was that, for the present, Mussolini was Austria's best friend, but that this friendship would last only if a rapprochement did not develop between Italy and Germany. The best guarantee against such a rapprochement would be a French-Italian understanding. It was in Austria's interest, therefore, to prepare the way for such an understanding by normalizing her own relations with France and France's allies, especially Czechoslovakia. However, these negotiations should not endanger the unity of the Rome Protocols and, therefore, should be led in harmony with the Italian and Hungarian foreign political designs. Due to the hard revisionist line of the Hungarian government, though, this seemed to be an impossible task, yet one worth trying. These facts again suggested a foreign policy change for Austria.

Maintaining Relations with the Little Entente

Austria had common borders with two Little Entente states— Czechoslovakia and Yugoslavia—and while Yugoslavia was more concerned with Italy, Czechoslovakia's main interest focused on Germany. Of course, both states were equally cautious toward Hungary and Austria.

Czechoslovakia recognized the danger that Hitler's Germany represented, and Benes made every effort to enlist the backing of powers other than France. He wholeheartedly supported Barthou's Eastern Pact and, with less enthusiasm, the Balkan Pact. At the same time, he prepared the way for the Czech-Soviet Assistance Treaty, which was signed in May 1935.

Since they saw Germany as their greatest menace, most Czech statesmen hoped to lessen the German threat with these treaties. They also considered the independence of Austria to be in their own interest. The Rome Protocols, which created an uproar in Rumania and Yugoslavia, were interpreted in Czechoslovakia as a counterbalance to the *Anschluss* and, therefore, were received calmly and even with approval.[27] A real rapprochement, however, between Czechoslovakia and Austria was blocked for several reasons.

First, Benes, "up to the time of the Second World War, was very much concerned with the danger to Czechoslovakia represented by Austria and Hungary. The ideological problems complicated matters even further. Benes seemed to detect something too rightist for his taste in the regime of Dollfuss."[28] President Masaryk, on the other hand, was more concerned with reality and on September 27, 1933, expressed his conviction to the Austrian ambassador in Prague that a confederation of Austria, Czechoslovakia, and Hungary would give the necessary security for all three states. "If the three of us would unite again, it would be best for the whole of Central Europe. To put it concisely, it was necessary to create something like a new Austria-Hungary."[29] Even if Benes would be willing to accept Masaryk's plan, Austria certainly could not change her foreign policy so radically without consulting her allies (Italy and Hungary). The Hungarian revisionist policy was considered a real threat to the integrity of Czechoslovakia. Benes was very much afraid that Hungary would gain sufficient support from public opinion in England and France for a major revision of the peace treaty arrangements.[30] Thus, because of the rigid convictions of Benes and Gömbös, Austria would have to choose between Czechoslovakian and Hungarian friendship. Since the signing of the Rome Protocols, Italy and Hungary represented Austria's real friends. It would be naive to give up this existing friendship for a "possible" Czech friendship.

Another, obstacle in the way of an Austrian-Czech understanding was the question of the Habsburg restoration. The Hungarian, Rumanian and Yugoslavian governments were very much opposed to a Habsburg restoration in Austria and would have welcomed a declaration of similar feeling by the Austrian government. Interestingly enough, while the Austrian leaders never considered the restoration possible, they refused to make such a declaration.[31]

Finally there was the question of the Austrian Socialist émigrées who enjoyed political asylum in Czechoslovakia and directed a strong propaganda campaign against Austria, not only from Czech soil but also in Austria proper. They printed and smuggled in the *Arbeiterzeitung*, which was outlawed in Austria.[32]

Czechoslovakia considered an independent Austria an important link in her own security. For Austria to have closer cooperation with Czechoslovakia was a risk that might involve losing the support of Hungary and possibly Italy, unless an Italian-French rapprochement could pressure Czechoslovakia into removing some obstacles standing in the way of a more friendly Austrian-Czech relationship, and unless Italy could pressure Hungary to change her revisionist foreign policy. Without an Italian-French and a Czech-Hungarian rapprochement, the continuation of Dollfuss' policy of a cold and correct political relationship with the Little Entente states seemed to be the best course in order to at least secure their economic cooperation.

Maintaining Relations with France

A friendly relationship with France was a vital matter for Austria. France had a commanding role in the League of Nations, and Austria badly needed the help of this organization, not only politically (as a safeguard for Austria's independence) but also financially. In June 1932, the League agreed to grant Austria a loan of 300 million shillings; however, because of technical difficulties, the loan was not put into effect until the summer of 1933.[33] Meanwhile, Dollfuss established his authoritarian regime, outlawed the Nazi Party and destroyed the Social Democratic Party,[34] none of which improved Austria's image in France. Then in 1934, he attached Austria to the Rome Protocols, which caused France to consider Austria a member of the opposition that caused the failure of the Tardieu plan.

With the changes in the French government in February 1934, Austria hoped for the sympathy of France. The Three Power Declaration on February 17 was a positive sign of the improving relationship. However, it was clear that, from the French point of view, the Little Entente was much more important than Austria. The French indignation following the Nazi Putsch in July compared with the vehement reaction of Mussolini, further indicated to Austria the reliability and value of French patronage.

The rapprochement of Austria with France was a desirable goal, but only in harmony with Italian foreign policy. Continuing Dollfuss' foreign policy toward France seemed to be a good solution.

Maintaining Relations with Germany

The Nazi Putsch and the murder of Dollfuss changed the situation to the advantage of the Austrian government. As the German military attache pointed out in his report from Vienna, "The moral setback suffered by the aggressor is considerable, the initiative has passed to the other side."[35] The European reaction to the Nazi Putsch, and especially the Italian troop movements toward the Austrian frontier,[36] forced Hitler to abandon his annexation plans (at least for the time being). Hitler assured Schuschnigg, through the newly appointed German ambassador, Franz von Papen, that Germany was "determined, for the sake of a *détente* in Europe, to respect Austria's formal independence."[37]

In order to support these intentions with tangible proof, Hitler ordered the reorganization of some Nazi paramilitary groups in Austria (such as the *Kampfring*) into Relief Societies to be "concerned only with the cultural, social, and economic care of its members."[38] As far as the Austrian economic grievances (tourist traffic) were concerned, it seemed wiser not to open the German-Austrian frontier for a while.[39] On the other hand, Papen asked Schuschnigg to allow the exchange of ideas (newspapers), but Schuschnigg's reply was vague and emphasized that he would not allow Austria to become a colony or province of the German Reich.

Dollfuss' policy toward Germany seemed to be successful, so its continuation was desirable. A good relationship with Germany appeared to be on the horizon. The cornerstone of this relationship, however, was not so much an Austrian-German mutual understanding as an Italian-German disagreement.

New Policy of German Appeasement

There were many well-founded reasons why Austria should appease Germany. The economic interests of Austria demanded the normalization of German trade relations. A great number of Austrians (those supporting the government and, even more so, the Nazis) agreed with Schuschnigg that the "Austrians were not only a German-speaking people, but actually a German people and as such, they could never accept an anti-German combine."[40] This romantic idealization of German loyalty never influenced Germany, neither in the time of Bismarck, nor in the period of Hitler; but, astonishingly enough, it seemed to be the right attitude for the Austrians to have. It is also true that a great number of Austrians were opposed to the *Anschluss* idea.[41] Strangely enough, the Nazis found allies in the disappointed Austrian Socialists, who could not forgive the government for the February days. They sought revenge "in overalls or in brown shirts" against the regime that brought horror to them.[42]

The Schuschnigg government's survival at home depended on finding a *modus vivendi* with Germany, thus eliminating German interference in Austrian domestic affairs. Hitler's response to this Austrian aim was controversial. On August 6, 1934, he explained to the Hungarian foreign minister, Kálmán Kánya, that "if the Austrian government was able and willing to prove that they constituted the absolute majority of the German people in Austria, then German resistance to cooperation with Austria would automatically wane." This sounded like a threat to Austria. In the same conversation, however, Hitler stated that "Germany did not aspire to the acquisition of territory through the *Anschluss* of Austria," since *Anschluss* would mean "Germany would have to take over all economic and financial commitments which today, as a 'poor Reich', she would not be in a position to do."[43] That sounded like a renunciation of the *Anschluss*, but it did not eliminate the possibility of future interference in Austrian domestic affairs.

Two weeks later, Papen told Schuschnigg that Hitler was "not only determined to respect Austria's formal independence, but he also recognized Austria's right to settle her own internal affairs independently." This sounded reassuring. At the same time, though, Papen emphasized that the National Socialist's ideological revolution must "have repercussions beyond the frontiers of Germany, especially in a country with the same culture, customs, language, and tradition." The statements together sounded ambiguous. However, Papen then added that "If the present policy [of the Schuschnigg government] and the severe persecutions and sentences continued, fresh revolts might perhaps result." This was a clear statement that Germany did not give up her idea of the *Gleichschaltung*. She wanted to continue to work for it, not necessarily through a forceful annexation, but rather through the "ideological revolution" and its "repercussions."[44]

Schuschnigg knew of the role of the German government in the Nazi Putsch from the results of the investigation of the murder of Dollfuss. After he had received this and other information about the real intentions of Hitler, he certainly had to realize that an appeasement policy toward Germany would not satisfy Hitler. Instead of appeasement, he had to prepare to block possible future German threats to the integrity of Austria. It was clear that to trust the independence of Austria entirely to Italian goodwill would be a gamble. The natural choice in the selection of other guarantors had to be France and Britain. From the beginning of the fall of 1934, Schuschnigg tried to enlist the support of these two powers by trying to pave the way for a French-Italian understanding.[45]

Thus, a rapprochement with Germany would only endanger Austria's independence. To acquire greater security, Schuschnigg had to enlist Britain and France among the guarantors of Austrian independence. This probably would demand from Austria the creation of a better relationship with the Little Entente, which could lead to the alienation of Hungary and Italy but nevertheless was a possibility to be explored. Austria would profit even more if a common understanding were to be created between Italy and France.

Complete Change in Foreign Policy

After the February revolt, the Social Democratic Party, as well as the Communist Party, continued to work underground against the Austrian "totalitarian" regime. They enjoyed if not the support of the majority of Austrian workers, at least the support of their sister parties in other countries. With their help, the *Arbeiterzeitung* and the Communist *Rote Fahne* were printed abroad and smuggled into Austria. The Social

Democrats and Communist underground, with the help of sympathetic foreign newspapermen, tried to undermine the authority of the Dollfuss regime and used every occasion to discredit it in the eyes of foreign governments.

It is no wonder, then, that after the murder of Dollfuss, the British government (hoping that France and Italy would do likewise) recommended to Schuschnigg reconciliation with the Pan-German Nationalists and Socialists.[46] However, neither the Nazis nor the Socialists wanted simple cooperation with the government; both wanted to oust Schuschnigg and establish their own power.[47] Therefore, even attempting a reconciliatory policy would be risky for Schuschnigg; but if the Great Powers were willing to guarantee the independence of Austria, it certainly would be a risk worth taking. The Great Powers, however, did not offer anything other than "all possible moral support."[48] The cooperation and support of the Little Entente states had the same condition.

It seemed that the Western democracies were demanding the right to interfere in the internal affairs of Austria, and Schuschnigg was being forced to choose between the dangers of German and Western cooperation, both of which demanded the establishment of a regime to their own liking. At that point, thanks to the support of Italy, a government crisis was avoided. Without Italy, it was clear that both Britain and France were willing to give Austria *only moral support*, and only at a very high price. Therefore, a complete turnaround of Austrian foreign policy was not feasible, and it seemed best to follow Dollfuss' policy toward France and the Little Entente.

Schuschnigg's resignation was also a possibility, with the government being handed to a Social Democratic-Communist coalition. In that case, most probably a bloody civil war would have erupted with the terror directed especially against the former supporters of the government: the clerics and the Nazis.

The reaction of foreign governments to such a situation is easily predictable. The Little Entente would have applauded the turn of events; Italy and Hungary would have turned hostile; Germany most probably would have taken more aggressive measures, possibly an annexation attempt; France and Britain would have morally supported the Austrian regime. In other words, the annexation of Austria, which did not happen until 1938, could have occurred in 1935. But, of course, Schussnigg did not resign.

Schuschnigg's Foreign Policy

In January 1936, Schuschnigg visited Czechoslovakia to discuss economic problems[49] concerning the two countries. At the same time, the Austrian foreign minister, Baron Berger-Waldenegg, hoped for a possible friendship treaty with Czechoslovakia, which caused great anxiety in Hungarian government circles.[50] The new Czech prime minister, Milan Hodza, received Schuschnigg with real friendliness and fulfilled as much of the Austrian economic requests as he could.[51] However, even he could not overcome the deep hostility of the Czech population toward Austria. Schuschnigg's visit did not bring positive political results in Czechoslovakia; moreover, the trip created hostility in Hungary, Italy, and Yugoslavia. The German diplomacy used this visit very skillfully. For instance, the German ambassador to Budapest warned Kánya that Schuschnigg had made unfriendly remarks to Benes about Hungarian revisionst aims.[52] Hungary, while still regarding Austrian independence in the interest of Hungary, began diplomatically to prevent the realization of an Austrian-Czech rapprochement.[53]

When Mussolini expressed the view that he did not think it was time for him to interfere as mediator in the Austrian-German disagreement,[54] Schuschnigg felt it necessary to explain the Austrian policy toward the Little Entente. Further, he attempted to regain the goodwill of Italy by stating that Austria would not seek closer connections with the Little Entente without the consent of Italy and Hungary.[55] Thus, Schuschnigg's efforts to try a new, broader foreign policy than that of Dollfuss' failed. Austria remained completely dependent on Italy. Then, when the Ethiopian War weakened Mussolini's influence in Central Europe, Schuschnigg felt Austria's only chance for remaining independent lay in the goodwill of Hitler. Ultimately, this appeasement policy also failed.

Wanting to continue along Dollfuss' line of thinking in the field of domestic policy, Schuschnigg had to follow the course that he did: strengthen the government forces and fight the Nazis as well as the Social Democrats. However, this domestic policy limited his foreign political alternatives to the Rome Protocols. The independence of Austria was based on the theory that the Italian-German misunderstanding would never be resolved. At the same time Schuschnigg considered it too risky to base his country's independence on the French-German misunderstanding.[56] If Schuschnigg wanted to be consistent, he should not have considered the Italian-German differences to be eternal either. Yet, under the circumstances, Schuschnigg cannot be blamed. Austria was an artifically created state. By 1936 none of her patrons was willing to use force in order to support the independence of their own creation. Little Austria became the toy of Great Power politics, and her fate was decided by forces too great to challenge or openly oppose.

Impact of the Austrian Crisis on French Foreign Policy

The attitude and actions of the Little Entente states during and after the Austrian crisis revealed the "serious gaps of opinions within the French Alliance system concerning Austria's independence."[57] Austria's neighbors closed their borders to her with the exception of Germany and Yugoslavia. "Hungary strengthened her border guards to carefully filter out the refugees who arrived from Austria."[58] Czechoslovakia alerted her troops along the Austrian border, as well as along the *Hungarian border*, and ordered the arrest of Austrian Nazi refugees.[59] Yugoslavia moved seven battalions to the Austrian border, gave asylum to fleeing Austrian Nazis, and declared that "they will act in accord with the Great Powers if the Austrian situation should become more serious."[60]

The marching up of seven Yugoslavian battalions was not, however, in accord with the desire of the Great Powers, nor was the Czech mobilization along the Hungarian frontier. Both events brought home to Barthou some important lessons. Austrian independence was not considered a vital interest to Yugoslavia if it meant the strengthening of Italy's influence in Central Europe. The asylum given to the Nazi refugees indicated that Yugoslavia was more concerned about this growing Italian influence than about a possible *Anschluss*. The Czecho-slovakian reaction suggested that the Czechs were more afraid of a possible Italian-Hungarian occupation of Austria than of an *Anschluss*. Barthou's foreign political designs lay in ruins; France's security system proved to be practically worthless. Her allies simply rejected French leadership when their immediate interests demanded a different solution.

French politicians in government circles, as well as the opposition, did not fully understand these implications of the Austrian crisis. It appears, however, that Barthou realized that a complete reexamination of his foreign policy was necessary along the following lines: Was the Eastern

Pact still a promising combination? Was the independence of Austria more important for France than the unconditional support of Czechoslovakia and Yugoslavia? Was it possible to find a compromise in this question with Czechoslovakia and/or Yugoslavia? Was Mussolini's support worth more than Yugoslavia's? Was there any possibility for a compromise between Italy and Yugoslavia?[61]

First, Barthou found the answer to all these problems in the Eastern Pact. The French diplomacy renewed its efforts to convince the Polish government that it would be to their advantage to accept the French designs. The strong French pressure on Poland resulted, however, not in reconciliation, but rather in further alienation. In August, the Austrian ambassador reported that the French-Polish relation was "spoiled."[62]

Incidents in Poland and in France, such as the arrest of the French directors of the Polish Textile Trust in Jirardow and the expulsion of sixty alleged Communist mineworkers from France, helped to deteriorate the relationship. The French ambassador in Warsaw, Jean Laroche, presented a strongly worded *démarche* demanding the release of the French directors of the Textile Trust. The Polish reply, which stated the government would not intervene, was so offensively worded that Laroche wanted to leave Warsaw, and he stayed only because of his government's strong advice. Barthou threatened the Polish ambassador in Paris with the end of French economic and political support if Poland continued a German rapprochement policy, to which the ambassador responded that France "cannot free herself" from the mistakes of the previous French governments, which treated their allies as "vassals."[63]

The situation ended in a hopeless deadlock with Germany (on September 5, 1934) and then Poland (on September 27, 1934) refusing to participate in the Eastern Pact. Barthou rescued what he could, but in the Little Entente, only Czechoslovakia paid attention to the German menace. Yugoslavia's main concern was Italy. Losing Polish support, and realistically evaluating the weight of any possible Soviet help, Barthou had to realize that the only rescue for France was represented in stronger British support and a closer relationship with Italy.

British support was looked upon as being of doubtful value. It is true that Stanley Baldwin stated in the House of Commons: "When you think of the defense of England, you no longer think of the chalk cliffs of Dover; you think of the Rhine—that is where our frontier lies."[64]

However, this statement did not mean that Britain was backing French policy. She opposed Barthou's Eastern Pact designs; she recommended reconciliation with Germany; she did not prepare herself to live up to her promises. Logically, then, Barthou interpreted the Baldwin declaration not as a guarantee of French security, but as a British design to use France's Rhine frontier for the security of Britain.

When the reaffirmation of the Three Power Declaration concerning the independence of Austria was published on September 27, 1934, Barthou was already preparing a visit with Mussolini, to settle, first of all, the problems existing between Yugoslavia and Italy.[65] The time was ripe as Mussolini wanted to have an understanding with France. In order to show his goodwill, he supported the French proposal to invite the Soviet Union into the League of Nations, while the Italian press conducted a strong press campaign against Germany. The only condition of an Italian rapprochement was the desire to avoid further alienating Yugoslavia, who displayed a growing pro-German sympathy.[66]

Barthou thus found the following answers to the problems created by the Austrian crisis: the idea of the Eastern Pact proved impractical; Austria's independence remained of primary interest to France; Czechoslovakia was inclined to consider better relations with Austria; the rapprochement with Italy became urgent and seemed feasible; there was a chance to find a compromise between Italy and Yugoslavia; and the League of Nations, with the Soviet Union included in it, would perhaps become a stronger instrument for France against Germany, as well as against any other attempt to modify the status quo.

Barthou did not have time to realize this new foreign policy of a French-Italian alliance fortified by the Little Entente and the Rome Protocols, with a sympathizing Soviet Union against a German-Polish alliance and a hesitating England. Just when he wanted to take his first step toward the realization of his new designs, Barthou was cut down by an assassin's bullet along with King Alexander of Yugoslavia. The assassination, on October 9, 1934, created a new international crisis and put in the governments of France and Yugoslavia new leaders, who once again had to make decisions concerning the grand strategy of their respective states in relation to the rest of Europe.

CHAPTER VI
THE THIRD CRISIS:
ASSASSINATION OF KING ALEXANDER

Foreign Policy of King Alexander

The main principle of Yugoslavian foreign policy under King Alexander was the maintenance of the status quo. This policy determined clearly Yugoslavia's enemies and allies. Italy was her strongest enemy; up to the spring of 1934, the King relied on French support against Italian aims. Next in the row of enemies stood Hungary, Austria, and Bulgaria. Hungary, encircled by the Little Entente, was weak economically and even weaker militarily. It was true that Hungary could not threaten Yugoslavia unless in alliance with Italy, and only if Czechoslovakia and Rumania did not honor their obligations determined in the mutual assistance treaties. However, what the Little Entente feared was not so much Hungary's military power as a possible Habsburg restoration,[1] or even the coronation of another person as king of Hungary.

The common tradition of the peoples living in the Danube Basin, the long (though not always peaceful) cooperation of the minority groups of the Habsburg Empire, the common economic problems of the area, and the nostalgia many people living in the Little Entente states felt for the "good old days" made the idea of a Hungarian kingdom very attractive, even with an empty throne. With a king on the throne, a chain reaction might be triggered which could lead to the dissolution of the successor states. At the same time, the Austrian activities concerning a possible Habsburg restoration were greatly exaggerated in the minds of the Little Entente leaders due to the misinformed reports they received from their ambassadors.[2] Hungary and Austria were also dangerous because of their aid and comfort to the Croatian refugees. Bulgaria, likewise a revisionist state, represented an even more vivid danger because of her support of the Macedonian revisionist and terrorist groups.

The fronts were therefore sharply drawn: Italy, Hungary, Austria, and Bulgaria were the enemies; France, the Little Entente, and the Balkan Pact[3] nations were the allies. It was a simple foreign policy, easily understood by every Yugoslavian patriot.

In the field of economic interests, however, the international relations of Yugoslavia could not be directed according to nationalistic principles alone. The best buyers of Yugoslavian grain, meat, timber, etc. were Italy, Austria, Germany, and Hungary.[4] France, with her well-balanced economy, did not need Yugoslavian raw materials or food products. Among her other allies, only Greece (food export) and Rumania (oil export) played any significant role. Thus, a basic contradiction developed between Yugoslavian political strategy and her economic interests.

King Alexander realized the precarious position his country was in and took the first steps toward the harmonization of political and economic policy. The King already had established secret negotiations with Mussolini in 1932.[5] After two years, through, Mussolini put an end to these negotiations by refusing to see Bogoljus Jevtic, when he came to Rome with a secret message from the King.[6] In the spring of 1934, a successful coup in Bulgaria put into power a pro-Yugoslavian government which began at once to restrict and liquidate the IMRO forces in Bulgaria.[7]

Similarly, a secret Hungarian rapprochement with Yugoslavia meant an end to the USTASHE movement in Hungary. The first steps of this rapprochement were taken in 1933 by Horthy, through his military attache in Belgrade. Horthy hoped that Hungary would come to an understanding with her southern neighbor, "thanks to the long common tradition and common fate" of Serbia and Hungary.[8] One obstacle to that understanding was the fact that the Croatian refugees who received political asylum in Hungary very often had committed terrorist activities in Yugoslavia before their escape.[9] In the summer of 1933, the Yugoslavian chief of staff suggested to the Hungarian military attache a very unorthodox method of solving the Croatian refugee problem: "It would do a great service to Hungary, as well as to the Hungarian-Yugoslavian rapprochement, if you would close your eyes for a night. During that night we would cross the border to Janka Puszta and would solve the Croatian emigrant problem."[10] Instead of accepting this proposal, the Hungarian government sent the Croatian refugees to Lausanne, where Eugen Kvaternik organized their immigration to other European countries.[11]

In September 1934, King Alexander met personally in Sofia with King Boris of Bulgaria, further promoting a mutual understanding between the two countries.[12] Communication lines were also opened secretly with Hungary, though seemingly without results.[13] This rapprochement policy of King Alexander with Italy, Bulgaria, and Hungary was in harmony with French political designs. France sought a rapprochement with Italy against the growing danger of Germany. A rapprochement between Hungary and Yugoslavia could ease the tension between Italy and Yugoslavia and promote a better understanding between France and Italy. However, this French policy made Czechoslovakia and Rumania suspicious. Benes and Titulescu worked against such an understanding, undercutting Mussolini's Four Power Pact to such a degree that the final text of the pact "pledged rather the maintenance of the status quo than the alteration of it."[14]

Meanwhile, both the IMRO and USTASHE lost ground in 1934 due to the skillful diplomacy of King Alexander. No wonder that both organizations looked upon him as their most dangerous enemy. In 1929, they had agreed upon joint terrorist actions to liberate Croatia and Macedonia;[15] it was time to again act in cooperation, now for the assassination of King Alexander. Thus, on October 9, 1934, during this confusing international situation, the shot at Marseilles was fired which killed Barthou and King Alexander and put Yugoslavian foreign policy at the crossroads.

EFFECTS OF THE ASSASSINATION

Question of Responsibility

Without going into great detail, certain aspects of the regicide need to be repeated and explained because they had a decisive effect on the foreign policy of Yugoslavia. The assassin, later identified as Vlado Gheorghieff Tchetnozemsky, was caught quickly by the police, severely injured, and died the same day. Although often described as an USTASHE, Tchetnozemsky was a member of the Macedonian IMRO and had come into contact with the USTASHE only after 1931.[16] His accomplices, captured a few days later, were Croatians and probably members of the USTASHE. The French investigation discovered that their Czechoslovakian passports were forgeries. They traced the two men back to Lausanne, where it was found that they once used Hungarian passports to register at a hotel.[17] The first results of the investigation thus directed every attention towards Hungary.

Then, the League of Nations' investigation discovered that the assassination was planned by the USTASHE's Ante Pavelic and Kvaternik, both of whom escaped to Italy. Mussolini refused to extradite them because the French had never extradited anyone implicated in an attempt against the Duce's life.[18] Increasingly, it appeared that Italy might be more involved in the case than Hungary. A Little Entente press campaign, led by Czechoslovakian and Rumanian papers, began against Italy and Hungary; however, neither England nor France wanted to endanger the French-Italian rapprochement which, since the assassination of Austrian chancellor Dollfuss, had reached very hopeful stages.[19] Even French-Italian military cooperation against a German attack was worked out on the drafting boards.[20] On October 15, 1934, Pierre Laval was appointed successor to Barthou. In his inaugural speech he blamed Hungary, alone and by name, for the assassination.[21] Unless the Little Entente states, among them Yugoslavia, wanted to create a breach with their French patron, they would have to accept Laval's statement.

Hungary fought against the charges by every means available, revealing to Eden and Laval at a secret meeting the story of the passports as it really happened.[22] However, Benes and Titulescu went so far in their accusations against Hungary that the public revelation of the truth (excluding the responsibility of Italy) "would have mortally damaged their credibility and trustworthiness."[23] Therefore, a compromise solution was worked out, at the suggestion of Eden; and on December 10, 1934, the League of Nations Council adopted the resolution without change.

The League resolution stated that "certain Hungarian authorities may have assumed at any rate through negligence, certain responsibilities relative to acts having connection with the preparation of the Marseilles crime."[24] This referred to the undeniable fact that the Hungarian passports of the two Croatian terrorists were genuine. The Hungarian government was asked to take appropriate punitive "action at once against any of its authorities, whose guilt could be established."[25] With this resolution, the whole passport affair was forgotten and accepted as closed. The truth of the matter, however, was that the Hungarian authorities had issued the passports, not only to the men involved in the assassination, but to some thirty other Croatian political refugees.[26] Although the Hungarian government, even the Intelligence Department of the General Staff, was innocent in the preparation of the regicide,[27] in such a tense atmosphere the revelation of the Hungarian government's role in providing the passports could have created an embarrassing situation.

Reaction in Yugoslavia

King Alexander was succeeded to the throne by his son Peter II, who was only eleven years old. In his name, according to the King's will, a regency was to govern Yugoslavia until 1941. The members of the regency were Prince Paul, the cousin of King Alexander; Radenko Stankovic, minister of education; and Ivan Perovic, governor of Croatia.[28] The most important persons after the regents were General Pero Ziffkovic, Prime Minister Nikola Uzonovic, and Foreign Minister Jevtic.

General Ziffkovic was an ardent Serbian patriot and, at the beginning of the royal dictatorship, was prime minister and advisor to King Alexander.[29] Later, he was appointed commander of the Royal Guard and was also chief of the Serbian secret military organization.[30] He felt that the assassination created a favorable condition for him, on the one hand, to restore his own importance versus the civilians (especially against Jevtic who followed the moderate, reconciliatory foreign policy of the late King) and, on the other hand, to direct a mortal blow against the Hungarian revisionist policy. Yugoslavia had no plans for the invasion of Hungary, except in cooperation with the other Little Entente states.[31] The time seemed to be right to put that cooperation into effect.[32]

Prime Minister Uzonovic, an equally ardent Serbian patriot, believed that the Yugoslavian unity created by the assassination could be further strengthened by directing the attention of the Yugoslavians toward the external enemies of Yugoslavia, that is, against Italy and Hungary. Public opinion was especially hostile toward Italy. On October 28, 1934, in his first speech as prime minister, Uzonovic indicated that he would demand the complete revelation of the guilty persons connected with the assassination, that their responsibilities would be established and "indispensable sanctions applied."[33]

Prince Paul, the regent, seemed not to have much influence on foreign policy during his first days in power, though he was probably well informed. General Ziffkovic's membership in the newly appointed government indicated a turn toward strengthening the royal dictatorship, while the release from prison of Vladimir Macek—leader of the Croat (Separatists) Peasant Party—suggested a reconciliatory tendency toward the Croatian minorities. Yugoslavian foreign policy was still undecided. Only one thing was certain: no matter what direction the Yugoslavian policy would take, the criminals involved in the regicide had to be punished.

Foreign Minister Jevtic could be considered the only realistic politician at the time. While he was a good Yugoslavian patriot and believed in the undisputed preeminence of the Serbians in the leadership of Yugoslavia, he recognized that in terms of the international situation, a hasty Yugoslavian action could bring grave consequences to his country. He was ready to compromise and sought support not only from the Little Entente and Balkan Pact states, but from France as well. The following Laval-Jevtic negotiations led to an agreement between the two countries. Prime Minister Doumerque, in a speech to the Chamber of Deputies on November 6, 1934, reported: "Being aware of the dangers, which are threatening Europe, it became necessary [for Yugoslavia] to harmonize its government's actions with the actions of the Government of the [French] republic."[34] Thus, Yugoslavian foreign policy was forced to fall in line with French interests.[35]

There was only one episode during this period which could be considered an independent Yugoslavian action: the deportation of thousands of Hungarians from Yugoslavia. However, this was done by General Ziffkovic without the blessing of the Yugoslavian government, and when Eden expressed his dislike to Jevtic, the expulsions ceased.[36]

Reaction In France

Doumergue left no doubt in the speech he gave at Barthou's funeral[37] that he wanted to continue the existing French foreign policy. The appointment of Laval as foreign minister was the best manifestation of this desire, because Laval was known in diplomatic circles as a "stern and energetic politician." who wanted to create a close cooperation with Mussolini.[38] At the same time, he was known as a man who was firmly convinced of Germany's war guilt, but was "not an enemy of the German people."[39]

His first problem was the Yugoslavian reaction to the regicide of Alexander. It was so overwhelmingly bitter and aggressive against Hungary that French government circles were afraid Yugoslavia would send "an ultimatum to Hungary following the pattern of the Austrian-Hungarian ultimatum of 1914,"[40] led with similar results. Even more dangerous was the possibility that the Yugoslavian reaction toward Italy would once again raise the question for France of which was more precious, Yugoslavian or Italian friendship. France had to avoid this issue because she needed the friendship of both states. The best solution seemed to be to refer the problem to the Leaque of Nations, try to steer the new Yugoslavian leaders toward moderation,[41] and secure the continuous friendly attitude of Mussolini. This, however, was about all that Laval could do.

France, not having a common frontier with Yugoslavia nor vital economic influence in the country, could impress her own designs only through the goodwill of some Yugoslavian politicians and groups. It was now Yugoslavia's turn to make an important decision, one which would influence not only her future, but also the future of the whole existing French foreign political system.

Influence of the Assassination on Yugoslavian Foreign Policy

The final resolution of the League of Nations and the entire handling of the assassination question taught Yugoslavia some very bitter lessons. Their king was murdered, the real criminals escaped punishment, and Italy was not even mentioned among those who bore responsibility. The League of Nations proved to be an instrument in the chess game of the Great Powers. Yugoslavia's most trusted friend, France, forced the Yugoslavs to close their eyes to the guilt of Italy in order not to disturb the possibility of a French-Italian rapprochement. Clearly, French interests were more important than Yugoslavian interests—and the truth. The Little Entente states, who at the beginning loudly stressed their sympathy and support, calmed down and were not willing to risk any move against the wishes of the Great Powers. England, through Eden, played a key role in the whole affair. Again, England's interests proved to be more important than Yugolsavia's. Only one conclusion could be drawn: "Yugoslavia felt isolated both diplomatically and militarily."[42] It became the primary aim of Yugoslavian diplomacy, then, to break out of this isolation.

From among the alternatives open to Yugoslavia before the assassination, this bitter experience eliminated the possible adjustment of commercial treaties to the traditional foreign policy and made even more desirable the adjustment of foreign policy to economic interests. A rapprochement with Italy, if Yugoslavia wanted to keep the friendship of France (and for the time being she certainly needed this friendship) became necessary. A better relationship with Hungary, for the present, was out of the question; but in case of an Italian-Yugoslavian rapprochement, it could become a feasible policy. The Bulgarian-Yugoslavian relationship had not changed, while a closer relationship with Germany seemed to be a necessary security step in case France should be willing to sacrifice vital Yugoslavian interests in order to please Mussolini. It was clear that a compromise solution had to be found. A new ally presented itself during the sessions of the League of Nations: the Soviet Union.[43] However, direct help from the Soviet Union depended on Rumania's permission for Soviet troops to cross her territory, and Rumania seemed unwilling to grant that permission. Therefore, a possible alliance with the Soviet Union represented only moral, and not too anxiously sought, support for Yugoslavia.

Alternatives for Prince Paul

Alexander's will appointed Prince Paul as First Regent. He was disinterested in politics and preferred to spend his time with his art collection. Educated in England and more at home in London or Paris than in Yugoslavia, Prince Paul now had to reexamine the internal and international situation and then design a domestic and foreign policy which would best serve the interests of Yugoslavia and *primarily Yugoslavia.*

Domestic Policy

Yugoslavia seemed to be well unified under the royal dictatorship of King Alexander, but in reality, the country was very much divided. "Yugoslav patriotism remained a phrase: Serbian and Croatian chauvinism survived; social discontent and political rivalries were repressed by force but were not removed."[44]

Prince Paul could continue the existing domestic policy, but that would mean conditions in the country would not improve. The revisionist foreign powers would be able to continue to use Croatian discontent to promote their aims, which would make Croatian émigrées heroes in the eyes of the Croats living in Yugoslavia. On the other hand, it would probably secure a reign without much disturbance and without greater crisis for the time being. In the long run, however, the continuation of this policy would undoubtedly lead to a greater alienation of the people, strengthen the opposition, and endanger the very existence of the Yugoslavian nation-state.

The assassination of King Alexander created an unexpected unified response on the part of every minority group in Yugoslavia.[45] The continuation of an oppressive policy would certainly destroy this unity again. This unanimous indignation offered another alternative for the direction of domestic policy: promote better understanding between political factions and reconcile the alienated minority groups. Such a program would certainly speed up progress in the field of social and economic achievement and would strengthen the Yugoslavian state. The basic problem was represented by the Croatian minority. If they could be reconciled, then the Croatian emigrees would lose their influence, and the revisionist propaganda would become ineffective. This would enable the government to pursue its foreign political aims with more vigor and aggressiveness.

The possible disadvantage of such a reconciliatory policy was the demand of the Croatian minority for a greater share in the political life, even for autonomy. Compromise was possible, but it would signal to the minorities that Prince Paul was willing to give up the idea of a Yugoslavian nation-state and accept the idea of federalism, which undoubtedly would weaken the authority of the royal government. Some extremist groups would probably demand not only autonomy but complete separation, endangering the very existence of the Yugoslavian state. To give a greater voice to the people would possibly mean also that Yugoslavia might have to take into consideration some changes in her traditional foreign policy.

Comparing the advantages and disadvantages, the reconciliatory policy had great promise, but the pursuit of this policy had to be very cautious in order to avoid the greater dangers.

Foreign Policy

Following the traditional line of foreign policy—friendship with France, the Little Entente, and the Balkan Pact states, while maintaining a strong pro-status quo attitude toward Austria, Hungary, Italy, and Bulgaria—was one of the alternatives that Prince Paul could select. Though he possibly did not know about the rapprochement attempts of King Alexander, he had to be aware of the existing contradiction between Yugoslavia's foreign political and commercial treaties. In case of an international crisis or war, the very existence of the Yugoslavian economy would depend on the goodwill of hostile nations. Ending this dualism was the primary interest of Yugoslavia. The harmonization of foreign policy with the economic interests of the country could be pursued by adjusting the commercial treaties to the traditional foreign policy, adjusting foreign policy to economic interests, or finding compromise solutions if a radical solution would be impractical.

Adjusting the commercial treaties to the traditional foreign policy would be almost an impossible task. Yugoslavia simply could not find markets enough in the friendly countries, and finding new markets in neutral countries would take considerable time. A hasty action most certainly would create an economic depression, if not a crisis. Such a crisis would sharpen internal political conflicts, would destroy the unity created by the indignation over the King's murder and, therefore, would play into the hands of the enemies of Yugoslavia. This alternative was completely impractical for the existing situation.

Adjusting the foreign policy to the commercial interests would demand a rapprochement with Italy, Bulgaria, Hungary, and Germany.

Rapprochement with Italy

Rapprochement with Italy would be possible because of the French-Italian rapprochement, already an open aim of France. It would give Yugoslavia two Great Powers as friends. The question was, what would Italy be willing to do to express her goodwill toward Yugoslavia. The primary requirement as far as Yugoslavia was concerned was that Italy denounce her revisionist policy.[46] However, the events preceding the assassination of King Alexander pointed in the opposite direction. According to the French designs, it was Yugoslavia, not Italy, who was expected to make sacrifices for a better understanding, sacrifices which Yugoslavia was not willing to make.[47] This French action made Yugoslavia skeptical of a sincere French friendship.[48]

There were further drawbacks to a rapprochement with Italy. It would create a sharp division of opinion within Yugoslavia. Italian support given to the USTASHE was an open secret. Italy was not expected to change this attitude, which meant that Mussolini's interference in Yugoslavian domestic political affairs would continue. Thus, the advantage of such a rapprochement was great, but only if France could convince governent was involved in the assassination of King Alexander, Yugoslavian public opinion simply would not allow a rapprochement policy.

Rapprochement with Hungary

Rapprochement with Hungary would be an easier matter. The Hungarian government indicated her willingness to cooperate with Yugoslavia by liquidating the Croatian refugee organizations during the summer of 1934. On the other hand, the revisionist policy of Hungary had not changed. Even more discouraging, during his visit in Belgrade in 1934, Barthou displayed a great reserve in replying to a strong anti-Hungarian speech by Uzonovic.[49] It was evident that France wished to moderate Yugoslavian hostility toward Hungary. However, even if Hungary would be willing to modify her revisionist aims, rapprochement would endanger the friendship of Yugoslavia's natural allies, for Czechoslovakia and Rumania would reconsider their policy toward Yugoslavia. Both countries were strong militarily and represented real force on Yugoslavia's side. To exchange their alliance for the friendship of a militarily weightless[50] Hungary would be insane. Finally, Hungary too might have been involved in the assassination of King Alexander. In that case, a rapprochement with Hungary would be out of the question.

Rapprochement with Bulgaria

The attitude of the new Bulgarian government was encouraging. Their attempted liquidation of the IMRO and the friendly visit of King Alexander improved the relationship of the two countries even further.[51] This rapprochement did not oppose French interests and gave hopes that it would strengthen the Balkan Pact and meet with the approval of Rumania.

Rapprochement with Germany

During the funeral of King Alexander in Belgrade, the Yugoslavian public opinion and press displayed an unparalleled sympathy toward Goering and the German delegation.[52] This was the second occasion that Yugoslavia openly demonstrated her sympathies toward Nazi Germany.[53] Yugoslavia did not have a common border with Germany, so Germany did not have territorial aims. Germany was Yugoslavia's best business partner, and Germany did not exploit the Yugoslavian economy. She charged competitive prices and did not restrict the types of goods sold.[54] Since the signing of the Three Power Declaration and the Rome Protocols, it was clear that Germany's interests were not the same as those of Italy and Hungary. In case of German-Yugoslavian rapprochement, Germany could become a valuable ally, putting a break on Italian, as well as Hungarian, ambitions—a relationship from which Yugoslavia would benefit greatly. On the other hand, Germany was the main enemy of France, so a German rapprochement would certainly not meet with French approval. Therefore, "it would hardly be possible in the near future for pro-German sentiments to find expression in practical politics."[55] At least not as long as France remained the strongest power in Europe.

Rapprochement with Austria

The relationship with Austria was quite cold. The USTASHE committed terrorist actions against Yugoslavia from Austrian territory,[56] though without the knowledge of the Austrian government. Also, Yugoslavia granted asylum to the Nazi terrorists after the murder of Dollfuss, an act which created hostility in the Austrian public and government. Because of his pro-Habsburg convictions, Schuschnigg was looked upon by the Little Entente as a person who might attempt a restoration and create with it the greatest possible threat to the integrity of the successor states. Austria enjoyed the patronage of Italy, a fact which multiplied the dangers for Yugoslavia. A reconciliation seemed impossible.

The Nazi attempt to overthrow the Austrian government proved Hitler's great interest in the domestic and foreign policy of Austria. With a possible growth of German influence in Austria, the restoration of the

Habsburg Monarchy in Austria would be improbable. Therefore, the reconciliatory policy was out of the question for the time being, and the help of Germany was needed for the neutralization of Austria.

Evaluation of Prince Paul's Policy

Many historians[57] think that the times, problems, and challenges were too great for Prince Paul, and he just could not live up to his obligations as a statesman. The alternatives open to Prince Paul for both domestic and foreign policy have been discussed above. A comparison of the optimum alternative with the chosen policy may give a more objective description of his qualities as a statesman and a diplomat.

Domestic Policy

An analysis of the alternatives for domestic policy suggests the following solution: a reconciliatory domestic policy (loosening of the royal dictatorship) with great caution in order to avoid the dangers represented by the autonomist, separatist movements of the minority groups, especially the Croatians.

Prince Paul took the first step toward reconciliation with the release from prison of Macek, who expressed his desire for a better understanding with the government. In 1935, Jevtic, a strong Serbian chauvinist, was replaced as prime minister by Milan Stojadinovic, who belonged to the Radical Party[58] but who held more liberal views than did his predecessor. The government then released 10,000 political prisoners, moderated dictatorial methods, and sought an understanding with the Croatian Peasant Party.[59] The main obstacle to complete reconciliation and understanding lay in the Royal Constitution; however, in this area, neither Stojadinovic nor Prince Paul entertained any serious plans for dramatic change.[60]

Judging these actions from a contemporary with the decisions, and considering the knowledge that Prince Paul and his aides had about the general situation of Yugoslavia, there can be only one conclusion: in 1935 the regency tried to pursue the most promising and best domestic policy for the benefit of Yugoslavia.

Foreign Policy

The unchangeable facts of international politics at the time were: Yugoslavia needed French patronage, as well as the alliance of the Little Entente; Yugoslavia had to make small concessions to Italy in order to preserve the goodwill of France; Yugoslavia did not have to and could not make concessions to Hungary because it would cause alienation of the Little Entente, as well as of the Balkan Pact, and so would weaken the Yugoslavian position; and Yugoslavia's economic interest demanded a closer, more friendly relationship with Germany.

Thus, a compromise foreign policy seemed to be the most feasible for Yugoslavia, and the regency followed such a policy. Yugoslavia strengthened her friendship with France and the Little Entente by cooperating with them during the investigation of the Marseilles crime and not accusing Italy. With this action, the door was left open for a possible Italian-Yugoslavian rapprochement. The regency made a firm stand against Hungary, thereby forcing the Hungarian government to tone down her revisionist policy and propaganda, as well as forcing her to follow a stricter line concerning the Croatian refugees. The regency expressed sympathy to Germany; in this manner, they paved the way for both better economic and political relations, doing so in order to harmonize Yugoslavian foreign policy with her economic interests.[61]

Those historians who argue against this compromise solution argue in the knowledge of later developments. However, King Alexander, Prince Paul, and the Stojadinovic government had no crystal ball to see into the future. The actions (or rather *inactions*) of the Western Powers, the failure of the Eastern Pact, and the French-Italian rapprochement all brought home one lesson to Yugoslavia: her interests were only secondary in the eyes of her allies and protectors. With reason, the leaders of Yugoslavia had to look for alternate solutions and selected the ones, which, at the time, seemed to serve best the interests of Yugoslavia.

A small power seldom has a chance to decide her foreign policy independent of the great nations. Yugoslavia could and did make such a turn toward Germany, which meant that the interested Great Powers acted completely against Yugoslavian interests or—paid no attention to developments in Central Europe and the Balkans.

The regency selected the best foreign policy for Yugoslavia. Prince Paul indeed lived up to the challenges of the contemporary situation, and those historians who condemn him[62] have disregarded the simple fact that he could not foresee then the developments which followed in later years.

The assassination of King Alexander was a terrible crime. However, it was more than that. It speeded up the regrouping of the European nations; it weakened small power confidence in the great champions of the status quo; it opened the Danubian region for German penetration, which naturally led to a growth of German political influence; it signaled the beginning of a race in Central Europe and on the Balkans for the goodwill of Germany; it undermined the solidarity of the Little Entente; and it made questionable the real value of the mutual assistance treaties.

Laval Takes the Initiative

The assassination at Marseilles created a domestic political crisis in France, and the Doumergue government resigned. The new government of Pierre Flandin obtained the confidence of the Chamber on November 13, 1934. Although the Right accused his cabinet of "murdering the national unity" and the Left believed that his cabinet was "too far on the Right," the Flandin government could rely on the majority of those deputies who felt that the new ministers were the "defenders of the strict republican orthodoxy."[1]

The most important personality change occurred in the post of the war minister where General Maurin replaced "Old Marshal" Pétain. Laval, Barthou's successor in the Doumergue government, retained his post within the new cabinet. The Flandin government began its activities successfully. The new military budget submitted by General Maurin received unanimous approval (a phenomenon which had been absent in the Chamber for a long time) on November 24, and Laval's foreign political *exposé* was accepted on November 30.[2]

The government stressed that it would continue the work of Barthou in the field of foreign policy expressing the hope that "France and Italy, with England in reserve" would be able to solve many of Europe's problems with mutual agreement.[3] However, this statement alone proved that Laval did not completely share Barthou's political views, at least not in the judgment of priorities. Barthou had worked anxiously first to keep the friendship of the Little Entente, then to convince England of the necessity of a more active participation in continental affairs, to enlist the support of the Soviet Union against the growing German menace, and to secure the cooperation of Mussolini. It was this last aim that Laval considered most important.

By rearranging Barthou's list of priorities, Laval proved to be a more realistic diplomat. He was anxious to avoid hurting France's relationship with the Little Entente and emphasized that his projected negotiations with Italy would not be in the spirit of his aims if they did not "guarantee, at the same time, a rapprochement between Italy and the Little Entente, especially Yugoslavia."[4] The assassination of King Alexander, however, created such a public uproar in Yugoslavia that this goal was hardly attainable. Laval valued the Italian friendship more and, with the help of Eden, settled the assassination problem without offending Italy, while at the same time leaving the door open for a Yugoslavian reconciliation.

Laval used a more moderate approach toward Germany.[5] He assured Hitler that "the French-Soviet preliminary agreement for mutual assistance is not intended to be a two-sided agreement;" he expressed his hopes that Germany would find it possible to join the Eastern Pact "as one among equals;" and he declared that "France will recognize the result of the [Saar] Plebiscite as binding and unalterable."[6]

Laval also commented very favorably on Baldwin's November 28, 1934, speech to the House of Commons in which he expressed British disapproval over German rearmament plans and concluded that "now the British government agrees with France in the principles of preservation of peace in Europe."[7] Everything seemed to work in Laval's favor. His declarations and activities even impressed the Germans, and Hitler found some signs in Laval's activities pointing toward a *détente* in German-French relations.[8] The Polish government, however, thought that the French "went too far with Germany."[9]

Laval moved ahead rapidly in his attempt to realize the rapprochement with Italy. On December 14, 1934, he learned that Mussolini was anxious to see him; four days later, in a speech in the French Senate, Laval expressed his confidence in the success of the upcoming negotiations with Italy.[10] At almost the same time, Laval learned that Germany disliked his designs concerning Italy and the Eastern Pact.[11] It was natural to expect that Germany would try to thwart a French-Italian rapprochement, just as it was natural for Laval to visit Mussolini before the Germans could succeed. The visit to Rome, announced on January 2, took place on January 4-8, 1935.

Advantages and Risks to France of Rapprochement with Italy

In order to appreciate the importance of the Laval-Mussolini meeting, it is necessary to understand the advantages Laval hoped for and the risks involved. The basis for the negotiations was given as the common interest of France and Italy in the preservation of Austria's independence. However, the Austrian crisis had already proved that a bilateral agreement between France and Italy would not be respected by Yugoslavia and Czechoslovakia, since they were not willing to "accept a factual protectorate of Italy in Austria."[12] Thus, the differences existing between Italy and France played a secondary role. Laval's primary concern while negotiating with Mussolini was the preservation of the goodwill of France's client states. However, this demanded concessions only on the part of Italy, and why should she give such concessions? Mussolini had his own problems with Austria and Hungary. Schuschnigg flatly rejected the idea of having foreign troops on Austrian soil in defense of Austria.[13] Since the Treaty of Trianon, Hungary had feared the realization of Benes' dream for a corridor on Austrian or Hungarian territory in order to make direct communication possible between Czechoslovakia and Yugoslavia,[14] even though Yugoslavia's participation in the guarantee of Austrian independence could lead to that very situation. For Mussolini to disregard completely the sensitivity of Austria and Hungary would mean the loss of Italian influence in Central Europe.

Both Laval and Mussolini objectively evaluated the interests of their individual countries. Therefore, it was clear from the beginning that both were ready to compromise only on points not involving their own national interest.

France wanted Mussolini's friendship not only for the sake of Austrian independence, but also for France's own vested interest. The French Army Council had already concluded (in May 1933) that the French army could not face both the German and Italian forces without grave risks.[15] A rapprochement with Italy would secure France's rear in case of a conflict with Germany. Though the French army had great shortcomings, it still contained 577,000 men.[16] Adding the tremendous defensive strength of the Maginot line, it was more than a match for the German army, which was in a state of transformation with a projected strength of 300,000 men.[17] From the strategic point of view, then, rapprochement with Italy was a question of primary importance for France. It is interesting to note that the critics of Laval's foreign policy, as well as his defenders,[18] failed to point out this strategic factor which was perhaps the most important aspect of the French-Italian rapprochement.

The security of France was worth the risk involved, that is, the further alienation of Yugoslavia. However, Yugoslavian alienation would be risked only if Laval gave in to the revisionist demands of Mussolini. The recognition of Italian revisionism would lead to the alienation of not only Yugoslavia, but the whole Little Entente as well. Even that would not be too high a price to pay for the security of France. Laval, however, skillfully avoided that danger.[19]

Laval's meeting with Mussolini was an immense success for the French diplomacy. The Rome Agreements which resulted consisted of a general declaration, worded in such a way that it could not offend anybody. It was a *procès verbal* concerning Austrian independence that projected consultations in case of a new Austrian crisis, a protocol concerning disarmament that condemned unilateral rearmament, a treaty on Africa concerning territorial revisions and special rights secured for both parties in Tunisia, and an exchange of letters about Abyssinia.[20]

The most important results of the Rome Agreements were the harmonization of French, Italian, Yugoslavian, and Czech standpoints concerning the independence of Austria; and the secret military clause which secured for France both the chance to strengthen her German frontier and the cooperation of the Italian army and air force in case of war against Germany.[21] The details of this military cooperation were worked out not only between France and Italy, but also between these two Great Powers and the Little Entente.[22] This military plan represented a sharp deviation from the existing French strategic principle of strictly defensive operations. It renewed the old conception of the cooperation of French-Italian-Czech forces against Germany, known as the Foch Plan at the time of the Versailles peace negotiation.[23] However, the changed political situation necessitated several alterations which did not change the basic idea of the plan, but made its execution more difficult. To avoid a possible clash between Italian and Yugoslavian forces, it became necessary to insert a French army corps between them. The objective of the Yugoslavian, French, and Italian right flank was the occupation of Vienna in cooperation with the Czech forces.[24]

This simple change in the original Foch Plan created numerous difficulties. It delayed a swift reaction to German aggression because of the long transportation route involved (ca. 350 miles from the French border) which, since the French army was not motorized, planned on using the railroads. The French military trains would cross the transportation lines of the Italian army, causing many possible chances for delay and confusion. Supplying the French army with ammunition, should the operation drag on, presented more problems. Transportation from France was difficult, while supplies in Yugoslavia were not at hand in satisfactory amounts. Supplies from Italy were not feasible because of the differences in weapons. The march up of the Italian army corps to the right flank of the French army projected less difficulty. The route did not cross French transportation lines, and the corps was mainly comprised of air force units assigned to operate over the territories of southern Germany.

The plan seems complicated and difficult. Yet, it was feasible in 1935, especially since Germany was not satisfactorily armed even at the time of the Rhineland occupation in 1936. The plan was good in its conception, *but its success depended on future political decisions* which the two governments might possibly make.

With these political and military agreements, France again became the commanding power in Europe. What concession had Laval given for such a great success? As Mussolini put it, "nothing but a desert in Africa."[25] The free hand given to Mussolini in Abyssinia cost even less. France had no essential interest in that country, "and Mussolini agreed with Laval to expand by peaceful means."[26]

French public opinion, as well as the Chamber and the Senate, was pleased with the results of the meeting.[27] The success of the Rome Agreements concerning Central Europe, however, depended to a great degree on the approval of other states, such as Germany, Hungary, and the Little Entente. They expressed certain scepticism, but Laval and Mussolini hoped that their objections would be overcome in the Danubian Pact.[28]

Reaction to the Rome Agreements

The announcement of the Laval-Mussolini meeting created nervous reaction in Central Europe. The Hungarian *Budapesti Hirlap*, undoubtedly wanting to calm down the nervousness of the revisionist, published a comment which stated: "Hungarian revisionist aims will not suffer any setback in Rome because the mutual non-interference treaty will guarantee only the independence of the states, but not their borders."[29] Yugoslavia, having expressed her confidence in Laval, expected that "Mussolini will try to further reduce the role of the Little Entente in Central Europe."[30] Titulescu felt it necessary to call an extraordinary meeting of the Little

Entente Council.[31] Czechoslovakia proved to be the most optimistic, as diplomatic circles in Prague expected Italy to realize that the support of Hungarian revisionism would harm her own interest. "If Italy would sign this agreement, she would notice that instead of losing something, she would gain a great deal in the future through a friendly cooperation with the Little Entente."[32]

It is noteworthy to compare these expectations of the Danubian states with the aims of France and Italy, both of whom wanted to secure the independence of Austria. France wanted to strengthen her military-strategic position against Germany, and Italy wanted to gain a free hand concerning Abyssinia.[33] *What the Danubian states felt important remained to be unimportant in the eyes of Laval and Mussolini.* Yet, an agreement depended on the approval of these small states, unless Laval or Mussolini or both were willing to give up their influence in the Danubian Basin. It seems that Laval was the more faithful patron, as he constantly consulted the three Little Entente states, while "Italy had merely kept Hungary informed in general terms without consulting her."[34] Gömbös sent warnings to Mussolini: "If the Laval-Mussolini agreement would guarantee the present borders in Central Europe, and this kind of guarantee would be against Article 19 of the League of Nations charter, Hungary would be forced to change her policy and place her confidence in the future in Germany instead of Italy."[35] At the same time, Czechoslovakia expressed great satisfaction that "Italy will not be the enemy of the Little Entente in Central European affairs anymore."[36]

The official text of the Rome Agreements was published on January 13, 1935, and was celebrated by the French press as a great victory for Laval. Without question, it was his victory, for the agreement not only included the guarantee of independence for the Danubian states, but also recommended a Danubian Pact in which the participating states would accept the mutual obligation to respect each other's national frontiers.[37]

Meanwhile, the upcoming Saar plebiscite[38] held the attention of Western Europe, and very few statesmen noticed the comments of the Hungarian semi-official paper: "The success of the Danubian Pact depends on the joining of Germany and Hungary, but *that is questionable.*"[39] (italics added)

THE DANUBIAN PACT

A Franco-Italian Proposal

The Italian-French communication of January 6, 1935, recommended to Austria and her neighbors (except Switzerland) the conclusion of a noninterference treaty, with the door also left open for France, Poland, and Rumania to join. The participants in the pact were not to interfere in the domestic affairs of other countries and "not to stir up or support any action which was directed against the territorial integrity or against the political and social order of any of the contracting countries;" the treaty also provided for consultations among the participating states "in case Austria's independence and integrity should be menaced."[40]

The Danubian Pact was to be based on the cooperation of Austria, Czechoslovakia, Germany, Hungary, Italy, and Yugoslavia. It was strange to expect that these states would join in a single pact, and wishful thinking on the part of Laval and Mussolini to hope that it would work. However, such cooperation was to them the most feasible solution for satisfying the demands of particular French and Italian interests.

The envisioned Danubian Pact also disregarded economic considerations. Due to German trade activities, the influx of German products into Central Europe, grew from 20.3 percent in 1934 to 22.2 percent in 1935, while the German market for Central European products grew from 18.3 percent to 24.7 percent.[41] The percentage of German participation in the trade of these countries was so high[42] that the smallest German economic pressure or restriction on trade would produce catastrophic consequences. On the other hand, Central European trade relations were so insignificant with Italy and France that these two countries could not exert any political concessions using economic pressure.[43] Laval faced the same problem as Barthou did with the Eastern Pact: French allies were much more independent than France thought, and they would follow the French political designs only if they believed that these designs would also serve their own interests.

On France's part, the Danubian Pact was an attempt to create an alternative for her Polish, Rumanian, and Yugoslavian allies who bitterly opposed those articles of the Eastern Pact that wanted to secure the right for Soviet troops to pass through their territories. The Danubian

Pact left out the Soviet Union, thereby eliminating the reason for that opposition. This also made it easier for Germany to join the pact. The projected noninterference treaty provided a means to stop not only Nazi propaganda in Austria, but also the support of revisionist propaganda among the Hungarian minorities of the Little Entente states. In other words, the Danubian Pact was an alternate plan to secure the status quo in the Danube Basin. Italy's participation in it created the impression that France gave up her claims of influence in that region; but in reality, the pact indirectly assured the preservation of this influence through the cooperation and consent of Italy. The pact was even more important from the military point of view in that the reorganized French army could launch an attack on Germany with hope of success, since the bulk of the German army would be engaged with Italian troops.[44]

Italy was hoping that the Danubian Pact would secure the independence of Austria even better than the Three Power Declaration by eliminating Yugoslavia's jealousy and creating an atmosphere of cooperation within the Danube Basin. Mussolini still very strongly opposed a possible *Anschluss.* On February 13, 1935, he wrote a long article for the *Popolo d'Italia* in which he analyzed the history of Austria and concluded that Austrian independence was a "particular Italian problem, but not exclusively Italian, for it is also a European problem."[45] The Danubian Pact, in Mussolini's mind, was the best solution for Austria, certainly a better solution than his alternative plan; that is, if the European powers were not willing to limit Hitler's expansionist schemes, then German expansion should be directed toward Poland instead of Austria.[46] Receiving the green light from Laval for the "peaceful solution" of the Abyssinian conflict,[47] the Danubian Pact seemed to secure Italy's influence in Central Europe, even if Italy turned her full attention toward Africa.

Reaction to the Proposal

Germany

Germany received the Danubian Pact plan with less hostility than she had received the Eastern Pact proposal. Hitler thought that "a settlement could be reached in spite of considerable difficulties with the problem of the definition of intervention."[48] What made Hitler more conciliatory toward the Danubian Pact was the absence of the Soviet Union, because he was unwilling to sign a treaty of mutual assistance with Russia.[49] On the other hand, the preservation of the status quo and the principle of noninterference were still unacceptable to Germany. Hitler did not flatly reject the Danubian Pact; he only expressed his reservations and demanded further clarifications.[50] These demands were phrased in general terms, yet they clearly expressed Germany's lack of enthusiasm about certain aspects of the pact; primarily the strengthening of ties between Austria and other states, especially Italy; and the creation of sort of an Italian-French protectorate over Austria.[51] The request for clarification on such points as the inclusion of Switzerland and Britain, the precise definition of nonintervention, and whether or not the pact would be concluded within the framework of the League of Nations (of which Germany had not been a member since October 1933) hardly camouflaged Hitler's desire to abort the Danubian Pact.

The Soviet Union

The Soviet Union naturally saw in the Danubian Pact an attempt to exclude her from European affairs. The Russians realized that they would become dispensable from the French point of view if the Danubian Pact succeeded. However, it was a delicate situation. Litvinov and Vladimir Potemkin, the Soviet ambassador to France, had to frustrate the French plans in order to gain the closer cooperation of France. Very skillfully, they did not openly oppose the Danubian Pact but only expressed scepticism. Potemkin thought that "the Rome accords had only relative values, and that the Little Entente would not join the Danubian Pact without stipulations," he guessed that the Little Entente would demand the connection of the Rome Agreements with the Eastern Pact and the Balkan Pact.[52] Furthermore, he did not see any possibility for the realization of the Danubian Pact because of the political situation in Yugoslavia where General Ziffkovic seemed to have much greater influence within the government than Jevtic. If true, this meant there was no hope for a Hungarian-Yugoslavian reconciliation.

At the same time, both Litvinov and Potemkin pushed Laval for a separate French-Soviet mutual assistance agreement. Their negotiations lead to the Franco-Soviet Mutual Assistance Treaty in which both countries agreed that in the event "of an unprovoked attack on the part of a European state, the U.S.S.R., and reciprocally France shall immediately give each other aid and assistance."[53] With this agreement, signed on May 2, 1935, the French diplomacy overplayed its hand for security. First it had exchanged the Eastern Pact for the Danubian Pact; that is, it exchanged Soviet cooperation for Italian cooperation. Then, after securing the friendship of Mussolini, Laval returned to the old formula, alienating Mussolini and completely confusing the small Central European states.

The Little Entente

The Little Entente states made clear their attitude concerning the Danubian Pact in a common declaration agreed upon at the Laibach Conference in September 1935. In the declaration, which read like an ultimatum, they stated their conditions[54] for joining the Danubian Pact. Anxious to keep the status quo concerning Hungary, they demanded the exemption of the question of Habsburg restoration from the general operation of the nonintervention principles. They demanded the renunciation of revisionism by the Hungarian government as the price for recognition of Hungary's right to rearm. They demanded the Hungarian government give up its protection of Magyar minorities on their territories, and they wanted the firm pledge of Hungary against a possible Habsburg restoration. Finally, they wanted Hungary to sign both a non-aggression and a mutual assistance treaty.[55]

Perhaps the strongest opposition of the Little Entente was expressed in their desire to see France promote the Eastern Pact over the Danubian Pact. Jevtic even demanded the connection of the Danubian Pact with not only the Eastern Pact, but also the Balkan Pact. Jevtic remarked that "France forces Yugoslavia to follow her own interest like Poland does."[56] Thus, the success of the Danubian Pact was doomed by Laval's naive belief that the Little Entente would unconditionally follow the desires of France.

Austria

Schuschnigg protested against the exclusion of Austria from the French-Italian negotiations.[57] He rejected the consultation article of the projected Danubian Pact and desired a more positive mutual assistance treaty. In February 1935, however, Schuschnigg decided to act according to the resolutions of the Rome Agreements. He visited France "to save Austria's existence as an independent state."[58] Schuschnigg described the visit as friendly, and he received the impression that Laval understood the Austrian position. Yet, in the Danubian Pact question, Laval was not willing to force his allies further for the benefit of Austria, while Schuschnigg was unwilling to give a formal pledge that Austria would not restore the Habsburgs to the throne.[59]

The outcome of Schuschnigg's visit to London was not much better. Sir John Somon, the British Foreign Secretary, assured him that "England's attitude concerning Austria's independence had not changed and would never change."[60] Simon asked about the possibility of both a plebiscite concerning the *Anschluss* problem and a change in the Austrian form of government. Schuschnigg found the plebiscite idea, as well as the abandonment of the Austrian-type Fascist government, impractical. As it happened in France, so in England, positive support was not available for Austria because of ideological differences.

Hungary

The official text of the Rome Agreements very much disappointed the Gömbös government. Instead of defending Hungarian revisionist aims, Italy conceded to the demands of Laval and the Little Entente and agreed to a treaty which guaranteed not only the integrity of the Danubian states, but also their national frontiers. The plans for the Danubian Pact signaled the coming of further trouble. The demands to cease revisionist propaganda, the nonintervention treaty, and the opposition of Germany to the Danubian Pact indicated that Italy and Germany were once again on a collision course. Gömbös' dream of an Italian-German-Austrian-Hungarian block seemed even further from reality than before. Hungary once again had to examine her own realistic interests before joining or opposing the Danubian Pact.

CHAPTER VIII
THE FOURTH CRISIS: HUNGARY'S DILEMMA

THE GÖMBÖS GOVERNMENT, 1932-1933

Ideological Basis

Gömbös was appointed prime minister on October 1, 1932 by Regent Horthy, who could not agree with some of Gömbös' political convictions. Horthy, however, did not have much choice. The economic crisis and the severe measures introduced to fight against it produced great dissatisfaction among the small farmers, unemployed civil servants, and jobless university graduates. This discontent took the form of a Radical Right movement and the leader of that movement was Gömbös. The ideology of the Radical Right was a mixture of nationalism, national socialism, anti-Habsburg feeling, anti-Semitism, and authoritarianism. All of these convictions had a well-founded basis.

Nationalism was fed by the decisions of the peace treaties and prevailed in an ardent, aggressive cult of the glorious Hungarian past, as well as in revisionism. Its most devoted followers came from the ranks of middle-class intellectuals and public servants who fled to Hungary from territories annexed by the other successor states.

National Socialism became popular due to economic hardship and was considered an alternate solution to the Marxist Socialism attracting young anti-Communist intellectuals and small peasants. The devotion of the peasantry was not accidental. Hungary was a land of large estates owned by aristocrats, bankers, rich businessmen and the Church. While her neighbors introduced land reforms right after the war, Hungary's land reform program projected the distribution of only a small portion of the great land estates (7.5 percent of the total land), and even this reform was of no real benefit to the landless peasants since the land was alloted in small plots of 1.6 hold to only 298,000 peasants out of a total of nearly 3 million.[1]

Anti-Habsburgism had a long tradition in Hungary. Though the Compromise of 1867 and the thoughtful policy of Emperor Francis Joseph helped the Hungarian people to forget the former differences between themselves and the Habsburgs, memories of the 1848-49 Hungarian freedom fight still lingered.

After World War I, the restoration attempts of King Charles of Habsburg were defeated by Horthy and his followers. During the 1920's, the "Hungarian kingdom without a king" was greatly influenced by the conservatives, who nourished pro-Habsburg sentiments. On the other hand, the new generation of politicians, the middle-class, and a great number of the professionals, not having personal memories about the Habsburg monarchy, fell prey to the not so truthful anti-Habsburg propaganda. Gömbös and his followers believed that the Hungarian people were the victims of the former Habsburg aristocracy, and in order to improve social conditions, they wanted to destroy the aristocracy's power. According to their belief, a Habsburg restoration would make the realization of this goal impossible. As prime minister, Gömbös officially promoted anti-Habsburgism[2] because of both personal and ideological reasons.[3]

It is interesting that at the same time, the peasantry looked back to the monarchy with a certain nostalgia. According to peasant tradition, the kings were always "for the people" and helped fight against the despotism of the landed estates.[4] However, the political representatives of the peasantry, the leading members of the Smallholder Party, were against the restoration.

Anti-Semitism also had some practical basis. After World War I, under economic pressures, the Hungarian middle class became increasingly interested in industrial and commercial life, as well as in the free professions. Yet, 54 percent of the merchants, 48 percent of commercial personnel, 46 percent of physicians, 41 percent of veterinarians, 41 percent of factory owners, and 34 percent of newspapermen were Jews.[5] "The domination of the economic life of the nation by an alien element became a subject of increasing resentment.[6] The fact that the overwhelming majority of arrested Communists in 1920 and in the following years were Jews[7] gave added impetus to this anti-Semitism.

An admiration of authoritarianism was created by Fascist Italy and Mussolini's support of Hungary's revisionist aims. In 1927, Hungary and Italy signed a friendship treaty directed against Yugoslavia.[8] In order to give strength to that treaty, Mussolini supported Hungarian rearmament by providing a credit of thirty million liras. Mussolini's friendly gestures naturally attracted the admiration of Hungarian nationalists.

Economic Situation

As in the other European countries, the economic crisis represented the main concern of the Hungarian government. Hungary needed markets for her agricultural products and needed industrial products to satisfy the needs of her population. The denunciation of the Trade Treaty by Czechoslovakia in 1929 marked the beginning of the end of the prosperity created by the Bethlen government. While in 1930 Czechoslovakia bought 16.8 percent of Hungary's total export and Czech products represented 21 percent of the total import, in 1931 these figures fell to 4.2 percent export and 9.2 percent import.[9] On March 31, 1932, Austria denounced her commercial treaty with Hungary. It was again a heavy blow as Austrian trade represented 30.1 percent of Hungary's exports and 15.5 percent of her imports. In a personal letter to Hitler on April 22, 1933, Gömbös requested Germany's urgent help.[10] His expectations were not in vain as Germany's share in Hungary's exports grew from 11.2 percent to 22.2 percent by the next year.[11] As a result of the German trade, unemployment decreased and industrial production was revitalized.

At the same time, due to heavy borrowing by the Bethlen and Károlyi governments, Hungary was indebted to the League of Nations, as well as to private banking interests in Britain, France, and the United States. It was urgent to give these circles some security that Hungary would not imitate nazism. To the great surprise of the Hungarian Right, Gömbös moved swiftly in that direction. He initiated negotiations with the representatives of the Jewish Neolog community, concluding an agreement in which the Jewish leaders "recognized and approved Gömbös progressive policy" and Gömbös indicated he had "revised his views on the Jewish question."[12]

By the end of 1933, Gömbös had a relatively united country behind him as far as domestic policy was concerned. His economic policy tied Hungary closer to Germany, but kept the United States and England friendly. With the declining external and internal pressures at the turn of the year, he was relatively free to select the foreign political moves which would serve Hungary's interest the best.

Alternatives for Hungarian Foreign
Policy at the End of 1933

Gömbös basic political convictions partly promoted and partly opposed the foreign policy of the preceding aristocratic governments. He enthusiastically accepted their revisionist program, but rejected the possibility of a Habsburg restoration. These two principles already put some limitations on his choices for alternative solutions in the field of foreign policy.

Equally important was the influence of Regent Horthy and Foreign Minister Kánya. Horthy never lost his admiration for the seas and considered the great naval powers unchallengeable. He openly expressed the conviction that "What was true in the last war is no less true this time, namely that sea power will win the war."[13] It was well known in both government circles and the general public that Horthy was an Anglophile. Though legally he had no authority to interfere with the foreign policy of Hungary,[14] his position gave him the chance to influence Gömbös to at least display a certain caution in not alienating England.

Gömbös appointed Kánya to the post of foreign minister on February 4, 1933. Free from the influence of any ideology, Kánya had no scruples concerning diplomatic morality or loyalty; and "he knew exactly what he wanted for Hungary, which was all the revision he could get for her."[15] His basic aim was to secure a free hand for Hungary, that is not to ally Hungary with the victors of World War I. Kánya's aggressive character impressed even Gömbös, moderating his enthusiasm for Hitler and Mussolini.

Taking into consideration the factors of revisionism, anti-restorationism, Horthy's Anglophile sympathies, and Gömbös' authoritarian admirations, the following foreign policy alternatives existed for Hungary at the end of 1933: continue Bethlen's foreign policy by, toning down revisionist claims, becoming firm allies with Italy, and trying to find a *modus vivendi* with the other European countries, including the Little Entente; start a more aggressive foreign policy, creating political and military alliances with the other revisionist states (Italy, Germany, Poland, Austria, and Bulgaria) and trying to realize revision, by force if necessary; accept the status quo, give up revisionism and drift into the camp of France and the Little Entente; or reject every rigid line of foreign policy and pursue revisionism whenever the conditions favor it.

Continue Bethlen's Foreign Policy

Developments in Germany, as well as the cancellation of the Czech and Austrian trade agreements, made this line of foreign policy obsolete. Before 1933, Germany had accepted the Versailles Treaty, at least as far as her western borders were concerned, by joining in the Locarno Pact. During this period, she was a member of the League of Nations, economically weak, cooperative and peaceful in international politics, and militarily insignificant. By 1933, however, Germany's policy had become aggressive and openly revisionist. She began to play a more important military role and was an economically desirable trading partner for every nation, especially the countries of Central Europe and the Balkan states.

These changes in German conditions made the Little Entente nervous, primarily Czechoslovakia, and it gradually turned the attention of France toward the problems of Central Europe. To discount the role of Germany would be impractical from the Hungarian point of view, especially since the economic well-being of Hungary to a great degree depended upon her trade relations with Germany. An alliance with Italy, however, remained important and needed to be incorporated in other diplomatic designs.

Start a More Aggressive Foreign Policy

This would involve creating political and military alliances with the other revisionist states, that is, Italy, Germany, Poland, Austria, and Bulgaria. Here again, events already canceled out some of the realistic possibilities. Bulgaria, abandoning her revisionist policy, began to cooperate with the pro-status quo Balkan states.[16] Austria was completely alienated from Germany because of the German supported antigovernment propaganda in Austria and Germany's financial pressure tactics.[17] Long and hard diplomatic negotiations were needed to stop Dollfuss from continuing a rapprochement with the French sponsored group. Italy was determined to stop the growing German influence in Austria, and Mussolini openly expressed his displeasure over Gömbös' visit to Hitler.[18] The only improvement in relations within the anti-status quo camp was achieved by the German-Polish rapprochement.

Also, there existed in Hungary a great dislike for the idea of closer cooperation with Germany. The people (especially university students), utterly disappointed because of Hitler's demands concerning the rights and privileges of the German minority in Hungary, organized demonstrations against Germany; and the Hungarian press attacked not only Germany, but also Gömbös because of his visit to Hitler, commenting on the visit as an unfortunate step "in a time when Germany was going to be completely isolated."[19] A too radical and open pro-German policy could create a problem, even a government crisis, since Gömbös followers were in a minority within the government, and he did not possess the unconditional support of Horthy.[20]

From the economic point of view, closer cooperation with Germany was certainly a requirement. In 1934, Germany was to carry 20.35 percent of Hungary's total foreign trade so that with a friendly Germany, Hungary would depend on friendly countries for 54.22 percent of her trade and on hostile countries for only 13.77 percent. A hostile Germany on the other hand, would force Hungary to depend on friendly nations for only 33.87 percent of her trade and on hostile nations for 34.12 percent.[21]

The policy to ally Hungary with the block of anti-status quo nations for the time being lacked all realism since *no such block existed.* However, if such a block were to be created in the future, economic as well as revisionist political considerations recommended that Gömbös join the block.

Accept the Status Quo and Reject Revisionism

When Kánya visited the French capital on September 15-18, 1933, Daladier suggested Hungary reject revisionism and join the camp of the pro-status quo. Daladier noted that France would welcome a more friendly attitude on Hungary's part concerning Benes' proposal of trade benefits for Hungary in return for the renunciation of revisionism, but Kánya's answer was that "any Hungarian government would fall at once if it would accept such suggestions."[22]

The Hungarian government included revisionism in its political platform in order to gain popular support.[23] Even the leaders of opposing parties agreed with the government on that point. Tibor Eckhardt, leader of the opposition Smallholder Party and vice-president of the "Hungarian League for Revisionism, was no less revisionist than Gömbös."[24] Pál Auer, one of the strongest opponents of Gömbös and unrestricted Hungarian nationalism, emphasized, during private conversations with Benes, the disadvantages of the annexation of Hungarians by Czechoslovakia, recommending instead a peaceful revision of borders following ethnic lines.[25] Hungarian school education, as well as parental influence nurtured revisionist sentiments in the younger generations and in that way secured continuous mass support for revisionism throughout the interwar period.

Kánya was right in his response to Daladier, who himself understood that the realization of anti-revisionist policy was an impossible task.[26] This policy was not feasible from the Hungarian point of view for both domestic and foreign political reasons. The *only* advantage that Daladier offered to Kánya for Hungary's renunciation of revisionism was support of Hungary's rearmament demands in the Little Entente states. What Hungary needed most of all, though, was a helping hand in her economic situation. No such offer was made because France was not in a position economically to help Hungary. Moreover, a renunciation of revisionist policy could result in loss of trade with Germany and Italy. Without French guarantees for the replacement of that loss, the acceptance of such an offer would be a naive, unrealistic policy.

Reject All Rigid Lines of Foreign Policy and Pursue Revisionism Under Favorable Conditions

This policy had to take into consideration all possible means through which revisionism could be achieved, including war, review of the peace treaties in the League of Nations, agreements with the Little Entente, agreements with the individual successor states, and decisions of the Great Powers (Britain, France, Germany, and Italy).

The first alternative could be dismissed at once. Hungary's military-geographic position excluded any chance for success in case of an armed conflict with any of the Little Entente states. It would be different if there were no Little Entente, for then Hungary could pursue a more aggressive policy against these states individually and one at a time. The aim of such a policy for the time being ought to be directed, therefore, against the unity of the Little Entente, as well as against the understanding between France and the Little Entente.

The alternative of revision through the League of Nations promised even less success. France and the Little Entente states were able to block all attempts in the League directed toward revision of the treaty and successfully prevented the League from fulfilling its obligation as guardian of minority rights.[27] However, for the sake of international publicity and for propaganda purposes, it seemed wise to seize every opportunity in the League of Nations to stress Hungary's grievances.

The help of the Great Powers in achieving revision did not seem feasible after the experiences of the Four Power Pact and after the Kánya-Daladier negotiations. Yet, the attitude of some English politicians created slight reason for hope. With the enlistment of Lord Rothermere's support for Hungary's revisionist aims, the Hungarian public was led to believe that the support of English public opinion could be secured. In fact, this belief was based on illusion.

A revision through agreements with the Little Entente depended upon the possibility of finding at least *one* acceptable basis to start more friendly diplomatic relations. This basis was created by the attitude of the Little Entente states toward the Habsburg restoration problem. King Alexander of Yugoslavia preferred a German-Austrian custom union to a possible Austrian-Hungarian-Italian one.[28] Benes preferred "an *Anschluss* to an Austrian-Hungarian union," he felt that a restoration would endanger the security of Czechoslovakia, but he was not afraid of the Germans, with whom the Czechs had had a cordial neighbor relationship for centuries.[29] Titulescu, while not objecting to a possible *Anschluss*, remarked that "in case of an Austrian-Hungarian unification, Rumania will order mobilization."[30]

The Little Entente and France had approached Hungary in 1932 to take part in the Tardieu Plan.[31] This plan envisioned the establishment of tariffs, on the basis of the most favored nation principle, among the Danubian states (Austria, Hungary, and the Little Entente) and the creation of an economic block, a kind of custom union under French tutelage. The plan failed, not because of Hungary but because of German, Italian, and British opposition.[32] However, it was also unacceptable from the Hungarian point of view because the plan demanded as a precondition the renunciation of Hungary's revisionism.[33]

Unless Hungary was ready to denounce revisionism, there was no hope of finding any solution for reconciliation with the Little Entente states as a block. Hungary was not ready to and could not take such a step. Hungarian political leaders in the government, as well as in the opposing camp, could work only on some kind of alternative compromise. The

idea was to renounce at least part of the revisionist demands against
one country, but keep the demands intact against the other countries.

Reconciliation with Yugoslavia

In Horthy's judgment, Yugoslavia was the best choice for Hungarian
friendship, and he had publicly stated this conviction in August 1926.
He had frequent private contact with King Alexander through Admiral
Prika, with whom Horthy served in the KUK Navy and who was now
the adjutant general of the Yugoslavian King. It was even more important
that Jevtic shared Horthy's views concerning the necessity of rapprochement between Hungary and Yugoslavia. He said to Hennyey, the
Hungarian military attache, during the presentation of his credentials:
"I am convinced that you will have a good time in our country, because
there are no real differences between the two people."[34]

Not only sentimental and personal emotions suggested a rapprochement
with Yugoslavia, but also realistic considerations. Yugoslavia had the
smallest group of Hungarians,[35] and the political refugees escaping from
Yugoslavia to Hungary were mainly Croatians. Furthermore, Yugoslavia
and Hungary had mutually important trade relations. There were signs
of goodwill on both parts. The private information that Horthy had
received gave him "every reason to believe that King Alexander would,
as soon as circumstances permitted, accept the proffered hand of friendship."[36] This friendly hand was offered as early as May 1933 when the
Yugoslavian ambassador in Budapest paid a visit to Kánya and expressed the
friendly feeling of Yugoslavia toward Hungary, suggesting the creation of the
Italian-Hungarian-Yugoslavian alliance against the threat of an *Anschluss.*[37]

At the same time, though, the public relationship of the two countries
seemed hopelessly hostile, and this hostility prevailed in newspaper
articles as well as in complaints at the League of Nations.[38] These press
attacks, however, did not play too important a role. In Yugoslavia, the
press was firmly under the government's control, and it could change
the tone of articles from one day to another. In Hungary, mainly the
government press published extreme revisionist articles, while the
opposition press followed a more liberal line and advocated a pro-French
and proreconciliatory policy.[39] If stopping the press campaign was in their
interest, both governments could do so with ease.

Reconciliation with Czechoslovakia

On September 27, 1933, President Masaryk proposed a Czech-Austrian-Hungarian union, adding though, that the "probability is very small that the Hungarians *will come to their senses.* If Hungary would follow a realistic policy we could discuss—no doubt with positive results—some kind of border revisions."[40] (italics added) The wording of this proposal certainly was not apt to awaken Hungarian sympathies. Its substance was even less acceptable: it projected a coalition of three states who were members of the former Habsburg Monarchy, in which Hungary for centuries (before the compromise of 1867) played second fiddle to the other two. The proposal reminded Gömbös of the possibility of a Habsburg restoration, and that alone was enough to elicit his opposition to the plan.

The attitude of the Czech government toward the Hungarian minorities also did not promote a possible better understanding. "There were the usual complaints, often justified, about insufficient educational facilities, the impossibility of entering the civil service, and the tactless behavior of officials of the majority nation in purely Magyar districts."[41] It was natural for the population living in such districts to turn to the Hungarian government for protection, although according to international law, the Hungarian government had no right to protect foreign citizens. However, the activities of the Hungarian minority group provided a constant chance for hostility between Hungary and Czechoslovakia.

Reconciliation with Rumania

This seemed to be the least desired and least possible alternative because Rumania held the greatest part of former Hungarian territories with the largest Hungarian population: 1,354,000 according to the Rumanian census and 1,900,000 according to the Hungarian census of 1910. The greatest number of political refugees living in Trianon-Hungary were represented by those escaping from Transylvania. These refugees were among the most politically active and influential (Bethlen, was a Transylvanian) people working for revision. On the other hand, Titulescu, the Rumanian foreign minister, was one of the strongest anti-revisionist statesmen. He was instrumental in the defeat of the Four Power Pact and in the preparation of the anti-revisionist Balkan Entente.[42]

The Foreign Policy of Gömbös

The success of any of these foreign policy alternatives depended entirely on the consent of Italy and Germany. Hungary could not afford to lose Italian sympathies, what with Mussolini being the only statesman who openly supported Hungary's revisionist aims. Also, Hungary could not afford to lose Hitler's goodwill, since Hungarian foreign trade was greatly dependent upon import-export business with Germany. It was important to learn Hitler's attitude and harmonize Hungary's foreign policy with him.

During a visit in Berlin on June 17-19, 1933, Gömbös learned from Hitler that Germany could not support Hungarian revisionist requests directed against Rumania and Yugoslavia, but could cooperate with Hungary against Czechoslovakia.[43] Furthermore, Hitler expressed his dissatisfaction with Dollfuss. Gömbös asked Hitler if a more moderate policy would not be possible vis à vis Austria, but the reply was disappointing.[44] The Hungarian leadership, however, sympathized with Hitler's conceptions and did not want to get involved in that "fratricidal struggle."[45] Nobody could expect Hungary "with a sane mind to take the side of Germany in the Anschluss question," wrote Kánya after the Berlin visit.[46]

Hungarian revisionist propaganda was somewhat effective in the Western world, especially in Britain and France, but it created a negative response in Central Europe. The Little Entente feared that Hungary might convince the Great Powers that they were very unjust to Hungary during the peace negotiations.[47] As a result, Benes and Titulescu nipped in the bud every French idea of a possible revision and led a continuous anti-revisionist press campaign, which proved to be more successful than the Hungarian propaganda.[48]

During the last months of 1933 and into January 1934, there were rumors about the possibility of a German-Little Entente Non-Aggression Pact. Gömbös asked Germany for clarification, even writing to Hitler, but Germany decided not to reply.[49] These German actions were just as disturbing as Hitler's attitude toward the German minorities question in Hungary,[50] all of which recommended to Gömbös a cautious rapprochement with Germany.

During his visit to Rome on July 25-28, 1933, Gömbös learned about Mussolini's plans for Central Europe. The kernel of this plan was "tight cooperation between Austria and Hungary," which would be realized both commercially and politically. At the same time, Mussolini assured Gömbös that Italy remained "in strong opposition to a Habsburg restoration." This Austrian-Hungarian agreement, strongly supported by Italy, would be extended eventually to neighboring states, first of all to the Little Entente and Germany.[51]

The effects of Hitler's and Mussolini's plans on all the alternatives for Hungarian foreign policy were disastrous. Germany wanted an *Anschluss*, and Italy opposed it. Germany wanted close cooperation with Hungary for the dissolution of the Little Entente and the destruction of Czechoslovakia, and Mussolini wanted a reorganization of the whole Danube Basin through reconciliation and understanding with France. Both Germany and Italy opposed a possible Habsburg restoration. *None* of the foreign policy alternatives was feasible without alienating one or another Great Power. Consequently, there remained only one remote chance of promoting Hungarian foreign political aims—the creation of an understanding between Hitler and Mussolini. Until that time, only one road was left open for Hungary: to try and retain her freedom of action without offending either of the two powers.

Thus, Gömbös *did not bind* Hungary to *unconditionally* follow the Italian or German political line. Communist-controlled Hungarian historians were not allowed to say this before 1968-1969,[52] although it was accepted as "historical fact" by many prominent experts in the free world as early as 1945.[53] Gömbös and Kánya saved Hungary's freedom of action to follow a policy which would serve Hungary's interest the best. They kept this point of view throughout 1934 and were ready to play Germany and Italy against each other if they believed that such a policy would benefit Hungary.

EVENTS OF 1934

The German-Polish Non-Aggression Pact

Following World War I, the official relationship between Hungary and Poland was correct, but very cool. Though the two countries had had friendly connections for centuries before the war, and the two peoples mutually cherished the memories of old times, the peace treaties placed the two countries into opposing camps. Poland's rebirth was the work of the Versailles Treaties, while the Trianon Treaty mutilated Hungary.[54] The result of this was that old friendly relations were manifested mostly in negative actions: Poland did not ratify the Trianon Treaty and did not participate in the French or Little Entente diplomatic designs directed against Hungary, while Hungary did not see any practical value of closer Polish-Hungarian cooperation.[55]

The circumstances began to change with the increasing Polish-German tensions in 1931-1932, and the tensions created by German revisionist aims and propaganda concerning the Danzig Corridor. Mussolini indicated in a conversation with the secretary of the League of Nations that he would welcome an eastward shift in German expansion because this direction would be the least threatening for Italy.[56] The Four Power Pact earned the unconditional opposition of Poland and could have strengthened her relations with the Little Entente; however, during his visit to Prague, Beck discovered that the smaller states of Central Europe, with their "ultra-submissiveness to the Great Powers" represented an obstacle to the formation of a solid anti-Four Power Pact front.[57] As early as April 1933, Pilsudski believed that the only alternative left for Poland under such circumstances was direct negotiations with Germany. These negotiations led to the successful conclusion of the German-Polish Non-Aggression Pact on January 26, 1934.

At the same time, Beck tried to establish personal contact with the Hungarian government, but his visit was canceled because of the protest of the Yugoslavian government.[58] The Czech government was alarmed, too, and began to look suspiciously at Poland. After the signing of the German-Polish pact, the Czech General Staff considered Poland one of her main enemies.[59] From the Hungarian view point, the pact meant one more potential revisionist ally against Czechoslovakia; therefore, the Gömbös government sent a committee to Warsaw "to renew the friendly relations."[60] The visit did not promote political negotiations, however, and Polish-Hungarian relations remained unchanged. Pilsudski rejected the idea of a Hungarian-Polish alliance, but he promised "never to make war on Hungary, and to do his best to restrain Rumania."[61] Polish policy did not influence Hungarian foreign policy during the course of 1934, although from that time on, Hungary looked upon Poland as a probable ally against Czechoslovakia.

Negotiations with Italy

The German-Polish Non-Aggression Pact created a certain degree of alarm in France, and the new government was anxious to show a united front of Great Powers against the possible renewal of German aggressiveness in Austria. This anxiety produced the Three Power Declaration regarding Austrian independence, signed on February 17, 1934, by Britain, France, and Italy. The mood changed with this declaration, and France turned her attention toward the planned Eastern Pact. Italy seemed to have firm control over Austria and Hungary, especially since the three states planned to further regulate their relationship in a formal treaty.

Yet, there were certain signs which indicated that the supposed Italian influence was not as strong in Hungary as in Austria. Hungary signed a new German-Hungarian commercial treaty on February 21, 1934. This treaty put Hungary into the German economic orbit, with Germany holding 20.35 percent of Hungary's foreign trade. However, Gömbös did not feel that this treaty placed Hungary in an inferior position. On February 14, 1934, he thanked Hitler in a personal letter for "the attention" of the German trade delegation, but at the same time he reasserted his own political independence. While stressing the common revisionist interest of Germany and Hungary, he asked Hitler to order the German minorities in Czechoslovakia, Rumania, and Yugoslavia to cooperate with the Hungarian minorities and not to take, under any circumstances, an anti-revisionist position. He also demanded the discontinuance of German Nazi propaganda and the financial "support of the German minority groups in Hungary."[62]

During negotiations between Kánya and the German ambassador in Hungary, Kánya stated that while Hungary would not participate in any agreement directed against Germany, the Hungarian government would watch with great concern the alienation of Germany and Italy because of the Austrian question. Kánya also added that if, because of the Austrian-German problem, an open conflict would break out between Germany and Italy, "the Hungarian government would be forced to follow *a brutal Hungarian policy.*"[63] (italics added) Kánya's expression was vague; however, it made the impression he had hoped for: the German ambassador understood it as a possible threat of Hungarian-Italian cooperation against Germany.[64]

Though there is no reason to suppose that Mussolini did not know about these German-Hungarian negotiations,[65] yet he felt it necessary to send his political director, Suvich, to Hungary. During his February 21-23, 1934 visit, Suvich found both reassurance and disheartening forebodings. Hungary followed Mussolini's recommendation and Gömbös, against the advice of Horthy, established diplomatic relations with the Soviet Union.[66] Although ready to cooperate fully with Austria and Italy in the field of trade, Hungary expressed her desire to keep out of an anti-German formation; and Kánya was unmoved by Suvich's statements about Mussolini's growing nervousness.[67] These controversial actions indicated that Gömbös, through trying to maintain Mussolini's goodwill, started a new, more independent foreign policy.

Gömbös clarified this new policy in a private conversation with Mussolini during the closing negotiations of the Rome Protocols.[68] Gömbös stated the basic axiom of his foreign policy as: *"Hungary feels her calling is to practice a particular policy, relying on Italy for the area south of the Danube and on Germany for the area north of the Danube."*[69] (italics added) This statement left Mussolini speechless. It sounded like a declaration of independence, and truly that is what it was.

Then Gömbös expressed his doubts concerning the trustworthiness of Dollfuss, who wanted to keep the door open for an understanding with France and the Little Entente and wanted "his connections with us only apparent."[70] Not hiding his dissatisfaction over Dollfuss' Habsburg policy,[71] Gömbös stressed that Hungary was happy with the existing situation and a restoration in Austria would find the Hungarian government strong enough "to defend its position." Mussolini argued that Hungarian interests demanded the preservation of an independent Austria. Gömbös agreed, but stated that Hungary needed Germany's cooperation against Czechoslovakia. For this reason, he asked that the Rome Protocols be kept an open treaty, allowing for other powers to join. Mussolini agreed, and Kánya hurriedly instructed the Hungarian minister in Berlin to call the attention of the German government to that article of the Rome protocols. Kánya hoped that Hitler would agree to transforming the protocols into a wider cooperation of Austria, Italy, Hungary, and Germany.[72]

Gömbös' foreign political conceptions were triumphant and created a more advantageous position for Hungary whereby Hungary continuously enjoyed the support of Italy against Yugoslavia and Rumania while being permitted to cooperate with Hitler against Czechoslovakia. At the same time, Gömbös worked himself into the position of mediator between Italy and Germany. The Hungarian revisionist policy had had no realistic chances before. However, Gömbös had succeeded in creating a situation which hopefully could lead to some kind of revision, because now Hungary enjoyed the support of both Italy and Germany. Further, while securing this support, Gömbös was able to avoid any commitments which would alienate one or both of these nations or would secure the right for them to interfere in Hungary's domestic affairs.

Gömbös' triumphant feeling disappeared during the summer. The Hitler-Mussolini meeting of June 14-15, instead of creating a favorable atmosphere for the promotion of a Rome-Berlin-Budapest-Vienna understanding, brought disaster. Although Mussolini sympathized with Hitler's revisionist policy, he firmly asserted Italian opposition to an *Anschluss*, while Hitler expressed the view that an Austrian-German reconciliation could not take place as long as Dollfuss held power in Austria.[73] The fatal blow to Gömbös' designs was the murder of Dollfuss.

Nazi Putsch in Vienna

Gömbös' anxiety grew during the summer because of conditions in Austria. All the European papers reported the frequent Nazi terror actions and their effects on Austrian politics. Dollfuss sought a reconciliation with the moderate Social Democrats to strengthen his own position against the Nazis.[74] There were violent disagreements within the government over the possibility of including Legitimists in the government, and news of an impending government crisis circulated in the most diverse Austrian circles; Gömbös learned about a *coup d'état* in preparation against Dollfuss and tried unsuccessfully to warn him about the danger.[75]

In Gömbös' judgment, the Nazi Putsch on July 25 and the murder of Dollfuss represented a severe setback to his political designs. The vehement reaction of Mussolini and the hostile press campaign in Italy, the bellicose mood in Yugoslavia and the fact that she opened her borders to the Nazi escapees, and the resurgence of anti-German feelings in Hungary all signaled the collapse of any possible Italian-German-Austrian-Hungarian cooperation.[76] In Hungary's view, the danger could come from two directions—from a powerful Germany as next door neighbor, or from a new Italian rapprochement with France. The threat of a strong Germany was eliminated by the swift actions of Mussolini. Hitler, at least for the time being, gave up the idea of an *Anschluss*. An Italian-French *detente* however, seemed closer than ever.

Mussolini had indicated in the summer of 1933 that he would like to see a reconciliation with France. Gömbös did not believe that this reconciliation was possible without Italy giving up the support of Hungarian revisionism, while Mussolini believed that he could convince France to give up the support of the Little Entente and win her consent to some kind of revision.[77]

Barthou's visit to Rumania and Yugoslavia in June 1934, his speeches in the two capitals, and his final declaration upon arrival in Paris proved to Gömbös that a French-Italian rapprochement would mean the end of Hungarian revisionist hopes. After all, Barthou stated that: "The revisionist policy is not only unjust and contrary to the desires of peoples, but also magnifies the danger and carries the germs of war."[78] Also, the French press celebrated the fifteenth anniversary of the Versailles Treaty with long editorials stressing that though the treaty was denounced by Germany, nevertheless it had served the European peace. All of this gave the impression that France and the Little Entente were strongly united and Mussolini's designs were in need of more realistic foundations. However, on July 6, Barthou reversed himself by stating that revision was possible according to Article 19 of the Charter of the League of Nations, and if the international conditions were right, "France is ready to cooperate."[79]

Then came the Austrian crisis. Yugoslavia openly turned against France while Czechoslovakia and Rumania supported her. The chief of staff of the Hungarian army, General Vilmos Röder, evaluated the situation for the government and stressed that, in case of an *Anschluss*, the Little Entente would not follow French leadership; Czechoslovakia had already made military preparations against Hungary instead of against Germany.[80] Röder supposed that in case of an aggressive German action in Austria, the Little Entente would act in harmony against Hungary according to their military plans[81] and would not follow French advice concerning moderation. The Hungarian General Staff demanded diplomatic preparation for the reoccupation of Burgenland in case of an *Anschluss* and suggested much closer cooperation with Italy.[82]

In essence, the General Staff recommended that Gömbös assure Mussolini's support and, at the same time, keep the door open for a German-Hungarian understanding; because in spite of Germany's fast political retreat,[83] the Austrian question was not yet solved.

Gömbös, a former professional army officer, accepted this evaluation. The Italian friendship was already secured and it did not suffer any setbacks during the Austrian crisis, but the German situation became very delicate. There were signs, ironically coming from Yugoslavia, which suggested a better understanding with Hitler. During Barthou's visit, King Alexander revealed that he preferred a German-Yugoslavian rapprochement (in order to secure his country against Italy) to the Italian-Yugoslavian reconciliation which Barthou suggested.[84]

A German-Yugoslavian understanding would mean a diminution of chances for revision against Yugoslavia. However, an Italian-Yugoslavian rapprochement would have the same effect. The Hungarian foreign policy, therefore, decided to demonstrate to Italy the importance of Hungary over Yugoslavia.[85] The same decision was reached concerning Germany, with Kánya going so far as to demand Hitler's gratitude for Hungary's opposition to the Danubian Pact while also striving to convince Hitler to give up his plans directed against Austria.[86] To all of this, Hitler gave controversial replies. Although he stressed that "his friendship with Mussolini did indeed matter more to him than the whole of the Austrian state," Hitler concluded that he could not "see eye to eye with Austria where foreign policy was concerned."[87] In such circumstances, a stronger pro-German policy would be unwise.

Thus, although Gömbös did not give up his hopes for the realization of an Italian-German-Austrian-Hungarian block, he became more cautious as a result of the Austrian crisis and strengthened his relations with Italy. He still pursued an independent policy, but he now stood much closer to Mussolini than before the crisis.

Assassination at Marseilles

Threads of the assassination investigation led to Italy, Germany and Hungary. To find Italy, and particularly Mussolini guilty ran contrary to the interests of France, while to find Germany guilty was against the interests of Yugoslavia for both economic and political reasons.[88]

However, the uproar in the Yugoslavian press and public opinion made it clear to everyone that the question of responsibility could not be ignored. If they could not name the real criminals, they would have to find a convenient scapegoat. This scapegoat was found, on the basis of super-ficial evidence, in Hungary. The attitudes of the different governments in this matter no doubt influenced Gömbös' foreign policy to a great degree. France openly took the side of the Little Entente and Yugo-slavia, although Laval secretly tried to moderate Yugoslavian aggressive-ness.[89] Germany unconditionally took the side of Yugoslavia, and the German press hinted at Hungary's responsibility.[90]

When Gömbös learned that the German government judged an anti-revisionist political rapprochement with Rumania feasible, he sent the German foreign minister an ultimatum in which he warned Germany that if she "did not abandon her friendly relations with Yugoslavia soon, Hungary, together with Czechoslovakia and Austria, would form a Danubian confederation and close the Danube Basin" to Germany.[91] The German reply was brusque: the Hungarians could do what they wanted, but the matter would not be discussed any further.[92] Gömbös, not being able to do anything else, retaliated by delaying the promised special school system for German minorities in Hungary.[93]

Italy stood firmly behind Gömbös during the whole Marseilles crisis. Mussolini assured Gömbös at their October 7 meeting in Rome that if the Yugoslavians were to invade Hungary, "he would mobilize the whole Italian nation and would cross the Yugoslavian border with his troops."[94] It was good to know that Italy protected Hungary with such fervor. Yet, it was disquieting to see that France and Italy became such close friends. It was also discouraging to learn that Yugoslavia again returned to the French side and servilely followed Laval's advice. Finally, Eden's friendly attitude[95] suggested to Gömbös a possible regrouping of the Great Powers, unifying Britain, France, and Italy while isolating Germany. The circum-stances and her national interests clearly demanded Hungary's siding with this group, which she did.

Gömbös' neutral, independent policy had failed. He ended up where he began: Hungary's only friend was Italy and the realization of the revisionist demands seemed to be further away than ever. Yet, Gömbös did not give up hope and patiently waited for the opportunity to promote again his favored dream, that is, the creation of a Berlin-Rome friendship to the benefit of Hungarian revisionism. These were trying days for Gömbös. Then, at the beginning of January 1935, Laval surprised the world by announcing his upcoming visit to Rome, a trip which could lead to a possible French-Italian rapprochement.

Gömbös' Foreign Policy and
the Problem of the Danubian Pact

In the field of domestic policy, the Gömbös government gained respect and popularity because of its successful maneuvers during the Marseilles affair. The Rákosi trial[96] beginning in January 1935, created a Communist scare and further strengthened the government's popular support, as well as the position of rightist, anti-Communist, revisionist forces. At the same time, the outcome of the Saar plebiscite raised hopes for the realization of Hungarian revisionism.

These successes encouraged Gömbös to dissolve the Parliament on March 6, 1935, and declare new parliamentary elections.[97] The elections, held in April, further indicated to Gömbös which foreign political alternatives were the most popular in Hungary. The Gömbös party, with a strong revisionist ·program, gained an overwhelming majority. Districts with open ballots, as well as those with secret ballots, gave their unconditional support to this policy; and the government press emphasized as an important success the setback suffered by the Legitimist (Habsburg restorationist) Party.[98]

Gömbös then had to select the course for Hungarian foreign policy from the following alternatives: give up revisionism and unconditionally join the Danubian Pact; moderate revisionist aims and, while relying on Italy, continue to live day-by-day hoping for the best; exchange Mussolini's support for the possible support of Hitler; or try again to bring about a reconciliation between Italy and Germany, fulfilling the dream of Hungary's domination of Central Europe in cooperation with Germany north of the Danube and Italy south of the Danube. The results of the elections *canceled* out the feasibility of the unconditional acceptance of the Danubian Pact.[99]

Reliance on Mussolini's sole support seemed to be a dangerous course, for it would demand Hungary's adherence to the Danubian Pact. The whole Laval-Mussolini cooperation indicated to Gömbös that Mussolini was willing to bargain with the Little Entente as well as Laval in order to secure Austria's independence, and during this bargaining he was susceptible to forgetting Hungarian interests. Equally important, Gömbös learned that Mussolini's concern for Central Europe as a whole was declining, and the Italian-French agreement "could not have been postponed any longer. . .because of Italy's interest in Abyssinia."[100] Neither Horthy nor Gömbös saw the Italian friendship as eternal and judged it only a necessity created by circumstances.[101]

Hungary needed and welcomed Italy's support during the Marseilles affair, but soon the danger was over. In order to continue the Hungarian foreign policy of revisionism, Gömbös needed the support of a Great Power. If Italy was not available anymore, he would have to turn again to the other revisionist power—Germany. Gömbös began to change his tough attitude and use a conciliatory tone toward Germany as early as January 1935 when he ordered his Berlin ambassador to call German attention to "the fact that the [Rome] agreements were obviously directed against Germany, and therefore *the Hungarian government has the gravest doubts about them.*"[102] (italics added) However, this rapprochement attempt was not received with great enthusiasm in Germany.

Meanwhile, the Germans tried to gain special privileges for the German minorities in Hungary, which Gömbös refused to grant. The German minority entered its own candidates in the Hungarian parliamentary elections, and Gömbös practiced the "same terror" against them that he used against the rest of the opposition. Hungary sharply protested the maps drawn by pro-Hitler Hungarian youth groups since they had marked the German borders just north of Lake Balaton. Hitler still had not answered Gömbös' friendly letter sent a year before and found Gömbös' plan to visit Germany "untimely."[103]

The greatest obstacle to a German-Hungarian rapprochement, however, was the German-Yugoslavian rapprochement.[104] It not only tended to curtail Hungary's revisionist aims, but also threatened Hungary with the possibility of being sandwiched in between two unfriendly nations. Servilely following the German line was clearly against the interests of Hungary, but gaining Germany's goodwill was necessary to make revisionism feasible against Czechoslovakia. The old dilemma had not changed: Hungary needed the support of Hitler as well as Mussolini.

The success of Gömbös' foreign policy conception depended on a rapprochement between Italy and Germany. Although, the primary obstacle to this cooperation was the Austrian question, the differences between Germany and Italy were even more exaggerated by the Danubian Pact. As Gömbös recognized, in order to bring about any rapprochement, it was necessary to torpedo the pact without openly offending Mussolini. These were the considerations that made Gömbös state the following demands as preconditions for Hungary joining the Danubian Pact: closing of the Marseilles affair;[105] recognition of Hungary's right to rearm; security for the improvement of the Hungarian minorities' conditions in the Little Entente states; rejection of the mutual assistance treaties; and adherence of Germany to the Danubian Pact.

With the help of the Danubian Pact, Mussolini wanted "to secure calmness in Central Europe" for "possible military operations" in Abyssinia.[106] This made Mussolini touchy concerning the Hungarian demands. Yet, slowly, he gave in to these demands, especially when he experienced rigidity on the part of the Little Entente.[107] Gömbös' foreign political plans worked successfully *vis a vis* Mussolini.

Gömbös continued this policy until his untimely death in October 1936. Looking back to his political activities, we may suppose that, had Gömbös lived, he would have produced a new turn in his foreign policy since Germany's emergence created a situation that was not as "simple as Gömbös, in his early enthusiasm, had imagined."[108]

CHAPTER IX
THE END OF COLLECTIVE SECURITY

The year 1935 began with the diplomatic victory of Laval over Mussolini during their Rome meeting on January 7. One week later, on January 13, France suffered a public opinion defeat when the people of the Saar Valley voted overwhelmingly for a return of their territory to Germany.

On March 16, Germany reintroduced general conscription and denounced the obligations of the Versailles Treaty. Mussolini's reaction, prompt and direct, was mobilization, while France lengthened the duration of military service from one to two years.[1] As usual, the French Left opposed the government's measures, not because they were a mistake, but simply because *the government* did something. In contrast to the strong French reaction, the British note to Hitler was relatively mild since Britain was anxious to continue negotiations for a naval pact with Germany.[2] Hitler rightly evaluated that France and Britain did not represent a solid block in the way of his designs.[3]

On April 11-14, 1935, the Stresa Conference was called to deal with the problem of German rearmament and the question of Central Europe. It again proved that France and Britain agreed only on one point: they did not want any kind of open confrontation with Germany that could lead to war. Mussolini, seeing the passivity of his partners, came away from Stresa disappointed. He unsuccessfully tried to make an agreement with Great Britain and France concerning the exact limit of the concessions they were prepared to give to Germany.[4] A few days later (April 16-17), the Council of the League of Nations met and condemned the German action, though no punitive measures were adopted. The Western world accepted the German renouncement of Versailles and the German rearmament program as a *fait a compli*. Hitler had won his first gamble.

The paths of the three Great Powers seemed to diverge even further during the remaining months of 1935. France signed a mutual assistance treaty with the Soviet Union on May 2; Great Britain signed the naval accord with Germany on May 18; and Mussolini launched the Ethiopian campaign on October 3, which signaled the end of French-Italian cooperation.

Ethiopian Crisis and Sanctions

"The two principal arguments advanced by Italy to justify her action against Abyssinia were the vital needs of the Italian people and their security in East Africa."[5] Mussolini and the other leaders of Fascist Italy openly stated this goal, but the European statesmen did not pay too much attention to their announcement. Economic conditions in Italy became very critical by the end of 1934: the lira was threatened with devaluation, the government's budget was burdened with a heavy deficit, the balance of trade was unfavorable, and the balance of international payments was in the red.

On the other hand, Italy's international authority stood at a high point. The Laval-Mussolini meeting and the Stresa Conference seemed to secure Italy's European interests and Mussolini, according to his interpretation, received French and English consent for the realization of his East-African designs.[6] The only authority which could have opposed Mussolini's plans was the League of Nations, seemingly under the firm control of England and France. The League represented only moral authority, though, in practical cases she proved impotent. But how could Britain ask for the League's moral condemnation of Italy when, with the signing of the Anglo-German Naval Pact on June 18, 1935, she herself violated the basic principles of the Covenant? What right had Eden to lecture Mussolini on the question of morality and imperialism?[7] How could France oppose Mussolini's designs after recognizing, only six months earlier, Italy's colonial claims and agreeing to the Libyan transaction? How could his Stresa partners turn against him, when Mussolini had proven his loyalty by taking definitive, practical steps against their common enemy: Germany? Did not Italy have well-founded and legitimate grievances against Abyssinia? Most probably Mussolini answered these questions for himself without hesitation: they cannot, they will not turn against Italy. Yet, the unbelieveable happened and the League voted economic sanctions against Italy on October 14, 1935, two weeks after Mussolini launched the invasion.

However, the economic sanctions did not include an oil embargo, did not prohibit the supply of steel and chromium, and did not close the Suez Canal to Italian troop and supply transports. The conquest of Abyssinia was a relatively easy task and the santions were disregarded by

Mussolini.[8] His pride was more important, and it was badly hurt when, during the League debate, he was stamped an imperialist aggressor and was isolated from the "civilized" nations of the world. Only Austria, Germany and Hungary continued normal trade relations with Italy. Mussolini reacted with not only protests, but also economic counter-measures, a stepped up propaganda campaign against Great Britain, and military preparations against the Mediterranean movements of the British navy.[9]

In the meantime, Britain and France, as well as the League, tried to bring about a negotiated settlement. Italy was not interested. Though the economic sanctions hurt, military victories gave her enough confidence to continue the war. Laval and his government could not survive the Ethiopian crisis, for the French people clearly understood the consequences of his vacillating policy. It left France "at loggerheads with England and Italy."[10] The German remilitarization of the Rhineland made it urgent for Flandin, his successor, to restore the good relationship with Italy, without losing the goodwill of Great Britain.

Remilitarization of the Rhineland

In May 1934, four officers of the French army were found guilty of communicating to German agents secrets about French strategic defense plans. In March, June, and August 1935, German spies (some of them officers of the French army and navy) were arrested and tried for their activities in garrisons located near the Rhineland. In February 1935, the German intelligence service strengthened its personnel in Aachen, Trier, and Saarbrücken in order to increase the information collected about French forces stationed along the border.[11]

By the fall of 1935, the French Deuxième Bureau began to report information which caused uneasiness in the French General Staff, and the French intelligence services concluded from data collected in Germany that "Germany actively was preparing for the reoccupation of the demilitarized zone."[12] The government was not willing to believe these reports, but the General Staff became more and more alarmed. By the end of February 1936, they knew that the Germans would use the recent ratification of the Franco-Soviet Pact as justification for the occupation of the Rhineland. Now even the government was alarmed, especially when

General Maurin, Minister of Defense, reported that the French forces, in view of the strength of the Germany army, would be able to perform only defensive assignments in case of the German occupation of the Rhineland. Then, on March 7, 1936, the long expected happened:[13] German troops moved into the demilitarized zone, and the French forces offered no opposition at all.

Georges Bonnet harshly evaluates France's attitude and passivity during the time of the Rhineland occupation: "Destiny had given her [France] a final chance to safeguard her future, safeguard peace and the future of Europe, and she missed it."[14] No less severe is the judgment of historians, who have generally concluded that France missed the last chance to stop Nazi expansion in Europe.[15] However, French politicians and military leaders of the time had less information than do historians today. Because of that, judgment cannot be passed without reconstructing the general situation existing on March 7, 1936.

Conditions in France

French foreign relations were in bad shape. The old alliance system did not work anymore. The Little Entente existed on paper, but the only member France could rely on in case of war against Germany was Czechoslovakia. Britain pursued her own policy toward Germany, and since the Anglo-German Naval Accord, she was less than willing to follow a hard line policy against Germany. The Franco-Soviet Assistance Treaty lacked practical advantages as long as Poland refused passage for the Soviet troops. Poland, on the other hand, notified France on March 7, 1936, that she would not hesitate to carry out her obligations as an ally.[16] After the Stresa Conference, a disappointed Mussolini concentrated his attention on the Ethiopian War, was willing to make a compromise with Hitler concerning Central Europe, and felt increasingly hostile toward the British and French designs.

Thus, France was very much isolated. It is understandable that under such circumstances the French government did not want to take any step which could create an uproar of indignation in the world. World public opinion was pacifist, especially so in Britain and France.

International law also opposed any one-sided French countermove against the German remilitarization of the Rhineland. Articles 42 and 43 of the Versailles Treaty and Article 2 of the Locarno Treaty were violated "only if German troops entered the demilitarized zone for the purpose of marching on the French border and invading French soil;" if this was not the case, then France could act against the Germans only "as the result of a decision taken by the Assembly or by the Council" of the League of Nations.[17]

Any unilateral action on the part of France would violate international laws which were designed originally to strengthen the security of France. Of course, France could disregard all these obstacles and take decisive action, if she was willing to risk a war. The decisive factors which deterred the French government from the use of force were the French domestic political situation and her military condition.

After the Albert Sarraut government took office on January 24, 1936, the old majority of the "Governments of National Unity"[18] disappeared because the Popular Front wanted to preserve the advantages of the opposition in the upcoming election campaign.[19] Thus, though the Sarraut government superficially enjoyed the support of a great majority of the Chamber,[20] in reality it was tolerated only because of the upcoming elections. The breach of national unity was completed when Sarraut ordered the dissolution of all Right wing organizations after February 13, 1936, and then some members of the "Camelots du Roi" organization assaulted Socialist leader Léon Blum. The Sarraut government thus found the Left, as well as the Right, in opposition.

The press continued to attack the government, undermining its credibility and authority.[21] The strongly pacifist public opinion found comfort in the official interpretation of the German moves since March 16, 1935, when Germany had reintroduced general conscription against the resolution of the Versailles Treaty. This view held that the German steps did not represent a direct threat to France.[22] Even the lengthening of the military service was denounced by both the political Left and the press.[23] The domestic political situation in France then did not suggest to the government that a strong stand and possibly a war against Germany would gain the approval and support of the Chamber of Deputies or public opinion. "A throughout pacifist state of mind preferred to believe that a collective manifestation will achieve infinitely more, than a gesture of France alone."[24]

Meanwhile, instead of improving, French military conditions deteriorated.[25] Though Laval's diplomacy had eliminated the danger of a two-front war, changes which occurred (or did not occur) in the French army organization made the army an instrument of doubtful value. On the morning of the German remilitarization, General Gamelin reported to Sarraut that though the French army momentarily held the upper hand, if France had to fight a long war alone, German superiority in numbers and industrial capacity would prevail.[26] This was a realistic, objective evaluation, and Sarraut was convinced that France *would* have to fight alone, since "neither the English nor the Belgians will march."[27] Even more disappointing was the opinion of General Maurin who stated that the French army's training, equipment, and mentality were strictly defensive; the army would have to call in all available forces for an offensive operation, not only for the attack but also for the occupation of the Maginot line, which would serve as a base for any forward movement.[28] The Deuxième Bureau estimated that the Germans had assembled more than 265,000 men in the Rhineland under disguised names, not to mention the strength of those troops which had entered the zone to serve in the garrisons.[29] Maurin, therefore, suggested that a general mobilization of French forces was necessary in order to fight against Germany and a general mobilization was estimated to cost about 30 million francs daily.[30]

Thus, the military conditions undoubtedly opposed the adoption of an aggressive policy and suggested to the French government the need to find an alternative solution. They found it in the appeal that they made to the League of Nations which, not having military forces of her own, could not do anything other than accept the *fait à compli* after morally condemning the German aggression.

Conditions in Germany

The international relations of Germany were good by 1936. The Polish Non-Aggression Pact seemed, to a certain degree, to secure Germany from the danger of a two-front war. Germany had gained strong control over the economy of Central Europe and thereby could greatly influence political decisions. The negotiations for a naval accord with Britain were proceeding well, and through these negotiations, Hitler had successfully separated Britain from France. Mussolini, who was embittered by the British and French reaction to the Ethiopian War, was no longer an unreconcilable enemy; and in case of a French-German conflict, he was expected to take a wait-and-see attitude.

The domestic situation in Germany was improving, too, as "Germany was able to restore a measure of economic order and to introduce a number of programs leading toward economic development."[31] Thanks to the improved economic conditions and to the policy of *Gleichschaltung*, Hitler became the unchallenged dictator of Germany. On June, 1934, he purified his own party of those who "deviated either to the right or to the left."[32] With the Nürnberg Laws,. he began to eliminate the Jews from the government and professions, as well as the economic and cultural life. Since the elimination of Jews created vacancies and opportunities for thousands of people, the Germans reacted to these measures with less indignation than expected. The renouncement of the armament clauses of the Versailles Treaty secured almost unanimous popular support for Hitler.[33] Finally, the reintroduction of conscription assured him the loyalty of the army.

However, the organization, training, and equiping of the projected thirty-six divisions (550,000 men) was a hard task.[34] Realizing very well that the reorganization period (1935-1937) would represent a time of weakness for the German army, the General Staff sincerely desired a period of peace and quiet.[35] It was therefore, a shock for them to learn that Hitler wanted to use the army as early as the spring of 1936. First of all, they were far away from the completion of the thirty-six divisions,[36] and even the already standing divisions were not ready for combat. The German General Staff knew that their untrained, undermanned recruit divisions were no match for the combined forces of Poland, Czecho-slovakia, and France, which represented ninety fully trained divisions on peace footing and 190 divisions in case of war.[37]

Hitler knew, however, that in a crisis, psychology is sometimes more important than the number of divisions. Yet, he was extremely nervous when the first German units entered the Rhineland. Curiously, while he knew that the German army was not strong enough to confront even Poland alone, he was anxious only about a possible British military intervention.[38] The German forces which occupied the Rhineland numbered about 12,000 men, while only three batallions crossed the Rhine and marched to Aachen, Trier, and Saarbrücken.[39] The batallion commanders were under strict orders to withdraw in case of French resistance, since the Germans "had not the military resources at their disposal for even a feeble resistance."[40]

Evaluation of the Rhineland Incident

The most striking feature of the whole remilitarization affair is the overcautious attitude of both the German and French General Staffs. It is an outstanding denial of the fashionable accusation that the generals were warmongers and militants, anxious to wage war whenever they had a chance. Their hesitation, of course, had different reasons. The German generals cannot be blamed for not being able to raise the number and combat value of their divisions in such a short period of time.

The French General Staff's caution was another matter. They had superiority in numbers, training, and equipment. Even the overestimation of German forces should not excuse them from their responsibility in advocating such a passive attitude. Their memories of World War I had to influence them greatly, and they most probably shared the conviction of Mussolini, that during World War I "1,400,000,000 men were required in order to defeat 60,000,000 Germans; the reason being that the rigid Prussian military training has made the soldiers *invincible*."[41] (italics added) They also misjudged the value of defense lines versus mobile military units. The consequences of these misjudgments were much greater than only the loss of the Rhineland proper. The whole French-Central European military cooperation was based on the assumption that French forces, using the Rhineland as a bridgehead, would launch a massive attack in order to link up with the Czechoslovakian and Polish armies against the Germans.[42] With the loss of the Rhineland, the French General Staff renounced this opportunity and, by so doing deserted their Central European allies. The judgment of statesmen and historians seems to be valid: in the Rhineland, France missed the last opportunity to stop Nazi expansionism.

However, the question remains were the conditions which were so important in 1936 the results of a sudden change (most particularly, the product of the one year since Germany had renounced the Versailles Treaty) or were they only the end products of a long evolution? If the latter, the question of responsibility can possibly be placed on the shoulders of those other than the General Staff. The commitments of France toward her Central European allies had not changed since the signing of earlier alliances, though some modifications were implemented in 1932 and 1933. The aims of the French grand strategy remained the same: prevent Germany from becoming a great power. The diplomacy, however, had failed to secure favorable conditions for the enforcement of this aim. By 1934, Barthou had to pick up the destroyed French alliance system and try to rebuild it. During the Laval ministry, Franco-Italian cooperation created the necessary international situation which made the French grand strategy feasible again. At the same time, though, this Franco-Italian rapprochement further ruined France's chance to rebuild her prestige in Central Europe. At the moment that France turned her back on Mussolini and found the guarantee for her own security in the militarily useless Soviet mutual assistance and British cooperation of doubtful value, all the preconditions for the grand strategic aim of German containment had disappeared.

One may argue that the French military leadership bears the responsibility for not preparing the army for what occurred on March 7, 1936; that they could be blamed for not rightly evaluating the lessons of World War I and for not accepting the advise of Charles de Gaulle. This argument is based on one mistake: France was not a dictatorship. The French General Staff did not decide the size of the army and did not have unlimited financial resources for the army. The Chamber of Deputies made these decisions. Their responsibility at least equaled the responsibility of the General Staff, even in the decision to build the Maginot line. While perhaps being amateurish and naive in military strategy, the deputies nevertheless knew that building the Maginot line could not promote the feasibility of their state's grand strategy. The undeniable fact is that the French governments and politicians abandoned their original plan concerning the containment of Germany (nipping in the bud any German attempt to disobey the Versailles Treaty) and were concerned only with the security of France, even at the price of selling out their allies. They felt absolutely secure, as far as their fatherland was concerned, behind the Maginot line.

Central European Worries

Since Austria and Hungary did not join the sanctions against Italy, while the members of the Little Entente did, the frontlines were not altered: revisionist states opposed the block of anti-revisionist states. The Austrian and Hungarian positions weakened, however, because of

Mussolini's increased preoccupation with the Abyssinian war. No wonder, then, that each made an effort to improve her own position and security.

Austria's main concern was the German menace. She tried to secure her independence *vis à vis* Germany by recruiting new friends without losing the old ones or offending Germany. To this end, Schuschnigg made an attempt at rapprochement with France and Czechoslovakia. The attempt started out with great hopes: France began a propaganda campaign which stressed the importance of Austria and encouraged her joining the Little Entente, while Schuschnigg's visit to Czechoslovakia and his negotiations there with Benes and Hodza paved the way for closer economic relations and produced a relaxation of the previously hostile mood.[43]

Hungary still considered Austrian independence in her own interest and, therefore, tried to find a *modus vivendi* for Austria and Germany. She suggested that Germany give guarantees for the independence of Austria in an official declaration.[44] At the same time, Gömbös continued to resist Germany's attempts to gain special privileges for the German minorities in Hungary.[45] The idea of Austria-Czechoslovak rapprochement was received with hostility in Budapest. Hungary still hoped for the realization of her revisionist claims, first of all against Czechoslovakia, and became suspicious of Schuschnigg's real goals in Prague.

In the meantime, Austrian public opinion, under the influence of pro-Habsburg Legitimist propaganda, increasingly accepted the idea that the best security against an *Anschluss* would be a Habsburg restoration.[46] The German propaganda machine did not hesitate to pick up the topic and elaborated on the dangers of a Habsburg restoration from the point of view of the Central European states. Göring even suggested that Germany and Hungary organize and cooperate in an anti-Habsburg front.[47] How successful the German propaganda was in planting suspicion in Hungary and the Little Entente states was proven by their numerous diplomatic documents during 1936 which dealt with the danger of the Habsburg restoration.

The Little Entente seemed to be still a strong alliance. Their energetic warnings against the Habsburg restoration, firm support of the League of Nations policy in the Abyssinian crisis, and enthusiastic reply to the sanctions against Italy gave the impression of unity. However, their economic dependence on Germany began to influence their individual policies. The Yugoslavian government followed a steady rapprochement policy with Germany, thereby harmonizing its economic interests with its political aims. Rumanian Foreign Minister Titulescu, while still following the directions of France, lost domestic support due to the economic effects of the sanctions and had to comply more and more with the foreign political concepts of King Carol. Benes looked with distrust at Hodza's negotiations and began to seek security for Czechoslovakia by creating a better relationship with Germany. Poland's foreign policy, after the death of Pilsudski on May 12, 1935, remained entirely in the hands of Colonel Beck and followed the line marked out by the Polish-German and Polish-Soviet Non-Aggression Pacts.

Then in March, all the Central European nations forgot their own problems for a few days and nervously watched the German remilitarization of the Rhineland, and the French reaction to it. But the French reaction was not what they hoped for. Instead of taking the initiative and acting as a self-confident great power, France hesitated and, after a week delay, filed complaints in the League of Nations.

From this French action (or better, passivity), the Central European states had to draw their own conclusions concerning their particular situations and interests. It was urgent for them to do so, especially in light of Hitler's new offer: a twenty-five year treaty guaranteeing western frontiers and, for his eastern neighbors, individual non-aggression pacts similar to that signed with Poland.[48] At the same time, he expressed the willingness of Germany to return to the League of Nations.[49]

Germany's surprise move and the connected new offers divided even the French government. Flandin, and Sarraut wanted "to go to the limit in resisting the Third Reich, including if necessary the use of armed force. . .with or without Britain."[50] Paul-Boncour, on the other hand, preferred negotiations and a strong diplomatic action, possibly sanctions, against Germany. His group tried to force Great Britain to join these measures by stating that Britain could not demand the continuation of sanctions against Italy, where only her transportation routes were involved, if she rejected sanctions when France and her allied states were at stake.[51] General Maurin saw military action feasible only in case of general mobilization[52] and British help. Eden's reaction to the German moves was mild, and he seemed extremely concerned about not offending Germany, while Mussolini declined to support the League of Nations because of the sanctions in effect against Italy.[53]

The fact is that Mussolini did not care too much about the Rhineland. What disturbed him was the German offer of non-aggression pacts which, if signed, would create a new situation in the Danube valley. He interpreted the German intention to return to the League of Nations as a stab in Italy's back.[54] The Soviet Union offered Flandin "support in any steps he might take, emphasizing the dangers of condoning Germany's action."[55] Beck, despite Poland's relatively good relations with Germany, notified the French government that he was ready to fulfill Poland's obligations toward France.[56] Hungary, on the other hand, applauded the German action and recommended Germany not sign a non-aggression pact for a period longer than ten years.

The Little and Balkan Ententes published a joint Communiqué in support of France, thereby demonstrating again their unity; but shortly after, they separated themselves one by one from the Communiqué. First Greece notified Germany that the Communiqué was drawn up at the insistence of Titulescu, and the Greek government would remain neutral in the Locarno question even though they had signed the declaration.[57] The following day, Stoyadinovich confidentially told the German ambassador that Yugoslavia "was fully determined not in any circumstances to participate in sanctions of any kind against Germany."[58] In Prague, while the government gave unreserved support to any action France might take, business circles were anxious not to take part in economic sanctions against Germany since "Germany is not only Czechoslovakia's largest market, but is also at the same time her biggest supplier."[59] Even Titulescu, believing it necessary to find an excuse for his actions, declared that "he would so much have liked to find a way to Germany's side," and he instructed the Rumanian press to avoid exaggerating the situation.[60]

Unprepared and hesitant, France found herself alone. Hitler was victorious. The Versailles Treaty and the system it had created were thrown into the storage room of history. For France's allies, the question raised by the Rhineland affair was: "How can we count on France for our defense after she was not willing to defend even herself?"[61] Answering this question became especially urgent for Rumania, whose King Carol now foresaw the possibility of "German troops marching through Rumanian territory against Russia."[62]

CHAPTER X
THE FIFTH CRISIS: FALL OF TITULESCU

In directing Rumanian foreign policy from 1932 to 1936, Titulescu's basic foreign political conception was the preservation of the status quo in alliance with other pro-status quo powers. This political principle determined Rumania's enemies and friends on the basis of realistic considerations as well as ideological convictions. Rumania wanted to secure her territorial integrity against Hungary, especially regarding the former Hungarian territories of Transylvania and Banat. Rumania was at odds with Bulgaria because of southern Dobruja, a former Bulgarian territory awarded to Rumania by the Neuilly Treaty of 1919. The Soviet Union was an enemy because she refused to recognize the Rumanian annexation of Bessarabia after World War I, and because of ideology since Rumania was anti-Communist.

Realistic interests and ideology also marked out Rumania's allies. Czechoslovakia and Yugoslavia were Rumania's allies *vis à vis* Hungary; Greece and Yugoslavia were allies against Bulgaria; and Poland was an ally against bolshevik Russia. To secure Rumania's entrance to the Mediterranean Sea, it was in her interest to nurture friendly relations with Turkey.

NEW DEMANDS FOR RUMANIAN FOREIGN POLICY

Economic and Ideological Changes

Economically, Rumania needed and received investment capital from the West. She imported industrial products and machinery and sold her agricultural products, timber, oil and raw materials on the international market. Economic interests demanded a good relationship with the United States, who had controlled all public telephone services in Rumania since 1930[1] and had a great share in the modernization of the Rumanian oil industry. In 1931, Rumania ranked fourteenth among France's trading partners, importing 565.633 million francs worth of merchandise and exporting 115.165 million francs.[2] Rumanian trade was also significant with the successor states. Rumanian exports to these countries amounted to 32.2% of her total exports while imports from this area represented 35.6% of the total.[3]

Economic interests suggested to Rumania a peaceful, friendly foreign policy toward the Great Powers and her neighbors since they shared about equally in Rumania's trade. Titulescu's foreign political conception, the preservation of the status quo, did not contradict the basic economic interests of Rumania.

The great depression, however, caused important changes in the Rumanian trade situation. Rumania's most precious export, oil, lost its French market in 1934 because of the Franco-Iraqi and Franco-Soviet commercial treaties,[4] although Rumanian oilmen found ready buyers in Italy. Rumania's wheat export fell, due to the increased wheat production in France, Germany, Czechoslovakia and Britain. The Balkan states (Bulgaria, Greece, Rumania, Turkey and Yugoslavia) held several trade conferences between 1930-1933, but after some initial success they discontinued negotiations because of their sharp political differences.[5]

Rumania, like the other Central European states, then turned to Germany and the two states signed a trade treaty on March 23, 1935. Thus, by 1935, Rumanian economic interests began to oppose Titulescu's foreign political conceptions, and the Rumanian economy became dependent on trade relations with the revisionist powers.

Ideological changes began to occur in 1930 when, on June 9, King Carol returned to Rumania. He preferred authoritarian rule at the expense of democracy and admired Mussolini's state-controlled economy over the capitalist free enterprise system. More important were the changes in the field of ideology represented by the growing rightist groups. Yet, Titulescu remained faithful to democratic ideas. Thus a gap developed between him and domestic political leaders, creating many clashes and misunderstandings.

The contradictions between these economic and ideological changes and Titulescu's policy remained hidden for a longer period of time than, for example, in Yugoslavia. In the questions of Hungarian revisionism, Habsburg restoration and Italian involvement in Balkan politics, Rumanian business circles and the extreme nationalist groups supported Titulescu's aims until 1935. Furthermore, these very same problems usually united the Little Entente states into a solid block, with French support, and so Titulescu never found himself fighting for a cause alone. During the exciting events of the early 1930's (Eastern Pact negotiations, unsuccessful Nazi Putsch in Vienna, assassination at Marseilles, German-Polish Non-Aggression Pact, Four Power Pact plans, Danubian Pact proposal), Rumania's interests were the same as those of her allies, and economic or ideological factors did not contradict her foreign political goals.

In 1935, however, Titulescu's foreign policy for the first time lacked the unlimited support of the king and public opinion, did not agree with the goals of Rumania's smaller allies, and received the disapproval of France. The Soviet-Rumanian negotiations for a mutual assistance treaty, the Ethiopian war and sanctions against Italy, and the crisis created by the Spanish civil war, produced a chain of dilemmas for Titulescu. Under the pressure of events, his actions and reactions became more and more controversial.

Soviet-Rumanian Negotiations

The signing of the Soviet-French and Soviet-Czechoslovak mutual assistance treaties in May 1935 "created the political and diplomatic atmosphere propitious to the conclusion of mutual assistance pacts between the [other] Little Entente States and the Soviet Union," so that in July, at the encouragement of France and Britain, Titulescu asked for and received full authorization to negotiate a mutual assistance treaty with the Soviet Union.[6] Why was the conclusion of such a treaty in the interest of Rumania?

Rumania and Poland represented the first line of defense for Europe against the spread of communism and against a possible Soviet invasion. At least that is how France interpreted the Polish-Rumanian alliance when it was created in March 1921, although this interpretation lost significance after the Franco-Soviet rapprochement in 1934. There were, however, more realistic Rumanian and Polish interests involved. Both had received large and precious territories from Russia after World War I. The Treaty of Riga legalized the Polish occupation of parts of the Ukraine, and the Soviet Union acknowledged her loss of these territories by signing the treaty. No such agreement existed between Rumania and the Soviet Union. On the contrary, the Soviet Union never recognized Bessarabia as an integral part of Rumania. No wonder, then, that Rumania had a feeling of insecurity and worried about a possible Soviet aggression. As a result, Rumanian foreign policy was directed against the Soviet Union and against communism.

Titulescu himself was an ardent anti-Communist, and the Rumanian government broke off non-aggression pact negotiations with the Soviet Union in 1932 at the recommendation of Titulescu.[7] No diplomatic relations existed between Rumania and the Soviet Union until May 1934. Though on this occasion both governments pledged to respect each other's sovereignty, the main problem remained unsolved: "Titulescu wanted to guarantee the *national independence* and the *territorial integrity* of Rumania" (italics added), but this was unacceptable to Litvinov.[8]

What changes had occurred within three years that Titulescu decided to renew negotiations with the Soviet Union? And this time, why negotiate for not only a *non-aggression pact* but also a *mutual assistance treaty*?

Possible Changes in the Demands of Rumanian Security

The use of the expression "mutual assistance treaty" indicates that Rumania needed *additional* security against *a third party*, supposedly the common enemy of both countries. But no such enemy emerged between the years 1932-1935. The basic principles of Titulescu's foreign policy remained the same: anti-revisionism and defense of the status quo. According to these principles, the Soviet Union was an enemy of Rumania, along with revisionist Bulgaria and Hungary. It was questionable if Rumania could use additional help from the Soviet Union against a very improbable Hungarian aggression when more than enough assistance was already available from her Little Entente partners. The same reasoning would be valid concerning Bulgaria since the Balkan Entente provided similarly ample assistance. *Only against Soviet revisionism* was Rumania *not well enough protected*, relying on the realistic help of but one country: Poland. Then what was the purpose of a Soviet assistance treaty if the Soviet Union was the only enemy Rumania feared?

Possibly Titulescu considered Hungarian revisionism and a Habsburg restoration such a threat to Transylvania that he wanted to enlist Soviet help, even if it cost the loss of Bessarabia.[9] But Hungary and the Soviet Union did not have a common frontier, so that Soviet assistance against Hungary could be realized only by Soviet troops crossing Rumanian territory. In the absence of Soviet guarantees for the independence and integrity of Rumania, these troop crossings represented such a great risk that no Rumanian citizen, not even Titulescu, would be willing to take responsibility for it.

Today it is accepted without argument that Rumania sought the assistance treaty with the Soviet Union *against Germany*, and generally *against the Fascist states*. But even if we accept the untrue generalization that Austria and Hungary were Fascist states, their military weakness excluded them as aggressors; and the geographic location of Germany made it impossible for her to attack Rumania directly. For such a confrontation of German and Rumanian troops, it would be necessary for Germany to invade Austria and Hungary first, or for Rumanian troops to go to the aid of Czechoslovakia.[10] The latter alternative required an excellent road and railroad system between Czechoslovakia and Rumania; no such transportation system existed in 1935.[11]

Realistic political considerations thus deny that changes in the demands of Rumania's security necessitated a mutual assistance treaty with the Soviet Union, unless Titulescu hoped that he could incorporate in the treaty Soviet guarantees for Rumania's territorial integrity. The words "mutual assistance" are misleading, "non-aggression" truly describes the purpose of the Titulescu-Litvinov negotiations.[12]

Possible Changes in Economic Interests

Is it possible that Rumanian economic interests had changed so that economic considerations demanded a rapprochement with the Soviet Union? By 1935 the amount of Rumanian imports from the successor states fell from 118 million dollars to 32 million dollars while her exports declined from 88 million dollars to 43 million dollars.[13] Similar depreciation took place in her trade relations with the Western democracies. Only Germany greatly improved trade with Rumania, actually saving her from a new economic crisis. German trade was so precious that Titulescu took pains in 1933 to explain to Germany that his attempts at strengthening economic relations with the Little Entene would not effect other previously signed trade agreements.[14] German-Rumanian economic relations continued to improve and were crowned on March 23, 1935, by a new trade agreement which made Germany the number one trading partner of Rumania.

Economic interests did not demand even a rapprochement with the Soviet Union, still less a mutual assistance treaty. As a matter of fact, any closer relationship with the Soviet Union could only hurt Rumania's economic interest. Germany followed the Rumanian moves very closely and from the conclusion of the Soviet-French mutual assistance treaty constantly sent inquiries to the Rumanian government about the Soviet-Rumanian negotiations, warning Titulescu not to take part in any encirclement attempt of France or the Soviet Union.[15]

Possible Changes in the International Situation

Germany was not the only country watching the Titulescu-Litvinov negotiations with suspicion. The Polish government was also concerned, especially Beck who, while not objecting to a Soviet-Rumanian non-aggression pact, expressed his conviction that a mutual assistance treaty would endanger the validity of the old Polish-Rumanian mutual assistance treaty.[16] Beck and Pilsudski feared Soviet strength and aggressiveness in spite of the Polish-Soviet Non-Aggression Pact. They could not agree with Eden who, after his Moscow visit in March 1935, informed them that the "USSR had neither the intention, nor the capability of undertaking aggressive actions and would not for a long time."[17]

The Soviet-Rumanian negotiations triggered a Polish-Hungarian rapprochement that ended in a government-sanctioned "gentlemen's agreement" (December 1935), which said: "Poland regards the Hungarian annexation of Ruthenia and with that the restoration of the hundreds of years old common Polish-Hungarian frontier as her own interest."[18]

Change occurred in the international situation of Eastern Europe *in reaction to* the Soviet-Rumanian negotiations. Titulescu lost the confidence of Poland and at the same time endangered the security of Czechoslovakia, his Little Entente partner. It was too high a price to pay for the goodwill of Litvinov.

Effects of Ideological Considerations

If the realistic political and economic interests of Rumania did not demand more than a non-aggression pact, why did Titulescu pursue with such obstinacy the mutual assistance treaty? In spite of the Soviet Union's disinterest and over the objections of his government, Titulescu followed "a rapprochement with Soviet Russia, which the Government had not desired."[19] Why?

Maybe he wanted to please his French patrons by following the example set by the Franco-Soviet treaty. Maybe he did not want Rumania to lag behind after Czechoslovakia also concluded a treaty with the Soviet Union. Maybe, like Barthou, he believed that no European security agreement could function properly without the participation of the Soviet Union. This direction is indicated by Oprea: "The conclusion of such a treaty sprang up from the necessity of integrating Rumania's foreign policy with the general anti-revisionist policy."[20] If that is true, Titulescu made a great mistake: he submitted the realistic demands of his country to the demands of ideology, since neither the general anti-revisionist policy nor Rumania's patrons *demanded* the conclusion of such a pact. They just *suggested* it. However, if Titulescu could have incorporated Soviet guarantees for Rumanian territorial integrity in *any kind* of treaty, he would have given the greatest service to his country.

During the long bargaining, Titulescu lost the sympathies of Poland and of the anti-Communist politicians in Rumania; but even the Polish assistance treaty could have lapsed without consequences if Rumania had a non-aggression pact with the Soviet Union. Nobody can accuse Titulescu of forgetting Rumanian interests during his negotiations with Litvinov. Titulescu never gave his consent to Soviet troop crossings in the absence of Soviet guarantees for Rumania's territorial integrity. He accepted Soviet assistance as far as war material and armament was concerned, but he never entertained Communist ideas and never advocated a one-sided pro-Soviet policy.

No pact was signed because of the Soviet conditions. But Titulescu had to attempt to conclude such an agreement. The negotiation's negative effects influenced Titulescu's personal career more than the future of Rumania. He tried and failed, that is all a historian may say about him concerning his actions during the period of May 1934 to the summer of 1935.

Ethiopian War and Rumania's Role in the Sanctions

Titulescu considered Mussolini one of the most dangerous enemies of Rumania, because he was the patron of revisionist Hungary, protector of Austria, and supporter of Bulgaria. During the Stresa Conference in April

1935, when Mussolini suggested the rearmament of Austria and Hungary against the German menace, Titulescu fought violently against the proposition. Under his leadership, the Little and Balkan Entente countries rejected the Stresa proposals at their Bucharest conference the following May.

Titulescu's anti-Italian feelings were coupled with a suspicion concerning the real aims of England, especially after he learned during his London visit in February 1936 that King Edward VIII was willing to support the restoration of the Habsburgs in Austria. Titulescu considered the Anglo-German Naval Accord of June 18, 1936 a great diplomatic success for Hitlerian diplomacy.[21]

Relations with France were better, but since the Laval-Mussolini agreement in January 1935, Titulescu also looked suspiciously at the French political plans. Then during the summer of 1935, the Ethiopian crisis foreshadowed the possible final breach between Rumania and France. During the crisis, Laval clearly took the side of Italy *versus* England and the majority of the League of Nations. He tried to convince even England to give up her opposing position. France felt that Mussolini "needs colonial expansion and it would be the best if he would do it at the expense of Negus' empire;" an Italian "victory without war in Abyssinia," would be in "the common interest of all powers who were concerned over the independence of Austria."[22] On July 10, Laval declared to the Austrian ambassador that he would stand unconditionally on the side of Italy, expecting that England would finally yield and a friendly solution would be found.[23] But Eden did not seem willing to yield.

The moment was critical for Rumania. What position should Rumania take? Should she join those who condemned Italy and applied sanctions or should she side with Italy? Perhaps she should remain neutral. Titulescu had to determine Rumania's interest *vis à vis* Italy before deciding which alternative to follow.

Participation in the Sanctions

Politically, Italy was an indirect enemy of Rumania only because of her support of revisionist Hungary. Economically, Italy was among Rumania's best trading partners. Ideology was a sensitive question: Titulescu was a firm enemy of fascism, while King Carol sympathized with it and many Rumanians preferred a more extreme rightist regime. If the sanctions were effective in the short run, there would be some advantages for Rumanian participation. Mussolini would lose power, authority, and respect, maybe even fall as the head of the Italian government. In that case, the new Italian government could be expected to cooperate closely with the League of Nations and give up the support of revisionism. Italy would then no longer represent any danger for Rumania.

On the other hand, if his government could survive a defeat in Abyssinia, Mussolini might very well continue in an even more aggressive manner to pursue his political designs in Central Europe. He might even try a rapprochement with Germany. But after a victory over Mussolini one could expect the solidarity of the members of the League of Nations to grow stronger, and with unity they would be able to stop any attempt which might endanger the democratic world and the status quo.

If the sanctions were effective, the only disadvantage for Rumanian participation would occur in the area of economic conditions. In the short run, the Rumanian economy would be able to bear the stress without real complications; with sanctions applied for a longer period of time, however, the Rumanian economy would suffer greatly, and the economic situation might well cause domestic political repercussions. Yet, in the case of an Italian defeat, the democratic forces in Rumania also would grow stronger and would be able to handle any crisis with ease. Furthermore, Rumania could hope that Britain and France would reimburse her for the economic sacrifices.[24] Thus, if the sanctions were strict and observed effectively by every member of the League of Nations joining in the sanctions would be desirable from the point of view of Rumania.

On the other hand, if the sanctions were ineffective, not the slightest advantage would be gained by Rumanian participation in them. Mussolini would return to the League of Nations (if he considered it necessary to remain a member) with greatly increased power, authority and respect. He would feel free to pursue a much more aggressive policy in Central Europe; and France, anxious to secure her rear in case of war against Germany, might yield to his wishes. Hungarian and Bulgarian revisionism would flare up again and the status quo—with it the Rumanian possession of Transylvania and southern Dobruja—would face the possibility of change. All the sacrifices and economic suffering of the Rumanian people would not be rewarded with the increased security of the country.

Titulescu's conclusion had to be that Rumania should join the sanctions only if the Great Powers projected a victory over Mussolini.

Opposition to the Sanctions

If Rumania opposed the sanctions and they were effective, she would find herself on the side of the loser. The majority of the League of Nations would turn against her. Her partners in the Little and Balkan Ententes in all probability would "excommunicate" her. What is even more important, and possibly also dangerous, a Rumanian stand against the sanctions would undermine the confidence of Britain and France, and the Soviet Union would probably turn outright hostile.[25] The only advantage to opposing the sanctions even if they might be effective would be that such opposition would save Rumania's economy from the hardship which participation in the sanctions would bring.

On the other hand, if Rumania opposed the sanctions and they were ineffective, she would gain the goodwill of Mussolini, maybe to such a degree that he would curtail revisionist propaganda against Rumania. She would be able to join the Rome Protocols (for economic purposes), but would be excluded from the Little and Balkan Ententes. The loss of French friendship and support would not be certain, but the loss of Soviet goodwill would. This latter probability alone should have prohibited Rumania from opposing the sanctions if she projected a possible failure.

Ideology also should be mentioned. No matter how strongly the Rumanian government would have demanded Titulescu take a stand against the sanctions, knowing his convictions and character, we can suppose, that he would have resigned rather than turn against his ideological comrades. Nor was a neutral position toward the sanctions possible since neutrality would be interpreted by every nation as opposition.

Titulescu's Actions

Rumania had to make a very hard decision. Realities suggested that she should take part in the sanctions if France and her other partners required it, but should stay away from the spotlight in order not to become the target of Italy in case the sanctions failed. However, Titulescu firmly believed that the best way to preserve the status quo was to restore the authority of the League of Nations.[26] Consequently he pushed Rumania into the forefront of the Ethiopian debates. Becoming the greatest defender of the authority of the League, he opposed French attempts at moderation and supported the inflexible British stand.[27]

Playing a leading role as the League's champion was certainly not in the best interests of Rumania. It was Titulescu's mistake to turn against France[28] and try to exchange French patronage for the very reserved and questionable support of Eden. His anti-Fascist outburst created uneasiness at home.[29] His aggressiveness with his Little Entente partners caused a certain alienation and gave Benes and Stoyadinovich reason to look after the interests of their own countries by being more conciliatory in the Ethiopian dispute. Benes told the French Minister in Prague that "Czechoslovakia can adhere only to a very reserved position concerning the conflict between Italy and the League of Nations," while Stoyadinovich, who unenthusiastically supported the sanctions because the Italian counter-sanctions hit the Yugoslavian economy hard, suggested that the Little Entente suppress the sanctions.[30]

Keeping his strong anti-Italian and pro-Abyssinian attitude even after the annexation of Abyssinia, Titulescu isolated Rumania from those countries which initially were for the sanctions but by May 1936 displayed a growing dissatisfaction with the *political* consequence of the sanctions, that is, the alienation of Italy from the Anglo-Franco-Soviet group. Litvinov was the most outspoken, stating that the Soviet Union preferred a rapprochement with Italy in order to obtain from Mussolini satisfactory *obligations* concerning European problems.[31]

Not so Rumania. Titulescu continued to flight for the "just cause of Abyssinia" alone and against the wishes of his own King and government. In October 1936, King Carol told the Czechoslovak Minister in Bucharest that: "it was not necessary" for Titulescu "to become the public spokesman of this policy to bring Rumania among the foremost advocates of the sanctions, we could very well remain somewhere in the middle or bottom ranks but decidedly not in front."[32]

What were the consequences of Titulescu's actions? Mussolini, after victoriously finishing the Abyssinian war, returned his attention to Europe. He was full of bitterness against the League, against France, England, the Little Entente—and Rumania. Yugoslavia, who had joined the sanctions, separated herself further from Czechoslovakia and Rumania. Litvinov still refused to guarantee Rumania's territorial integrity. Eden, now British foreign minister, disdained Titulescu. France still wanted a reconciliation with Italy instead of the revival of Eastern Security plans. Germany further tightened her economic grip on Rumania by offering and receiving markets and trade contracts.

Titulescu thus alienated Rumania's friends and allies, did not befriend her enemies, and unintentionally prepared the way for the faster growth of rightist political influence in Rumania. With these actions he also began to prepare his own downfall.

REMILITARIZATION OF THE RHINELAND AND RUMANIAN FOREIGN POLICY

Loss of Confidence in France

The Ethiopian war and the sanctions were only five months old when Hitler, exploiting the opportunity created by European preoccupation with the League of Nations' debates over the Ethiopian-Italian conflict, ordered German troops into the demilitarized zone of the Rhineland on March 7, 1936.

We should remember the legal status and strategic importance of this territory. According to the decision of the Versailles Treaty,[33] the Rhineland was under German civilian authority with the condition that no military troops be garrisoned, and no fortifications or other military installations be maintained or built on the territory.

The Locarno Pact in the Treaty of Mutual Guarantee reconfirmed this Rhineland demilitarization and continued the maintenance of the territorial status quo. These conditions were recognized by Germany and their observation was guaranteed by Great Britain and Italy.[34]

The Rhineland had great importance primarily from the standpoint of military strategy. French forces in possession of a fifty mile strip on the east bank of the Rhine River would have a large bridgehead which could serve as an ideal base to launch a major offensive against the heart of Germany; use of the bridgehead could save the Rhine bridges from possible destruction by enemy artillery fire and provide march-up territory for large, strategically important military units. French-Polish and French-Czechoslovak military cooperation was based on the concept that, in case of war, the French army would occupy the demilitarized Rhineland *before* the German army could and would attack the German forces *before* they could destroy the armies of France's Eastern Allies.

In case of a German defensive plan, German forces in possession of the Rhineland could benefit from the fact that the Rhine River represented a "natural defense line." A French attack would thus need greater, more careful preparation; superiority in numbers, war materials and equipment; and much more time to break through the German defense line. The losses suffered during this break through might negatively influence the realization of the whole global strategic plan.

Maybe the time factor is the most important aspect. According to the estimates of the French General Staff, an attack across the Rhine needed about a week, plus additional time for total mobilization without which the global strategic plan could not be put into operation.[35] During this mobilization period, adding to it possible delays caused by the problems of the river crossing, the overwhelming German forces could gain decisive victories over the Czechoslovak and Polish armies.

In case of a German offensive, possession of the Rhineland would enable the German forces to prepare for the river crossing from the very beginning of hostilities. After a successful crossing and break through, they could launch a general attack against the left flank of the French army, separate the allied Belgian and French forces, and continue on the offensive right to Paris.[36]

The French General Staff gave up the idea of an offensive plan in the early 1930's because of the unilateral disarmament steps of the consecutive French governments and because of the greatly curtailed army budget. But after the Laval-Mussolini agreement in January 1935 and during the following military negotiations with Italy, they considered the offensive plan feasible again since they could now use against Germany those troops which were formerly employed on the Italian frontier. The success of their offensive plan, however, still depended on the swift occupation of the Rhineland by local French forces garrisoned on the west bank of the Rhine.[37] With the German remilitarization of the Rhineland, this plan suffered a mortal blow.

Alternatives for Rumania

The authority of the League of Nations, on which Titulescu had based Rumania's foreign policy, was at the edge of complete collapse. If Germany could violate the Versailles Treaty and the Locarno agreements without serious consequences, the League of Nations could hardly survive. Taking into consideration the importance of the League, and the consequences if it could not deal effectively with this new crisis, Rumania faced the following foreign policy alternatives.

If France, in harmony with Czechoslovakia and Poland, would decide to fight a preventive war against Germany, Rumania could support this stand morally as well as with supplies, even with troops if necessary. If France would choose again the forum of the League of Nations to register her complaints, trying to bring Germany to her knees only with the help of the League, Rumania could join the club condemning Germany and participate in possible economic sanctions or even in some military counter-measures. Rumania could stay entirely out of the conflict since she did not have common frontiers with Germany and therefore was not threatened directly. Finally, Rumania could switch sides and enter in an alliance with Germany, leaving the League of Nations as well as declaring all her former treaties and obligations to be void.

Preventive War Against Germany

A preventive war, if ending in victory, would knock out the *second* most dangerous revisionist Great Power in Europe (from the Rumanian point of view, Italy was still the most dangerous one). Such a victory would strengthen the unity of the democratic forces all over Europe and would greatly improve the respect for the status quo. It would also make Mussolini more cautious and this would increase the security of Rumania *vis à vis* Bulgaria and Hungary. On the other hand, the disruption of economic relations with Germany (which no doubt would happen) could spell disaster for the Rumanian economy, already greatly crippled by the sanctions and Italian counter-sanctions.

If the war went wrong for France and her allies, Rumania would not be able to deny permission for Soviet troop crossings unless she would be willing to accept the consequences and face the complete overturn of the status quo. The crossing of Russian troops would undoubtedly make Rumania a theatre of war. Titulescu knew that the Russians had every intention of marching through Rumania against Germany "with or without the consent of the government in Bucharest."[38] If the German troops overran Czechoslovakia with speed, it was possible that the Germans would march through Rumania against Russia.[39] The alternative of a preventive war in case of defeat also projected a disaster for Rumania.

But a preventive war had little chance of being selected by the French government. France was strongly divided on the question of a proper reaction to Germany. The majority of the government, of the deputies, and of the people had no desire to act alone. The two guarantors of the Locarno agreements were confronting each other in Geneva over the Abyssinian crisis. English public opinion strongly opposed the idea of sanctions against Germany, not to mention the possibility of a war.[40] Mussolini, on the other hand, viewed the situation with malicious joy and suggested ways to Germany on how to avoid an open confrontation.[41] There seemed to be very little chance for a preventive war, an alternative which would be unacceptable anyway from the point of view of Rumania's realistic interests.

Supporting France in the League of Nations

Next to declaring war, the strongest step France could take against Germany would be the filing of a complaint with the League of Nations. If Rumania chose to support France, the only question would be the degree of involvement. Rumania could jump in the frontline of these debates or she could give her support only from the background as a member of the Little and Balkan Ententes. Since every sign coming from Paris indicated that France would not force a showdown with Germany, not even economic sanctions, and would accept the *fait à compli*, it was advisable for Rumania not to act too loudly. Taking a restrained position, Rumania could keep the support of France and her Eastern allies without infuriating Germany, who played a very important role in the Rumanian economy.

This alternative seemed to offer the most advantages for Rumania, although it denied Titulescu the opportunity to champion the status quo. It contained some elements of danger, however, since accepting the *fait à compli* would further weaken the military-strategic position of France, making the value of the mutual assistance treaty with her very questionable.

Staying Out of the Conflict Completely

This alternative was better than participation in a possible preventive war, but worse than simply supporting France's policy. A neutral position would alienate Rumania's friends in Western as well as East-Central Europe. It would provoke the hostility of the Soviet Union, whose representative expressed his country's willingness to assist France if she was attacked by any European state.[42] Such Soviet assistance, without Soviet guarantees for Rumania's territorial integrity, would realize the worst nightmares of the Rumanian government. Because of this possible Soviet step, the neutral position seemed unacceptable.

Course of Events after the Remilitarization

On March 8, 1936, George Tatarescu, President of the Council of Ministers in Rumania, called a meeting to discuss official policy in connection with the German remilitarization of the Rhineland. Titulescu was present at that meeting. The ministers decided to declare "their solidarity with the protest note, which France had issued against the German aggression; at the same time they expressed their hope in a possible intervention of Great Britain."[43] Their resolution clearly manifested the Rumanian desire to support France's policy from the background. The next day, the Crown Council decided to keep three divisions in a stage of alert in Transylvania and ordered the Minister of Railways "to speed up the preparations of plans for the transportation of war materials from Russia."[44]

The League of Nations' Council held sessions in London on March 12-13 to discuss the French complaints against Germany. Here Titulescu could not resist the temptation to play again a leading role on the international stage. Speaking in behalf of the Little Entente (and forgetting the resolution of the Council of Rumanian Ministers), he painted a grim picture of the future if the "League of Nations comes off defeated from the present crisis;" and he concluded his dramatic speech by saying, "we do consider that the Versailles and Locarno Treaties have been violated."[45] A few days later, he tried to smooth over his harsh words by instructing the Rumanian minister in Berlin to deny the "rumors" concerning his unfriendly attitude toward Germany. Titulescu even claimed to be the arbiter who found the compromise formula for the solution of the Locarno crisis.[46] What forced Titulescu to retreat—his own judgment, the hesitancy and passivity of the League of Nations, or a rebuff from his government—we do not know. It is doubtful, however, that his explanations created the desired effect in Berlin.

The whole Rhineland crisis was suddenly abandoned by the Little Entente when, on April 1, 1936, Austria announced the reintroduction of general conscription for her army. Though the Austrian step turned the attention of the Little Entente away from the Rhineland, the effects of the remilitarization were great. The general attitude of the Little Entente toward France was: "How do you expect us to believe, that you will come to our rescue, since you did not move when your own interests were so seriously threatened."[47]

As far as the Little Entente states inner relations were concerned, it is no wonder that they diverged so greatly in their views *vis à vis* Germany. Rumania and Yugoslavia did not have common frontiers with Germany. Their economies relied heavily on trade with Germany. Both tried to make a rapprochement with Italy, but for *different reasons.*

Stoyadinovich wanted to regain Yugoslavia's Italian market to counterbalance the "commanding role" Germany had obtained in Yugoslavia's economy during the sanctions. On the other hand, after losing faith in the validity of the Franco-Yugoslavian mutual assistance treaty (as a result of French passivity during the Rhineland crisis), "certain Yugoslavian circles" sought German support against the "Italian pressure."[48]

In Rumania, the Rhineland incident created a similar crisis of confidence concerning the value of French assistance. Titulescu asked Count Wladimir d'Ormesson, French minister in Belgrade "to send an SOS" to Paris demanding the French government "demonstrate as much decisiveness as possible against Germany in order to preserve France's prestige in those second class [sic!] countries, which are supporting her policy."[49] The same day, May 4, d'Ormesson sent an alarming report about the rightist ideas which were rapidly gaining followers in Rumania.[50] From the French point of view, this changing domestic political situation forshadowed a possible change in the foreign policy of Rumania, creating a dangerous new crisis and possibly causing the loss of an old ally.

Rumania's Turn to the Right

King Carol found himself powerless after his return to Rumania in June 1930. Not accepting the idea of remaining only a figurehead, he attempted to gain power "by formenting dissension within the political parties and breaking them one by one. He won over the more ambitious politicians with favors and flattery and set them against the old leaders."[51] By 1928 the National Peasant Party was hopelessly divided and unable to provide an effective leadership. Five years later, the Liberal Party met the same fate. Prime Minister Tatarescu, a Liberal, was at odds with the head of his party. As a result of their struggle, King Carol gained complete control.[52] But now he had to face a new opposition, the Iron Guard,[53] a movement which had grown strong enough to be a challenge instead of a nuisance to the corrupt ruling oligarchy.

Various conditions existing in Rumania led to the growth of this rightist movement. Rumania had a strong nationalistic spirit "arising from the old feeling of isolation in a surrounding sea of Slavs."[54] After World War I, a fear of her great neighbor Russia was coupled with the fear of Soviet revisionism and communism, triggering the birth of militant nationalism. The constant worry over the possible revision of the peace treaties *vis à vis* Bulgaria and Hungary promoted chauvinism. Another factor contributing to the popularization of rightist ideas was the traditional anti-Semitism "which has been endemic in Rumania since the winning of independence."[55]

Nationalism and anti-Semitism were appealing to the educated people, the "intellectuals and the hard-pushing bourgeoisie."[56] The great depression, and later Rumanian participation in the sanctions against Italy, created economic conditions which made the peasants and industrial workers susceptible to the corporatist ideas of the Iron Guard whose religious piety and messianic faith in their own important role in the future of Rumania "attracted also an extraordinary number of the lower Orthodox clergy."[57] The Iron Guard enjoyed the tacit approval of King Carol, who remembered gratefully the strong support he had received from them after his return, and obtained financial contributions from wealthy individuals who liked their strong anti-communism.[58] Some members also received financial donations from Nazi Germany.[59]

Though the Rumanian rightist groups did not unite in a single organization, their influence was great. In July 1931, Iron Guard founder C. Zelea Codreanu won a seat in the parliament, and in 1932 the Guard won five mandates; then, dissolved again one year later by the Liberal government, Codreanu's group was reorganized as the All for the Fatherland Party.[60] Still the old Iron Guard only under a new name, their "grass root" organizations (called "nests") exceeded 4,200 in 1935 and grew to over 34,000 by 1937.[61]

The year 1935 witnessed the organization of another strong pro-Nazi group, the National Christian Party, which was created by the fusion between the League of National Christian Defense and the old National Christian Party. Fascist groups were growing stronger and stronger in Rumania and also beginning to publish their own foreign political conceptions. The Iron Guard, being chauvinistic nationalists, defended the status quo in Central Europe and, "despite its acute hatred for democracy," found it necessary to cooperate with France and other powers who wanted to uphold the Versailles treaties.[62] The National Christian Party, on the other hand, after receiving Hitler's support, advocated a pro-German foreign policy.

Both groups found something in Titulescu's foreign policy with which they could not agree. The Iron Guard disliked his rapprochement attempts with the Soviet Union, while the National Christians condemned his hostile attitude toward Nazi Germany and Fascist Italy.

According to Oprea, historian of Communist Rumania, although dissatisfaction with Titulescu spread even within the Liberal Party, his foreign policy enjoyed the "approval of the King and of the government, it relied on the adhesion of most bourgeois political forces, it won the adhesion of the democratic parties and the active support of the Communist Party and of the mass-organizations led by the Communists."[63] This creates the impression that, with the exception of the rightist movement, everybody liked Titulescu's policy. This is an overstatement. None of these mentioned groups supported Titulescu's foreign policy without great reservations.

The King and the government agreed with Titulescu's rapprochement attempts with the Soviet Union, but disapproved his arbitrarily assumed role in the League of Nations during the Abyssinian crisis. The bourgeoisie cautiously approved his Soviet policy, being afraid of communism, and supported his economic policy *vis à vis* Germany, but were disgusted with his role in the sanctions against Italy. Even the Rumanian Communist Party[64] did not support Titulescu unconditionally and, following Stalin's instructions, advocated a rapprochement with the Soviet Union while staying away from the strong condemnation of Italy.

Titulescu *believed*, however, that he had all the support that Oprea listed as being firmly behind him. No wonder, then, that in the next hurdle of international competition, Titulescu continued his activities with unchanged conceptions. The events he would have to face were fast approaching. In Central European capitals, rumors were spreading about an imminent Habsburg restoration in Austria; reverberations of the Rhineland crisis persisted in Western Europe; the League of Nations was agonizing over the sanctions against Italy and was considering possible new sanctions against Germany; and a civil war was brewing in Spain. Given this situation, the Rumanian government and Titulescu's French patrons looked with great concern at his diplomatic activities.

TITULESCU'S FOREIGN POLICY IN 1936

Diplomacy in East-Central Europe

The Italian military successes in Ethiopia made it possible, and the German remilitarization of the Rhineland made it necessary, for Mussolini to turn his attention once again to conditions in Central Europe. In March 1936, Italy, Austria and Hungary renewed the Rome Protocols. During their meeting, Mussolini recommended to Austria and Hungary that they renounce the arms limitation clauses of the St. Germain and Trianon Treaties and that they strengthen their defensive forces against a possible German annexation attempt. Austria followed his advice in April; Hungary did not feel it necessary to take such a strong step—yet.

As was expected, the Austrian declaration of reintroduction of general conscription created mixed reaction in East-Central Europe. Prague received the news with regret and announced that Czechoslovakia would join her allies in protesting the Austrian action; political circles in Bucharest forsaw a very energetic reaction on the part of the Little

Entente; and Yugoslavia's Stoyadinovich forced his Little Entente partners to send a strongly worded protest note to Austria.[65]

In spite of this protest, the Little Entente states did not really oppose the Austrian conscription. They were afraid that if they did not protest, Hungary would follow suit and the renunciation of the Trianon Treaty "could create complications,"[66] meaning that the Little Entente states were ready to use their armed forces against Hungary. Czechoslovakia alerted the division garrisoned in Bratislava (Pozsony) and began troop concentrations on the Hungarian frontier, while Rumania made similar precautions.[67] This excitement of the Little Entente died down as soon as Hungarian Foreign Minister Kánya notified the Czechoslovak government that "Hungary does not intend to follow the example of the Austrian government."[68]

The reaction of the Little Entente was not so unanimous toward the German offer to sign separate non-aggression pacts with Germany's Eastern neighbors. While Titulescu and Stoyadinovich looked at the German offer with suspicion, Benes was anxious to explore the details of Hitler's offer and sought to obtain further special guarantees for the security of Czechoslovakia.[69] Czechoslovakia's interest in a separate security agreement with Germany was natural. Only Czechoslovakia had a common frontier with Germany and the military agreements of the Little Entente "were inoperative vis à vis Czechoslovakia threatened by Germany."[70]

The shock caused by the passivity of the Locarno Powers, the disillusionment with France's impotency, and the effects of the economic sanctions against Italy influenced the members of the Little Entente differently and led to the further deterioration of harmony. In an attempt to eliminate their misunderstandings and restore their unity, Czechoslovakia, Rumania and Yugoslavia held a conference in Belgrade on May 6-8, 1936. In the resulting communiqué, which included the usual cliches about the preservation of the status quo and peace, they expressed their desire to see the fast termination of the discussions of the Locarno Powers, reaffirmed their determination not to approve any changes in the peace treaties, and announced their desire for closer international trade cooperation with the states of the Rome Protocols and with Germany.[71]

The restrained tone of the communiqué clearly showed that the Little Entente sought a reconciliation with Germany for the sake of economic interests. However, Czechoslovakia wanted to obtain some guarantees for her own security directly from Germany. Rumania and Yugoslavia hoped to find German support against a possible Habsburg restoration in Austria, while Benes tried unsuccessfully to obtain a strong French protest against restoration. Thus, the Little Entente communiqué did not demonstrate the unity of the Little Entente any more than the French condemnation of German aggression changed the *fait à compli*.

In the meantime, enemies and friends of France were looking forward with equal interest to the results of the French elections, which were to be held on June 3. As was expected, the Popular Front received the overwhelming majority of votes and Blum formed a new government of the Left. The reactions of foreign powers to the French election results were predictable. Mussolini, while still considering a Franco-Italian entente as the best choice for Italy, no longer saw much chance to realize that entente, since the new French government was "composed of people who were Mussolini's enemies."[72] Italy began to send her troops back to the French frontier and restated her determination to continue her opposition to the *Anschluss.*[73] Meanwhile, the Little Entente, during its June 6-8 meeting in Bucharest, continued to try to coordinate the foreign policies of the individual member states and agreed finally on several points.[74] The final communiqué of this conference revealed that the Little Entente did not find a new cohesive force. They still relied on the unifying effects of their desire to keep the status quo, primarily against Hungary, and on their wish to prevent a Habsburg restoration in Austria. As far as their loyalty to France was concerned they now divided this loyalty between France and England, not excluding the possibility of quitting the French alliance system altogether and beginning to lean toward Germany.

It was a warning to the new French government, and Blum understood it perfectly well. Czechoslovakia and Yugoslavia waited patiently for the French declaration concerning the new Popular Front government's foreign political principles. Only Rumania's Titulescu felt it necessary to present again the anxiety of the Little Entente states. Addressing Blum during the June session of the League of Nations, Titulescu stated that the "small countries" have "some doubts" about whether or not they can "rely on France's help," for "if on March 7, you failed to defend yourselves, how are you going to defend us?"[75]

The French government's official declaration[76] did not help Titulescu and the Little Entente dismiss their misgivings about Blum. Not a single word was said about France's alliances, her obligations vis à vis her allies, or her willingness to fight a war in defense of the Little Entente. It did express the hope of reconciliation with Italy. Blum considered this absolutely necessary, for he had the impression that the British government (since the Abyssinian war) considered Italy the main enemy and "looked for means to secure Hitler's support against Mussolini."[77]

What did this new French policy mean for Rumania? The leader of the Iron Guard, Codreanu, did not hesitate to publicize his conviction: "There is no Little Entente and Balkan Entente. He who still believes in it has not understood anything yet."[78] Titulescu was also apprehensive, but he (nor the King and his government) was not yet ready to abandon the existing alliances with France and the Little Entente. Their fear of the Soviet Union still made Poland a desirable partner, their interest in the upkeep of the status quo still required the cooperation of the Little and Balkan Ententes, and their conception of Rumania's security still recommended that they be a close friend of France. At the same time, Rumania and the other Balkan states, with the exception of Yugoslavia, took the bait offered to them by Hjalmar Schacht, German Economic Minister. During his Balkan visits, Schacht presented a picture of good markets, profitable trade and German economic assistance.[79] Poland clearly saw the significance of this new German economic drive as Germany's desire "to become the only mistress of the Balkan and Near East markets," thereby establishing "her political hegemony on the Balkans."[80] We may add that, because of the political situation in Western Europe and the economic conditions of East-Central Europe and the Balkans, nobody could do anything about it.

A few weeks later, even those who paid some attention to Schacht's negotiations were preoccupied with the new international crisis: Civil War in Spain. Titulescu, busy with East-Central European politics and the problems of the Little Entente, jumped again on the stage of Western European politics. The Spanish Civil War proved to be more important for him than any of his former involvements in Great Power politics: it was his swan-song.

The Spanish Civil War

"In a broad sense the Spanish Civil War was primarily the result of general European ideas and movements upon Spain."[81] On the other hand, the nationalist revolt became a full-fledged civil war because the European powers were willing to participate in the conflict, supporting their Spanish comrades on the Left and Right and defending their own realistic interests. In most cases, ideological sympathies coincided with these realistic interests. In some cases, however, the two clashed.

Britain's foreign policy was to seek an agreement with Mussolini concerning the Mediterranean sea. Its purpose was the maintenance of the status quo, or at least the preservation of British superiority. That is why British reaction was restrained in the Spanish Civil War. Their patience was rewarded when Britain and Mussolini signed a "gentlemen's agreement" on January 2, 1937.[82] Of course, British public opinion was divided. The British Labour Party was against the Fascist powers and demanded an investigation concerning the observance of the nonintervention agreement, while "British financiers with interests in Spain were not enthusiastic for the republic."[83] But neither side could influence the foreign policy of the government, which became more and more disturbed by the prevailing Communist influence within the Spanish republican government.[84] In the end, Britain remained neutral as her realistic interests in the Mediterranean demanded.

Germany had no interests in the Mediterranean and Hitler was at first very hesitant concerning German involvement in the Spanish Civil War. On the other hand, seeing a Fascist regime installed in Spain was tempting: a France sandwiched between Nazi Germany and Fascist Spain could hardly oppose the future ambitions of Hitler.[85] Giving moderate help to the Spanish nationalists for the right price[86] was thus in the interest of ideology as well as realistic policy.

Italy was still suffering from the aftereffects of the Abyssinian war and the hardship caused by the sanctions, which were lifted on July 4, 1936, shortly before the war in Spain began on July 18. Mussolini was disappointed with the position France had taken in the sanctions, and the election of the Popular Front government in France made him even more suspicious; leftist Spain allied with a leftist France (and possibly with the Soviet Union) could spell disaster for his future Mediterranean designs.[87]

Intervention on the side of nationalist Spain seemed to be a necessity from the ideological as well as realistic political point of view.

The Soviet Union did not react at first. Instead, the Comintern drew up a resolution on July 21, 1936, supporting the republican side and recommending aid to them. The Comintern made its decision on the basis of ideological sympathies; the Soviet Union's realistic interests demanded caution. After the sobering effects of the failure of the sanctions against Italy and the remilitarization of the Rhineland, the main concern of Soviet foreign policy was the prevention of possible German expansion toward the East.

This new Soviet policy seemed to gain space with the conclusions of the French and Czechoslovak mutual assistance treaties with the Soviet Union and with the negotiations for a similar agreement with Rumania. But the establishment of a pro-Nazi, Fascist regime in Spain could make these treaties useless for what kind of help could the Soviet Union expect from France if she had to fight also against Spain?[88] A republican victory in Spain would certainly alienate Mussolini. Since the Soviet Union considered Italy the only power in Western Europe which could prevent the realization of German dreams in Central Europe, "Stalin seems to have reached one conclusion and one conclusion only about Spain: he would not permit the Republic to lose, even though he would not help it to win."[89]

France and Blum's Popular Front government were perhaps in the worst position. The ideology of the Popular Front, Blum himself, Foreign Secretary Yvon Delbos, and War Minister Daladier all recommended helping the republicans on the basis of ideological affinity; but French public opinion and the press opposed any intervention, being afraid that with the French army engaged in Spain, Hitler would strike against Czechoslovakia.[90] Britain also advised France to act with restraint.[91] After long agonizing discussions, Blum decided to put France's realistic interests ahead of ideological considerations. A year later (on November 29, 1937), Delbos bluntly told Eden: "The French government would prefer that the Spanish government should win. But they did not think, that their interests would necessarily be menaced if Franco won."[92] Thus, France joined the non-intervention camp.

In Central Europe, meanwhile, Germany's surprise move of signing an agreement with Austria on July 11, 1936, continued to attract more attention than the Spanish revolt. Czechoslovakia was afraid of the consequences of a coordinated Austro-German policy; Yugoslavia saw in an Austro-German *détente* the best guarantee against a Habsburg restoration; and Rumania's government thought it advisable not to play a "too active part in European affairs."[93] What were the special Rumanian interests and goals the government thought to serve best with a low profile in European affairs, that is, in the Spanish Civil War?

Rumanian Goals and Alternatives During the Summer of 1936

Rumania's basic political interest was still the same: preservation of the territorial status quo against Bulgaria, Hungary and the Soviet Union. But some of the old weapons which had been used to realize this goal began to deteriorate; some even ceased to exist, functioning only on paper.

After the French acceptance of the Rhineland *fait à compli*, Rumania lost faith in French protection.[94] The great personal antagonism which existed between Beck and Titulescu[95] caused Polish relations with Rumania to decline and made the reliability of an anti-Soviet Polish-Rumanian assistance treaty questionable. Rumanian economic interests demanded friendlier relations with Germany, but Titulescu's attempts to conclude a Soviet-Rumanian treaty made Germany suspicious.[96]

By summer 1936, Rumania's position had weakened. The over publicized Soviet-Rumanian negotiations produced only the negative results of alienating Poland and making Germany skeptical. The Rumanian General Staff advised the government to be cautious. They felt that the Rumanian army was ready to start military operations against Hungary only in cooperation with the other Little Entente states and against Germany only if they were absolutely "sure of French military support."[97] But the French General Staff was not too anxious to offer this support.[98]

Amidst such circumstances, Rumania's official policy was one of wait and see. The government tried to maintain a friendly attitude toward France and the Soviet Union through the person of Titulescu, who was well-liked in both countries. At the same time, the King and Tatarescu kept the door open for closer cooperation with Italy and Germany. Meanwhile, the Rumanian domestic political situation and public opinion showed a definite turn toward the extreme right. The King undoubtedly favored the Right and tolerated Iron Guard activities, but he also firmly protested the German financial support given to these rightists.[99]

The Spanish Civil War raised the question of whether or not Rumania should continue to stay away from European affairs, and if not, which side she should help. Ideological affinity recommended the support of the Spanish nationalitists. The fear of communism, which grew in Rumania in proportion to the spreading of ideas, advocated taking the same step. Such action would certainly please Germany and Italy. On the other hand, support of the nationalists would alienate France, the Little Entente and the Soviet Union. The Soviet help given to the Spanish republicans proved to the whole world that Stalin was willing to act in behalf of Communist interests. The Soviet Union stood at Rumania's doorsteps while Spain, Italy and Germany were far away. It would be risky to provoke the Soviet Union; even a mild reaction, (like discontinuing war material supplies,)[100] would hurt Rumania's security. Thus, an open declaration of Rumanian sympathies for Francoist Spain was out of the question according to the demands of realistic interests.

Though the rightist sympathies of Tatarescu's government would not approve, knowing the Rumanians' great realism, they undoubtedly would help the Spanish republicans if Rumanian interests demanded it. Supporting the republicans would produce satisfaction in the Soviet Union and would receive Blum's applause. At the same time, however, this policy most certainly would turn German suspicions to hostility and would block the way of a possible Italo-Rumanian reconciliation. Germany's goodwill was very important for economic reasons. To secure undisturbed German cooperation (and to have security against a Habsburg restoration in Austria), the Rumanian government had accustomed itself to the idea of *Anschluss* and in June 1936 notified the Germans of this decision.[101] Hitler reacted with favor and began to influence the Hungarian government to tone down her revisionist demands *vis 'a vis* Rumania.[102] Therefore, for Rumania to announce that she sympathized with the Spanish republicans would be contradictory to her realistic interests.

There was the possibility of a neutral position in the Spanish question. Since nonintervention was the slogan (supposedly also the principle) of the Great Powers,[103] joining this group would release Rumania from her responsibilities while securing the goodwill and approval of all the Great Powers. The neutral position was the best policy for Rumania. That was the alternative chosen by the Rumanian government and the choice was right.

Titulescu's Fall from Power

Before accepting the position of foreign minister, Titulescu demanded and received formal assurances from King Carol "that he would remain in charge of the department for a long time, *irrespective of cabinet changes.*"[104] (italics added) The security of his position and his long absences from home had two important effects on his personality and diplomacy: he increasingly felt that *only he* was designated to plan and direct Rumania's foreign policy and, therefore, he arrogantly disregarded the foreign political decisions of the government and Crown Council. At the same time, he grew less and less familiar with the domestic political changes occurring in Rumania.[105] By the time of the Locarno crisis, King Carol and the Crown Council began to distrust him, since his diplomacy often contradicted his instructions. Titulescu felt the changing mood and in April 1936, concerned about the security of his position,[106] he hurried home to regain the confidence of the King and to strenghten his connections with the government. After receiving a general outline of policy, Titulescu went back to Genève to participate in the debates over the sanctions against Italy; but again he was carried away by his own convictions and forgot the just received policy principles.

In the meantime, because of the fear of communism and under the influence of rightist propaganda, public opinion also turned against Titulescu. Codreanu disliked him personally and as early as 1931 accused him of corruption.[107] As his strength grew, Cogreanu criticized Titulescu's foreign policy (especially his negotiations with Litvinov) more and more vehemently. By the time of the Spanish Civil War, trust in Titulescu was so low that for the first time in his career, Titulescu received detailed instructions concerning Rumania's position: Rumania accepted the principle of "noninterference in the events taking place in Spain."[108]

In late August, however, Titulescu saw that the nonintervention principle was not being observed by the Great Powers. He had the firm conviction that the Spanish Civil War was actually the war of Fascists against all the peace-loving nations,[109] and seeing the violation of the non-intervention agreement, he chose to disregard his instructions. Deciding that Rumania did not need the one hundred cannons and fifty airplanes which she had ordered from France and were now ready for delivery, Titulescu directed this war material to be transported to the Spanish republicans.[110] Right after these orders to ship the armaments to Spain, King Carol and the Tatarescu government decided that they had had enough of Titulescu's independent actions. On August 29, 1936, he was dismissed.

French Illusions and Reality

During August 1936, Titulescu made a desperate attempt to secure for Rumania not only the reconfirmation of French support, but also a mutual assistance treaty with France, supplemented by a military agreement. France was not ready to take up new obligations, though. Blum sent Air Minister Cot to Rumania, but the negotiations did not produce any new agreements.[111] From the French point of view, the Little Entente was no longer an important unit. After experiencing Rumanian stubbornness in not granting permission for Russian troops to cross her territory, and witnessing the Yugoslavian rapprochement with Germany to such a degree that she approved the idea of an *Anschluss*,[112] even the Popular Front government of France abandoned the idea of collective security. The unlimited confidence of the Popular Front in the value of a Soviet alliance made the Little Entente even less important.

Blum also tried hard to come to an understanding with Great Britain[113] in the naive belief that Britain had the same feelings vis à vis Germany as France did. But the British government and public opinion still considered France the most powerful nation on the Continent and Germany the underdog.

The Popular Front believed that France's security was served well by Franco-English cooperation, the policy of reconciliation with Mussolini, and the Franco-Soviet mutual assistance treaty. In the whole of East-Central Europe, Czechoslovakia was the only state which was important in French eyes. Czechoslovakia was to serve as an airbase for French and Soviet planes in case of war. Yet the maintenance of this airbase would be impossible without the protecting shield of ground forces, and the forty-first line Czech divisions "excellently trained and equipped, ready to oppose Germany with the best armaments of Europe"[114] could hardly resist a German attack without the help of the Russian infantry.

Thus, the key question for French security lay in the attitude of the Soviet Union: would she help Czechoslovakia *against* the opposition of

Poland and Rumania, or would she act only with Polish and Rumanian consent to cross their territories.

Since there was no hope that Poland would ever give her consent, Rumania remained the only possible connecting link through which Soviet troops could be employed against Germany. In other words, France's security and the functioning of the Franco-Soviet mutual assistance treaty depended entirely on Rumania. France nurtured the belief that since Titulescu was a devoted friend of France, Rumania also remained their friend. Czechoslovakia shared the belief that Titulescu's "absence will in no way change Rumanian policy, which remains faithful to the precepts of its adherence to the Little Entente and to France."[115] Only the Soviet Union interpreted Titulescu's dismissal as a success for German diplomacy and expressed her doubts concerning the future possibility of employing Soviet ground troops in the defense of "collective security."[116]

The appointment of Victor Antonescu as Titulescu's successor did not give any reason for France and the Little Entente to have confidence in the future Rumanian foreign policy. Antonescu was selected by the King because he was an insignificant, colorless politician[117] and his character assured the King that he would follow orders. Antonescu disapproved of Titulescu's pro-Soviet policy and wanted to revive Polish-Rumanian cooperation; being afraid of a possible German-Soviet war taking place on Rumanian territory, he recommended France make a rapprochement with Germany; and wanting to pursue an independent Rumanian policy since he was disappointed with the weak performance of France, he sought to improve German-Rumanian relations.[118]

This kind of foreign political platform did not promise too much hope for France. On October 18, 1936, the French ambassador reported with alarm to Paris that the majority of Rumanian public opinion accepted the theory of Rumanian neutrality. "Rumania (they are convinced) has to practice an independent policy between the two blocs formed on the one part by the democratic states, on the other part by the dictatorships."[119]

This new Rumanian trend signaled not only the end of France's leadership in Central Europe, but also the end of the collective security system. Without the cooperation of Rumania and Poland, Soviet help became completely illusory. Without the cooperation of Rumania, there was no Little Entente. Without the Little Entente, Czechoslovakia was helpless. And without Czechoslovakia, France unknowingly became "an auxiliary power in the British diplomatic system."[120] The "Fifth Crisis" of the French diplomacy was not a loud, spectacular crisis. As a matter of fact, it happened almost unnoticed. Yet, this may be the most ironic in that France again lost a diplomatic battle in East-Central Europe, but without realizing that her own future was at stake. The Sarraut and Blum governments wanted to serve only France's realistic interests. But by disregarding the Rumanian developments and by forgetting Rumania's nationalistic interests *vis à vis* the Soviet Union and Germany, they further undermined the security of France.

CHAPTER XI
CRISIS UPON CRISIS

September 1936 was a bad month for the Popular Front and for France, not only because of foreign political developments, but also because of the domestic political situation which once again became explosive.

After the Matignon agreement[1] in June, the Blum government introduced almost revolutionary social and economic reforms at the expense of the capitalists. With these measures, the government pleased the poorer masses but alienated the bourgeoisie. On June 18, the government ordered the dissolution of rightist organizations (like the Croix de Feu, Jeunesses Patriotes, and Solidarité Française), which was applauded by the Communists but condemned by the middle class. After Blum's decision to join the policy of nonintervention in the Spanish Civil War, the extreme Left also turned against the government.

In the meantime, the financial situation continued to deteriorate. The gold reserves of the Bank of France had declined by some 16 billion francs since January of 1936. The government budget projected 1936 expenditures of 100 million francs on public works, 710 million francs on agriculture, 580 million francs on education and 300 million francs on public health.[2] After General Gamelin's alarming report on June 25, the government decided to spend an additional 600 million francs over the regular 1936 defense budget of 1,400 million francs.[3] The government's budget was heavily imbalanced and the situation forced Blum to break one of his most important campaign promises: he devaluated the franc. The indignation of the masses found an outlet again in demonstrations, strikes, and factory occupations. The workers refused to negotiate a new Matignon agreement; the Communist Party refused to vote confidence for the government and organized a new front of leftists to oust Blum.

During the spring of 1937, leftist and revived rightist groups both demonstrated against Blum's Popular Front government, which finally resigned on June 22, 1937, under the heavy pressure of political opposition (mostly in the Senate). Although the name Popular Front survived during Camille Chautemps' two governments (June 22, 1937-

March 12, 1938),[4] the leftist coalition, which had secured the elections for the Popular Front, began to melt away. With the onset of the Daladier ministry on April 10, 1938, a conservative era started in France, which naturally affected foreign political conceptions.

French Policy Toward the Great Powers
In 1936 and 1937

When he assumed power in June 1936, Blum inherited the policy of sanctions against Italy. Yet, the Ethiopian war had ended a month before, and realistic considerations suggested the graceful acceptance of the Italian victory. But Blum was not yet a statesman, only a party politician.

Two days after he entered office, Blum received a note from the Ministry of Foreign Affairs which described a meeting between a Paris-Soir correspondent and Mussolini. During the meeting, Mussolini said that "if the sanctions will be lifted, Italy will be ready to enter into mutual assistance agreements in Europe;" but, he added, even if the sanctions were not lifted, Italy would remain a member of the League of Nations unless the French government joined in a possible condemnation of Italy.[5] A few days later, Mussolini repeated his offer to former Minister of the Interior Louis Malvy[6] and the next day to Pierre Dupuy, owner of the *Petit Parisien*.

Blum's reply to Mussolini's friendly exploratory gestures was the reply of a proud Socialist Party member, not of a French statesman: "I cannot forget that Mussolini was the assassin of Matteotti."[7]

Friendly signals continued to come from Italy in spite of Blum's rejection. On June 24, 1936, Galeazzo Ciano, the new Italian foreign minister, expressed "in very warm terms, the desire of the Italian government to cooperate with France and with the League of Nations as soon as the sanctions will be lifted."[8] The sanctions were lifted on July 4, with France abstaining from voting in order to satisfy Mussolini and at the same time not offend England.

On June 25, 1936, Gamelin submitted his evaluation of the French military situation, ending his report with the conclusion that the maintenance "of our military agreements with Italy is an essential interest of France."[9] Four days later, the Permanent Committee of the National Defense held a regular session in Paris where the possible alternatives of a future war were discussed.[10] Considering the potential enemies, the ministers of the three branches of the armed forces agreed that a war against Germany could create an extreme situation in which Italy could later join Germany. On the other hand, France might hope for the active support of Britain and Belgium. Opinions concerning the role of Czechoslovakia were divided. Gamelin discounted the possibility of sending aid to Czechoslovakia and expressed the conviction that the Soviet Union and Poland would help the Czechs. General Maurice Pujo, Chief of Staff of the Air Force, opposed this idea, since only with the cooperation of the Czechoslovak army could the French forces reach Berlin. He had sixteen heavy transport planes at his disposal to give material support to the Czechs.[11] Finally, Gamelin announced that the ground forces of the army would be ready to wage war after 1937.

After reading these military evaluations, Blum's most important duty as a French statesman should have been to seek a fast reconciliation with Italy. But the outbreak of the Spanish Civil War provided a new reason for Blum to avoid such a step. He "seemed to me always preoccupied with avoiding doing anything which may irritate England."[12] He did not care if something irritated Mussolini. Upon the resignation of L.C. Pineton de Chambrun, the French ambassador in Rome, Blum addressed the credentials of the new ambassador to the "King of Italy," omitting Mussolini's new title: Emperor of Ethiopia. Mussolini refused to accept the credentials.[13]

Shortly thereafter, Mussolini decided to recall the Italian ambassador from Paris, leaving Italian representation in the hands of a *charge d' affaires,* and asked France to do the same, unless the French government was ready to recognize the "lawful title of the Italian Sovereign."[14] On the same day, October 9, Ciano assured Chambrun that his (Ciano's) upcoming visit to Germany would not produce any surprise political agreement; he emphasized that since the Laval-Mussolini meeting in January 1935, Italy looked upon France as her natural friend with whom she wanted to have good relations.[15] The next day, Chambrun left Rome, and *France sent no ambassador to Italy until October 1938.*

Parallel with this Italian alienation, Blum had other worrysome problems. The Assistant Chief of Staff of the Army, returning from a visit in the Soviet Union, reported that the military value of the Soviet army was very much overestimated by the French military personnel. He even questioned the honesty of the Soviet government concerning Russia's obligations *vis à vis* France as laid down in the mutual assistance treaty.[16]

October 1936 continued to create unpleasant surprises for France. King Leopold of Belgium announced the neutrality of Belgium on October 14, saying that Belgian policy must be exclusively and completely Belgian. He also spoke about the effects of the remilitarization of the Rhineland on Belgium's strategic position and called attention to the changed methods of warfare.[17] The Belgian declaration of neutrality turned the strategic plans of the French army upside down. Earlier in the year, the Belgian and French General Staffs had held combined meetings and worked out in detail the cooperation of the two armies against a German attack, the French army was to help the Belgians according to this plan.[18] But now the Belgian army would have to fight *alone*, and if defeated, the French army would have to defend the French-Belgian frontier *alone*. This individual border defense needed many more men than the cooperative plan called for, since there were no fortifications built on this frontier.

The final alienation with Italy and the reoccupation of the Italian-French frontier by Italian troops[19] put the French General Staff in panic. They now had the additional assignment of preparing defenses against Italy. The effects of these two diplomatic fiascos (with Italy and Belgium) made the original French plan of an attack on Berlin a utopian dream, and the plan to aid France's Eastern allies was abandoned.[20]

That was not the end of unfortunate incidents. At the close of 1936, Blum received a warning from Czechoslovakia's President Benes, the most faithful ally of France. Benes, in possession of some secret intelligence information,[21] stated positively that France could not trust the Soviet Union since the German and Soviet General Staffs were secretly in close cooperation.

In November 1936, Blum learned that his desire to please the English government at any price also had misfired: The English themselves began negotiations with Mussolini for the conclusion of an English-Italian "gentlemen's agreement" concerning the Mediterranean status quo. France felt bitter and frustrated, but she could do nothing, so Delbos assured Eden that "an improvement in Anglo-Italian relations was as much in the interest of France as of Great Britain."[22] The Italo-English accords were signed on January 2, 1937.

The fear of a possible German-Italian rapprochement also began to haunt the French mind in 1936. French newspapermen interviewing Mussolini constantly asked him if he would remain loyal to his January 1935 agreement with Laval and his policy of opposing the *Anschluss:*

In substance, Mussolini always gave the same answer: "Germany could guarantee me against the *Anschluss* for five years, but what comes after?"[23] Preserving the independence of Austria, and thereby curtailing the expansion of Germany in Central Europe, was in the common interest of France and Italy. In this respect, they were natural allies.

The Popular Front government, however, did not accept the validity of natural alliances. According to their interpretation, ideology and not realistic interests determined allies and enemies. They shared Clemenceau's conviction that "the men of the Right are easy to recognize: they are not only stupid, but the wickedest;" and they felt that "Fascism is a far less developed doctrine than democracy or Communism, both of which are based on reason."[24] Selecting their allies on the basis of such convictions, the Popular Front refused to believe in the sincerity of Mussolini's statements. Further, while preaching the desire to cooperate even with Germany in the interest of French security,[25] Blum, by his actions, excluded the possibility of any cooperation with Italy.

The reaction of the French press to the Abyssinian war and to the Italian involvement in the Spanish Civil War would have prejudiced against France a much less conceited man than was Mussolini. Taking into consideration his past experiences concerning the reliability of French assurances given for the protection of Austria, it is no wonder that Mussolini began to look for new, more satisfactory solutions and arrived at the conclusion that "It will be easier for Italy to help Austria if both Italy and Austria will have good relations with Germany."[26] On June 17, 1936, Schuschnigg began negotiations with Papen on the condition that Germany would publicly recognize Austria's independency,[27] and on July 11 an agreement was signed.

Ciano assured Chambrun that the Austro-German agreement was not connected with an Italo-German agreement.[28] The French ambassador to the Holy See doubted that Mussolini would start a rapprochement with Germany because of ideological sympathies or momentary interests. "He is a cynic and takes his benefits where he finds them, without being too much preoccupied with the trustworthiness of his *momentary* associates."[29] (italics added) Even Pope Pius XI believed that the only thing which might urge Mussolini to ally himself with Hitler was the continuous weakness of France.

The weakness of France *vis à vis* Germany did indeed continue, as did Blum's roughness towards Mussolini. The first decisive result of this

French policy occurred in October 1936 when, after his visit in Berlin, Ciano announced the formation of the Rome-Berlin Axis. It was yet a very weak axis. Mussolini agreed to the remilitarization of the Rhineland and to the continuing support of the Franco government in Spain; Hitler once again guaranteed Austria's integrity; and since both men had lost faith in the League of Nations, they foresaw the possibility of the cooperation of Germany and Italy outside of the League.[30] There was not a single word in the agreement which projected the creation of a united Fascist-Nazi front against the Western democracies.

Mussolini looked upon the Rome-Berlin Axis announcement with cynicism. After Goering's visit in Rome on January 23, 1937, the Italian ambassador to France told Blum: "Mussolini hates Hitler. He feels toward him an immense repulsion. If France and Italy could understand each other nothing could resist in Europe the block of eighty millions. What is necessary for that? Let Franco take over Spain. Mussolini pledges to obtain Franco's friendship for France."[31] Blum refused the offer, convinced that since the Italo-German agreement, no real rapprochement was possible between France and Italy.

Blum resigned on June 22, 1937, but Delbos remained the Minister of Foreign Affairs, securing the continuity of Blum's foreign policy. On September 25-29, Mussolini visited Hitler, and although their meeting was not decisive, still "If no formal military alliance was concluded, the Rome-Berlin 'axis' was strengthened."[32] France did nothing to put a halt to the evolution of events in this new direction.

French Policy Toward the Smaller States
In 1936 and 1937

The misfortunes of French foreign policy were caused by the sad fact that while the diplomatic service on the ambassadorial level lived up to its duties, the statesmen in charge paid more attention to domestic political struggles than to the desperate warnings of their foreign service personnel. Only Delbos made some attempt to revive French influence in Eastern Europe although he committed the same mistake as his predecessors by disregarding the natural interests of the individual states. No wonder his attempts ended with failure.[33]

During 1936 the Eastern allies of France—Poland and the Little Entente—displayed more and more signs of dismay over the real value of

French protection.[34] But they received little comfort. Only General Gamelin made an effort to reconcile Poland and Czechoslovakia, with the result that the Czech General Staff made a weak attempt to "decrease the antagonism between their own country and Poland."[35] The Polish government continued to practice a selfish policy, however, partly because Germany did not seem to make military preparations against Poland and partly because of the problem of Danzig and the Corridor.[36] In November, Beck finally received assurances from Germany that the Reich would prevent the reoccurrence of incidents in Danzig.[37] Meanwhile, Antonescu, the new Rumanian foreign minister, followed a more independent policy and sought a rapprochement with Poland and Italy, while Yugoslavia's Stoyadinovich wanted to secure Mussolini's direct friendship because of the French-Italian alienation.[38] Czechoslovakia, surrounded by unfriendly and hostile states,[39] tried to repair the crumbling Little Entente by suggesting a mutual assistance treaty with France, but the French reply was not too encouraging; the French government "was ready to examine, with the necessary cautions, forms in which the solidarity of France and the Little Entente might be reaffirmed."[40] Delbos felt that caution and discretion were necessary in order not to give Germany any excuse to denounce her yet remaining responsibilities. By the middle of November, it was clear that France was not overenthusiastic about the pact and the military clauses Czechoslovakia wanted to attach to it.[41]

There were two countries in Central Europe which belonged to the Rome Protocols and, therefore, were regarded by Laval as in Italy's domain: Austria and Hungary. The upkeep of Austria's independence was in the interest of France as well as of Italy. After the Austro-German accord, France displayed a great amount of unconcern about the future of Austria. Here again, not the diplomats but the statesmen had committed the mistake. As early as August 1936, the French embassy in Vienna began sending alarming reports about the spread of Pro-Nazi sentiments in Austria.[42] They reported that Schuschnigg was inclined to adopt a policy of appeasement at any price toward Germany in order to ensure German observation of the July agreement.[43] Daladier was told of the impossible task given the Austrian army regarding the improvement of Austria's defense and security without an increase in the military budget, and he knew about the Austrian concern over the Czechoslovak-Soviet Mutual Assistance Treaty, which the Austrians considered a threat to their own security.[44]

Yet, France remained passive, not only in 1936 but also in 1937. Parallel with the French passivity, new developments and initiatives for the reconstruction of East-Central European alliances came from the Little Entente and from Hungary. During 1936 and 1937, however, Delbos paid very little attention to East-Central Europe, and though French attention was concentrated on Germany's future plans, the *Anschluss* "took France completely by surprise."[45] With a little modification, this statement is true. The French politicians, engaged once again in a power struggle, were taken by surprise; the French diplomats were not. But the reports of the diplomats were like lonely shouts in the wilderness. As for the French army, according to General Gamelin, the *"Anschluss* was not a surprise for us."[46]

CHAPTER XII
THE SIXTH CRISIS:
ANSCHLUSS AND THE ENCIRCLEMENT OF CZECHOSLOVAKIA

While France was preoccupied with the problems of her own security *vis à vis* Germany and with the hopeless task of enlisting the unconditional support of Britain against the Germans, East-Central European affairs were more and more neglected. But France, being dependent now to a great degree, on the diplomatic decisions of Britain, could do nothing else.[1] Britain had no direct interests in Central Europe. Hitler was considered the less dangerous enemy since he was not interested in the Mediterranean,[2] and Mussolini was. Eden "more than suspected that Mussolini wanted to dominate the Mediterranean" and was convinced that the "British government should not give way to him."[3] So Britain directed the main attention of the League of Nations, as well as France, to the Spanish Civil War and the Mediterranean.[4]

This relative disinterest of the Great Powers in the affairs of Central Europe gave the small powers an opportunity to take a few independent diplomatic steps in an attempt to normalize their relations and improve their own security. The key country in these negotiations was Czechoslovakia.

ECONOMIC CONDITIONS IN CZECHOSLOVAKIA

Influence of Geography on Economy

There existed a great gap between the economic conditions of the Czechs and members of the minority groups. Bohemia and Moravia had been agriculturally as well as industrially the best developed lands of the Habsburg Empire.[5] Slovakia and Ruthenia, on the other hand, were high, mountainous regions unfit for production of great amounts of wheat. The majority of inhabitants gained their livelihood in double occupation: during wintertime they worked as lumberjacks, during summertime they migrated to Hungary and earned their living as sharecroppers. The new national frontiers eliminated this second income. Then in 1930, the Czech government denounced the Czech-Hungarian commercial treaty to protect the interests of the Czech peasantry. But this very protection given to the Czech peasants deprived the Slovaks and Ruthenes of their nearest natural grain market. Their worsening economic conditions did not make them very ardent supporters of the Prague government.

The peasantry in all three parts of the country generally lived better than under Austrian and Hungarian rule since Czechoslovakia had implemented a far-reaching land redistribution program at the expense of the mostly German and Hungarian great landowners. Maybe the best way to understand the size and impact of that land distribution is to compare the statistics of Czechoslovakia with those of Hungary. While in Hungary the large landowners represented only 0.7 percent of the landowner population, at the same time they controlled 49.3 percent of the arable land. In Czechoslovakia, the great landowners numbered 0.5 percent of the landowner class and held only 16 percent of the arable land.[6]

While benefiting many poor nationality groups, the expropriation of the great land estates aroused strong opposition from three groups. The former owners, the old aristocracy, naturally opposed it because of their material losses while the employees of the former landowners opposed it because they lost their jobs. Finally, national minority groups opposed it because the land distribution often favored the Czechs over the local poor minority group peasants.[7] The nationalistically biased policy in agriculture thus created further divisions within Czechoslovakia.

In industry, the Czech provinces did not experience difficulties. But the industry of Slovakia, being cut off from its natural market in Hungary, faced severe problems since transportation expenses made Slovak goods uncompetitive pricewise in the further parts of the country; eventually the entire Slovak heavy industry was completely closed.[8]

Foreign Trade

The Czechoslovak trade balance was favorable from 1920 to 1931. The economic crisis caused deficits for 1932 and 1933, but by 1934 foreign trade turned again in favor of Czechoslovakia.[9] Czechoslovakia transacted business with almost the whole world, but her principal buyers and sellers were naturally the European countries. Her overseas trade was managed through the German ports of Hamburg and Bremen, Italian ports, and the Polish port of Danzig. These seaports carried 5.6 percent of the total foreign trade in 1934 and 7 percent in 1935.

Czechoslovakia's best trading partner was Germany; although German trade had steadily declined since 1933, she still commanded first place in 1935. The potentially hostile revisionist states, also with a declining share of the Czech trade, controlled an average of one-third of the import-export business. At the same time, the undoubtedly friendly nations, though increasing their transactions, still controlled only about 20 percent of the Czech trade. Thus, Czechoslovakia had the same weakness as the rest of Central Europe: no matter whether or not they liked German domestic or foreign policy, economic interests dictated that these nations make economic contracts with Germany.

Benes' Foreign Policy

Just as it is impossible to separate the foreign policy of Poland from Pilsudski, so it is impossible to detach Czechoslovakian foreign policy of this period from the personality, convictions and ideology of Edouard Benes. Born into a peasant family, Benes received his education in Prague, Dijon, and Paris. In 1915 he escaped from Austria-Hungary and returned to Paris where he joined the Czech exile group and soon became one of its most important leaders, second only to Masaryk. Serving Czechoslovakia as foreign minister without interruption from 1918 to 1935, "Benes' prerogative to run Czechoslovakia's foreign affairs virtually at will was never seriously challenged."[10] His basic foreign political principle was the preservation of the status quo, not only from the point of view of territorial changes but also concerning the proportion of power between the victorious and defeated states.

Since Czechoslovaka was created of former Austrian and Hungarian territories, these states represented to Benes the natural enemies of his country, especially Hungary, because she challenged the Trianon Treaty and never seemed to accept the loss of Slovakia and Ruthenia as final. Benes tried to serve the security of Czechoslovakia against Hungary by signing a defensive alliance with Yugoslavia in 1920, a mutual guarantee of security with Rumania in 1921, and a friendship treaty with France in 1924. The Rumanian and Yugoslavian treaties were incorporated in 1929 into the Charter of the Little Entente alliance.

Against a possible revival of German aggressiveness in Austria or Germany proper, Czechoslovakia seemed to be well protected by the military clauses of the French treaty. A great asset for Czechoslovakia would have been the conclusion of a treaty with Poland, but neither

Pilsudski nor Benes could forget the past or overlook the disputed Teschen territory, and their rapprochement never went further than the signing of a commercial treaty in 1925. After the conclusion of the German-Polish Non-Aggression Pact in January 1934, the Czech General Staff considered Poland an enemy.[11]

It was almost impossible for Benes to come to terms with the potential enemies of Czechoslovakia because of his ideological convictions. "In the regime of Dollfuss and even of Schuschnigg, Benes seemed to have detected something too Rightist to his vision of a free democracy. Obviously the regime of admiral Horthy was much too authoritarian for his taste."[12] Even less chance remained for a conciliation with Germany. Though Benes believed in bourgeois democracy, to use a stylish expression, he sympathized more with Marxist democracy than with an authoritarian regime which had a free enterprise system. In his mind, political considerations on many occasions were more overriding than economic organization. So Czechoslovakia remained hostile to her neighbors, with the exception of Rumania,[13] and drew closer to the Soviet Union.

Outside of the above-mentioned bilateral agreements, Benes always fully cooperated with the League of Nations which, in his eyes, served only one purpose: preservation of the status quo. Up to 1935, Czechoslovakia's interests were well served by Benes' foreign policy. Then, after the resignation of Masaryk, Benes became President of Czechoslovakia with Hodza[14] as his prime minister and foreign minister. Great differences in their opinions and methods made any Benes-Hodza cooperation a rough task.[15] The personal incompatibility between Benes and Hodza grew worse as time passed, with harmony restored between the two statesmen only in the spring of 1938.[16] In 1936, Benes still believed that Barthou's idea of an Eastern Pact would best serve Czechoslovakia's interests. He believed unconditionally in the value of French patronism. Hodza, expecially after the reoccupation of the Rhineland, lost faith in France and wanted to decrease the German danger with direct negotiations and the Hungarian threat with a rapprochement to Austria and Hungary.

Due to this unfortunate personal antagonism between Benes and Hodza, Czechoslovak foreign policy became hesitant, losing its former decisiveness and determination exactly at the time when it was most needed: the German occupation of the Rhineland and the weak French reaction confronted Czechoslovakia with the bitter reality that her security had become dependent entirely on her own strength.

CZECHOSLOVAKIA IN 1936

Domestic Situation

The domestic political situation changed for the worse during the 1935 elections when the new Sudeten-German Party won "the second largest number of seats of all parliamentary groups, being surpassed only by the Agrarian Party."[17] Also, the world economic crisis started late in Czechoslovakia, and in 1936 the Sudeten-German industrial centers were still suffering its effects.[18] This economic problem promoted alienation between the Sudeten-Germans and the Czech population. The German minority was also aggrevated by the arrogant and "politically not too psychological" attitude of the Czech bureaucracy and administrative personnel.[19] But the Sudeten-Germans did not yet want to destroy the Czechoslovak state, nor did they enjoy Hitler's unconditional support. There was hope and time to resolve the antagonism.

The Slovak autonomists, under the leadership of catholic priest Father Andrew Hlinka, formed the Slovak People's Party which was "anti-Democratic, anti-Semitic and anti-Socialist."[20] Naturally, they sympathized with every group whose activity weakened the authority of the central Czech government. Father Hlinka sought connections with the Sudeten-Germany Party, but actual negotiations began only in February of 1938 and even at that time they were unsuccessful.[21] Without outside agitation and help, the dissatisfaction of a small group of Slovaks did not represent too much of a problem for the Czechoslovak state.

Ruthenia's autonomy also fell victim to Czech centralization. Here the centrifugal forces were the autonomists, the Communists, the Fascist-type Fenzig Party,[22] and an unorganized group of intellectuals who still nurtured Pan-Slavic sentiments and were directed by the Uniate priest August Volosin. Yet none of these groups represented any danger for Czechoslovak unity in absence of outside support. The Ruthen peasants were more interested in everyday problems than in politics.[23]

The Polish minority in Teschen was really a minority (80,000 Poles against 250,000 Czechs)[24] and remained relatively quiet. The Hungarians in the Southern regions of Slovakia and Ruthenia received encouragement, but no financial support, from the Hungarian government.[25] The

Hungarians were not a united group organized into a disciplined political party. A great number of them, while cherishing a certain nostalgic Hungarian nationalism, preferred to live in a democracy instead of under an authoritarian system. These people fought for the recognition of their minority rights *within* Czechoslovakia and opposed the dissolution of that state, being afraid of nazism. Their arguments were expounded by leading intellectuals, who warned their fellow citizens that Hitler's plans for *Lebensraum* included Hungary.[26]

In conclusion, it can be safely stated that in 1936 the domestic political problems of Czechoslovakia, including the minority question, were not too pressing. A friendlier, more conciliatory policy could have prevented the transformation of these groups into dangerous, disruptive forces.

Military Situation

From the military view point, the reconciliation of minority groups was of first importance. Czechoslovakia needed these minority group members in the army for the defense of the national frontiers. Even if the Czech General Staff mobilized every male adult, the length of the frontier would have made a successful defense improbable. Czechoslovakia had approximately 200 miles of frontier with Germany, about 500 miles with Poland, more than 350 miles with Hungary and close to 250 miles with Austria—almost 1300 miles of frontier with unfriendly neighbors and potential enemies.

The Czechoslovak army numbered 111,539 men in 1930, and although by 1934 the army was down to 98,984 men, this decline did not effect its combat value since the active officer corps remained virtually the same: 10,079 in 1930 and 10,059 in 1935.[27] The technical equipment, manufactured in the famous Skoda factories, was excellent and in satisfactory amounts. The Czechoslovak army's strategic plans were defensive against Germany, Austria, and Poland and offensive—but only in cooperation with the Little Entente—*vis à vis* Hungary.[28]

Taking military-geographic factors into consideration, these plans were realistic only within the framework of a greater military alliance system. Such a system seemed to function effectively, at least in peacetime, through the French and Soviet military agreements. France kept a permanent military mission in Prague which advised the Czech General

Staff in questions of training, tactics, and strategy. The Czechoslovak intelligence service collected and exchanged information with the French Deuxième Bureau, while French military engineers were busy building a small-scale replica of the Maginot line on the Czech-German frontier and enlarging the military air fields of Kosice and Uzhorod in order to facilitate the landing of heavier Soviet transport planes.[29]

Yet there were great shortcomings in this grandiose military cooperative plan: France did not intend to attack Germany even in case of war and wanted to remain behind the Maginot line. The Soviet army's help depended on the goodwill of Poland and Rumania, neither of which seemed inclined to grant passage rights to the Soviet army.[30] Because of these weaknesses in the greater military system, Czechoslovakian strategic interests demanded the effective division of potential enemies in order to prevent their concentrated attack against Czechoslovakia.

Thus, the military preparedness of Czechoslovakia was very good, but naturally limited.[31] The successful employment of her army in case of war depended on the capability of Czech diplomats who, at least temporarily, had to neutralize or if possible gain the support of one or more of Czechoslovakia's potential enemies. In light of the deteriorating harmony of the Little Entente and the passivity of France, this military demand became one of the most important assignments of Czechoslovakia's foreign policy in 1936. It was unfortunate for Czechoslovakia that the direction of her foreign policy was in the hands of the realist Hodza only for a short period of time and that Benes regained control, since he continued to believe blindly in the great value of the French and Soviet assistance treaties.

Foreign Political Situation

From the beginning, two fears stood at the center of Czechoslovakia's foreign policy: the fear of Habsburg restoration and the fear of Hungarian revisionism. After 1933, a new fear was added: fear of the revival of German aggression. Finally, the military situation in Czechoslovakia added an additional problem. Benes hoped to revive the Little Entente against the possibility of Habsburg restoration and Hungarian revisionism. He hoped to create an Eastern Pact against German aggression. Though he was unsuccessful, he did not give up hope and believed that Germany was interested only in an *Anschluss*. When Hodza took over the premiership, all these problems seemed to reach crisis proportion at the same time.

Habsburg Restoration, Anschluss, Revisionism

The possibility of a Habsburg restoration in Austria and/or Hungary caused near panic several times in almost all of the successor states, with the possible exception of Austria. Yet, the probability of its realization was very slim as long as the peace treaties were guarded well by the victorious allied powers. When the question was raised openly to Schuschnigg, he always stated that the problem was not timely, but he also always refused to exclude the possibility of restoration once and for all. Hungary straightforwardly rejected the idea.

The Little Entente states were afraid of a Habsburg restoration more or less for different reasons. Czechoslovakia, with its great German population, was naturally anxious not to see the return of the Habsburgs. Yugoslavia, not being able to reconcile the Croatian minority, feared the possible loss of Croatia, while Rumania opposed restoration for the same reasons concerning Transylvania. Yet the Little Entente statesmen privately admitted that the question of the Habsburg restoration did not cause them real headaches. They even denied that they were afraid of it. "Jan Masaryk said that the government of Czechoslovakia was not as afraid of it as Rumania. However if one asked the Rumanian politicians, it was supposedly Benes who was afraid of it."[32]

In 1936, Germany joined the Little Entente to oppose a Habsburg restoration. The question was raised again at that time by Prince Starhemberg, Vice-Chancellor of Austria, who saw in it a good solution to avoid the danger of an *Anschluss*, but Starhemberg soon toned down his pro-Habsburg speeches at the request of Britain, France and the Little Entente.[33] Germany remained suspicious, however, and worked out a cooperative military plan with Yugoslavia for the occupation of Austria in case a restoration occurred.[34] Regent Paul refused to take further responsibility for the preservation of Austrian independence and the Yugoslavian government announced that the continuous independence of Austria was not a question of interest to them.[35] Since the Little Entente states agreed completely on the Habsburg restoration question, it became a secondary problem for Czechoslovak foreign policy.

The danger of *Anschluss* was again interpreted differently by Benes and Hodza. Benes, who felt a restoration attempt would provoke an *Anschluss* did not believe that a German attack on Austria was imminent. "Hitler is not so blind. He knows that it would mean a general war and he does not want that in the near future."[36] Hodza, on the other hand, expected the continuation of German aggression in East-Central Europe. Foreign Minister Kamil Krofta, who was considered Benes' man, had no doubt that "Czechoslovakia cannot resist any power alone because of the geographic and ethnographic situation."[37] Benes and Krofta hoped for a better future, expecting that the Great Powers would resolve their differences with Italy and return their attention to Central Europe. Until then, both of them agreed to continue cautiously with Hodza's rapprochement attempt with Austria.

Austro-Czechoslovak Rapprochement Attempts

If Hitler had any plans for expansion toward the East, he knew that such a move would be a real gamble without the liquidation of Czechoslovakia which, from the military point of view, would be a hard task for the still not combat-ready German army: the Bohemian Forests, Ore Mountains and Sudeten Alps offered a natural defense line against a German attack. The southern borders of Czechoslovakia, on the other hand, were open plains and the tributaries of the Danube offered easy access to the heart of Czechoslovakia from Austria. These geographic facts made it necessary for Germany to realize the *Anschluss* before confronting Czechoslovakia.

By winter 1935, Schuschnigg and Hodza recognized that they had a common interest against Germany. The already existing economic interdependence of the two countries provided a good basis for attempts at a political agreement. The Austrian Foreign Minister was ready to sign a friendship treaty with Czechoslovakia if the conditions were right, i.e., if Czechoslovakia would give some guarantee to Austria against a German aggression. The exploration of such a possibility was the goal of Schuschnigg's visit to Prague on January 16-17, 1936. During their meetings, Hodza expressed his desire to facilitate a rapprochement with not only Austria but Hungary and Italy as well, going so far in his fervor to reach an understanding with Austria that he considered the possibility of a Habsburg restoration as an acceptable alternative.[38]

Naturally, both men were very cautious not to engender early opposition to their designs, so publicly they denied the political aspects of their meeting and gave, economic reasons for it,[39] but the rest of Europe doubted that the subject of the Hodza-Schuschnigg negotiations was only the improvement of trade. Opposition and support showed up simultaneously coming from different countries for different reasons.

Germany naturally opposed an Austro-Czechoslovak rapprochement since it would have made the annexation of Austria and the liquidation of Czechoslovakia a much harder task. To prevent that, Germany started a propaganda campaign against Schuschnigg, spreading rumors in Bucharest, Budapest and Belgrade that the *only purpose* of his visit was to obtain Hodza's approval for a Habsburg restoration.[40] At the same time, the German press stepped up its attack on Austria while the government openly doubted the "trustworthiness of Austria" from the German, Italian and Hungarian points of view.[41]

During and right after Schuschnigg's visit in Prague, Italy displayed a certain approval with Mussolini indicating that "It is natural" Schuschnigg seeks more allies against the *Anschluss;"* however, a month later, Mussolini suggested that Schuschnigg seek a rapprochement with Germany and Yugoslavia instead of with Czechoslovakia.[42] To dismiss Italian misgivings, the Austrian government assured Italy that Austria would remain faithful to the Rome Protocols, and Mussolini was satisfied.[43]

Schuschnigg's Prague negotiations caused even greater apprehension in Hungary. Hungarian foreign political principles opposed any attempt at rapprochement with Czechoslovakia without first satisfying Hungary's revisionist claims. The Habsburg restoration possibility created just as great a dissatisfaction for other reasons. Gömbös did not desire the *Anschluss,* but at the same time he sought Germany's support against Czechoslovakia. For these reasons, Hungary watched the Hodza-Schuschnigg negotiations with suspicion, and Kanya "did his best to raise difficulties in the way of the new [Hodza] plan."[44]

At home, Hodza was confronted with even greater problems. Believing that an *Anschluss* represented a lesser danger for Czechoslovakia than did a Habsburg restoration, Benes did not agree with Hodza's Central European conceptions, and this opposition made Hodza's position insecure.[45] Hodza slso met the opposition of his Little Entente partners. Yugoslavia agreed with Benes while Titulescu considered the idea of the *Anschluss* and the possibility of a Habsburg restoration like "a choice between the gallows and the guillotine."[46] In spite of this opposition, the rapprochement continued, gaining momentum under the effects of the German remilitarization of the Rhineland; but it was slowed down by the Austro-German agreement of July 11, 1936, which demanded Austria practice its foreign policy "in harmony with Germany."[47]

Reactions to this Austro-German agreement were mixed. London expressed satisfaction while France's only concern was the possibility of an Italo-German secret partnership connected with the Austro-German treaty.[48] Yugoslavia greeted the agreement with relief, seeing in it a very effective obstacle in the way of a Habsburg restoration.[49] Titulescu regarded it as the first step in Germany's building of an alternate route (to that of Poland) for an attack on the Soviet Union while Poland interpreted it as the first step toward the *Anschluss.*[50] Czechoslovak Foreign Minister Krofta agreed with the Polish interpretation and continued to urge the collaboration of the Danubian states against the German menace.[51] The anti-Nazi political leaders of Austria looked at the agreement as a "necessary evil" since the Germans would try to "swallow" Austria and then Czechoslovakia anyway.[52] Schuschnigg secretly shared this opinion.[53]

Thanks to the common views of Krofta and Schuschnigg, the Austro-Czechoslovak negotiations were not terminated. Conversations, visits, and diplomatic exchanges continued throughout 1936 and the next year ending only shortly before the *Anschluss* in March 1938. The failure of these negotiations cannot be blamed on Austria or Czechoslovakia alone. Both states had only limited freedom of action because of previous treaties and obligations. And what is even more important, both states had their own Great Power patrons who, instead of promoting a Central European peace, used their little client-states to strengthen their own international positions.

Hungarian Little Entente Rapprochement Attempts

Benes was very much afraid that the Hungarian revisionist propaganda would gain sufficient support in Britain and France to force a rearrangement of the peace treaties; Hodza, on the other hand, had a feeling that the Hungarian government "had to do all that talking" for home consumption, without seriously expecting any result.[54] As long as the Hungarian army remained weak and the Little Entente treaty's mutual assistance clauses were honored by all the member states, Czechoslovakia's foreign policy did not have to pay much attention to this problem. Revisionist propaganda could not have prevented a rapprochement if both countries' realistic interests demanded that rapprochement.

The passivity of France during the events of 1936 convinced the Little Entente states that they could not rely on the protection of their great ally. France lost credit in their eyes after the Rhineland occupation while the Soviet Union's sincere intentions were doubted more and more. A willingness on the part of Czechoslovakia to loosen her ties with the Soviet Union opened the door for a possible understanding with Poland, and domestic developments in Hungary raised hopes for the chance of creating a Danubian block. Gömbös, who dreamed about a Berlin-Rome axis, died on October 6, 1936. His successor as prime minister, Kálmán Darányi, represented the more conservative Hungarians (supported by the majority of democratic intellectuals and university students as well as a great number of people from every way of life, all with anti-German sentiments) who, seeing the German successes in Central Europe *vis à vis* Mussolini,[55] wanted to find a counterweight against this growing German influence and so looked for opportunities to establish friendlier relations with England, France and the Little Entente.[56]

Conditions seemed to be right to end the hostility of the successor states and introduce a new era of friendly relations. However, two factors blocked the way to a real success. One was Hungarian revisionism, and the rigid attitude of the Little Entente toward any change in the status quo. The other was the interference or passivity of the Great Powers, that is, France, Germany and Italy. It was clear that without compromises on the part of the Danubian states and without the blessings of the Great Powers, the Hungarian-Little Entente rapprochement attempt would fail.

The Darányi government, in contrast to Gömbös' policy, dropped the demands for territorial revisions. Instead, they demanded that the Little Entente states give full citizenship rights to the Hungarian minority groups living in their territories and discontinue their "de-Magyarization."[52] Of course, this new formulation of Hungarian foreign policy did not mean that the government gave up its revisionism, it simply showed that Foreign Minister Kánya correctly evaluated the effects of the German-Italian rapprochement and tried to adjust his policy accordingly. Also, Hungary did not follow the Austrian example of denouncing the arms limitation clauses of the Trianon Treaty, thus keeping the door open for rapprochement.

After failing to conclude mutual assistance treaties with Rumania and Yugoslavia against Germany, Benes proposed the creation of regional treaties; this suggestion did not meet such firm opposition.[58] Delbos gladly gave his blessing to the attempt at improving Little Entente-Hungarian relations,[59] so in January 1937, Czechoslovakia suggested a non-aggression treaty to Hungary. Czechoslovakia indicated this would be the price for her recognition of Hungary's rearmament rights; but Kánya refused, arguing that since a non-aggression pact with Hungary would not cancel Czechoslovakia's military alliances (directed against Hungary) with Rumania and Yugoslavia, such a pact would not change the existing situation and therefore, was unacceptable.[60]

Two days later, on January 21, Kánya received the Yugoslavian ambassador who proposed the conclusion of a Hungarian-Yugoslavian friendship treaty; Kánya saw this as feasible·if Hungary would not have to do the same with Czechoslovakia and Rumania.[61] On January 23, the Rumanian ambassador visited Kánya. He received the same reply to his inquiry as the Czechoslovak ambassador had, but Kánya also expressed the desire to improve Hungarian-Rumanian relations.[62] The same day, Kánya met with the German ambassador. Using his conversations with the Little Entente ambassadors as a threat, Kánya bitterly condemned the German press attacks on Hungary's revisionist policy, rejected the German-supported provocations of the "Federation of Germans in Hungary," and expressed dissatisfaction over the rumors of Hitler's anti-Hungarian feelings.[63] Further, Kánya threatened to seek a sincere agreement with the Little Entente if Germany did not change her policy toward Hungary.[64] German-Hungarian relations remained cool throughout the year.

The Hungarian replies given to the Little Entente ambassadors intended—without doubt—to destroy the Little Entente. But the German attitude would have forced Hungary to give further concessions, if the Little Entente states had stuck together. Instead, each member state tried to improve her own security individually, sometimes even at the expense of her partners. That way, they became pawns in the Central-European chess game of the Great Powers.

Italy, while approving the Austrian-Czechoslovakian rapprochement, disapproved of the Hungarian-Czechoslovakian one.[65] In spite of his rapprochement with Germany, Mussolini still did not trust Hitler's intentions in the Balkans and tried to create an Hungarian-Austrian-

Yugoslavian-Italian block which would serve as a dam to German expansion, with Hungary and Yugoslavia being the most important members of this block since they could oppose Germany's Balkan plans and so defend Italy's interest even after an *Anschluss.*[66] Mussolini was ready and willing to support Hungarian revisionism *vis à vis* Czechoslovakia. A stronger Hungary, in possession of Slovakia and Ruthenia, would represent a stronger obstacle to Hitler's expansion toward the Balkans. On the other hand, Hungarian revisionism toward Yugoslavia and Rumania would endanger the creation of an anti-German block. After strongly recommending to Hungary a rapprochement with Rumania and Yugoslavia, Italy herself began negotiations with Yugoslavia at the end of February 1937 and, on March 25, signed an agreement mutually guaranteeing the Italo-Yugoslav frontiers.[67]

Stoyadinovich kept these negotiations secret from his Little Entente partners as well as from France,[68] and with this secrecy he violated the constitution of the Little Entente which required member state consultation and information concerning treaty negotiations with a non-member state. Nonetheless, Czechoslovakia greeted the Italo-Yugoslavian agreement with joy.[69] During their Belgrade conference on April 27, 1937, the Little Entente decided not to continue negotiations with Hungary as individual states, but only as a block.[70] At the same time, they requested that Eden and Delbos mediate between the Little Entente and Hungary in order to normalize their relations. Both statesmen declined the honor: Eden did not want to create the impression that Britain wanted to interfere with the affairs of Central Europe, especially since "British-German relations were decisively improved and British-Italian relations also showed a betterment," while Delbos servilely followed Britain's example, as Eden hoped he would.[71]

Effects of the Italo-Yugoslavian Treaty

Today it is accepted "historical fact" that with the declaration of the *Axis* in October 1936, close cooperation existed between Hitler and Mussolini. Therefore, the Italo-Yugoslavian treaty of March 1937 is looked upon only as a link in the chain of Hitler's diplomatic maneuvers to destroy the unity of the Little Entente and isolate Czechoslovakia. While this interpretation seems to be valid and proven by the events of

1938 and later, it overlooks a very important nuance of differences which existed in 1937.

With the treaty, Mussolini hoped to pave the way for a Franco-Italian reconciliation, to release the burden of the Italian army *vis à vis* Yugoslavia, and to create a block against German expansion in Central Europe and the Balkans. A skillful British and French diplomacy could have grabbed this opportunity, but Britain's eyes were fixed on the Mediterranean and France still had strained relations with Italy. Though with the Italo-Yugoslav treaty Austria lost importance from the Italian point of view, Mussolini continued supporting Schuschnigg and publicly manifested his interest in Austria.[72] France, on the other hand, remained passive and happily agreed with the Austrian proposal *not to* publish any declarations concerning the French guarantees of Austrian independence.[73] This suggestion was understandable on the part of Austria, cautious not to join openly with Germany's enemy. Its acceptance by France was hardly understandable.

The Italo-Yugoslavian treaty provided the last opportunity for France to regain Mussolini's friendship and with it the directing role in the international affairs of continental Europe. France decided not to do this and continued instead to follow the directions of Britain, who was much more interested in the high seas than in the continent. One may only speculate on how the future of Europe would have turned out if a cooperating France and Italy would have pressured their respective allies into working for the realization of Hodza's dream of close cooperation between the Danubian states.

Czechoslovak Relations with the Great Powers

What could Czechoslovakia expect from the Great Powers? Her 1924 mutual assistance treaty with France was still in effect, but France seemed daily to become a less trustworthy ally. It was disappointing enough that France accepted the German *fait à compli* in the Rhineland without any serious counteraction, the real surprise came when Krofta learned from General Gamelin that France did not intend to use force to prevent the building of German fortifications there. Krofta expressed his anxiety that these Rhineland fortifications would decrease France's ability to give military support to Poland and Czechoslovakia. Gamelin indirectly agreed by saying that the end of the Abyssinian crisis would make the whole Italian army available for employment in Central Europe if France would need more help.[74] Gamelin's suggestion that Czechoslovakia attempt a rapprochement with Poland did not meet with the enthusiastic approval of the Czech statesman, but Krofta realized that Czechoslovakia needed Polish cooperation.[75]

Confidence in the value of French patronage also declined because of the activities of French embassy officials who suggested that the Czech government give territorial concessions to Hungary in order to pave the way for closer cooperation between the two countries against a possible *Anschluss.*[76] Hodza and Krofta realized that their suspicions about France were well-founded. They learned that Czechoslovakia's unconditional support of the League of Nations' sanction policy had weakened her international position since it alienated Italy, the power on which, according to Gamelin, their security now depended. Krofta thus felt that his policy of rapprochement with Italy was justified and his rapprochement with Austria was the right thing to do.[77]

The relations between Czechoslovakia and Britain were confusing. Although British diplomats praised Benes and appreciated his great efforts to organize a free, democratic state, the government never sent to Prague a representative of high standing since "some officials in the Foreign Office thought that some of the new Czech officials were rather low-middle class people who did not live up to the Englishman's ideal of a true gentlemen."[78] British public opinion did not care too much about the future of Czechoslovakia while the British ambassador to Prague was outright hostile, expressing public disapproval of Chamberlain's attempts to promote an Austro-Czechoslovak rapprochement and stating that "Czechoslovakia is a country which has no justification for existence, and therefore, no British or French soldier will march to protect her security."[79]

In July 1936, only two months after visiting Prague, Chamberlain expressed his conviction that the guarantee of territorial integrity under Article 10 of the Covenant of the League of Nations "ought to be subject to acceptance of any advice tendered under Article 19, which provides for revision."[80] Thus, the Czechoslovaks' hope or gaining British support for their security did not promise much success.

Due to the fact that Mussolini supported Hungarian revisionism, relations with Italy were never too good. After Czechoslovakia participated in the sanctions against Italy, their relations became less than friendly. Yet, Italy could have helped Czechoslovakia in more than one way. With skillful diplomacy, Krofta could have convinced Italy to give up supporting Hungarian revisionism and (according to Gamelin's information) also to guarantee Czechoslovakian security against Germany. Krofta sounded out the possibility of Italian cooperation as soon as February 1936, and it was a right step on his part.[81]

Since signing a mutual assistance treaty in May 1935, relations with the Soviet Union were very good. But public opinion was divided concerning the value of this treaty. Those who still followed the Pan-Slavic dream looked at the Soviet Union as a "big brother." The Communists naturally applauded the Soviet friendship. On the other hand, there were also many people who pointed out the great ideological differences between communism and democracy.[82] Krofta believed that the Soviet assistance had great value and the application of the treaty would not face obstacles since the "Russian army will come to help his country crossing Rumania with or without the consent of Bucharest."[83] On the other hand, he began to realize that the Soviet treaty alienated Poland, made Austria suspicious, and turned Germany and Hungary hostile. Krofta worked hard to eliminate these unpleasant effects of the Soviet treaty, and in April 1937, he finally assured his neighbors that "the Soviet-Czechoslovak treaty is not an axiom of Czechoslovak foreign policy."[84]

Diplomatic Steps to Satisfy Military Demands

The military-geographic situation of Czechoslovakia demanded the division of hostile states, their neutralization, and if possible the separation of one or two from the other unfriendly nations.

After 1933, Germany became the strongest member of the enemy group. The Czechs feared Germany, but Hitler was equally afraid of Czechoslovakia, which was "a dagger pointed at the heart of Germany."[85] To eliminate this danger, he tried to neutralize Czechoslovakia. Before 1936, however, the French alliance seemed to give Czechoslovakia enough security, the Czech army was stronger than the German army, and ideological differences prohibited Masaryk and Benes from accepting any German offer. But by the end of 1935, the situation was different. Germany was no longer a member of the League of Nations, she had renounced the arms limitation clauses of the Versailles Treaty, and she kept the whole of Central Europe under her economic control. Then she openly challenged the strongest army in Europe, the French, and reoccupied the Rhineland. Amidst such changed conditions, realistic interests demanded that Czechoslovak diplomats take into careful consideration the latest German offer and, if otherwise acceptable, not reject it only because of ideological differences.

Hitler made the offer through his diplomatic representatives and included it in a speech to the *Reichstag*: "The German government is willing to sign non-aggression pacts, similar to that with Poland, with the states bordering Germany in the East."[86] This offer presented a golden opportunity to Czechoslovakia; because if Germany remained neutral, the Hungarian threat in case of war could be taken care of by the Czechoslovak army alone.

But unfortunate coincidences delayed the Czechoslovak reply. On March 5, 1936, two days before Hitler's speech, Benes, Krofta, and some high ranking officers of the General Staff met with a military emissary from Moscow, who recommended the transfer of "some cadres of the Russian air force to Czechoslovakia." News of this secret meeting reached London. The British protested to Flandin, who in turn notified Prague that "that sort of thing was at the present moment most undesirable since it furnished unwelcome grounds for the Führer's anxiety." During the following days, the semi-official Czechoslovak press adopted a critical tone against the Soviet Union and Krofta's remark that "Czechoslovakia must be careful not to let herself be taken in by the Soviets" became widely known in Prague's diplomatic circles.[87]

Benes was thus cautious not to do anything which might meet with French disapproval, and so he waited for a decision from Paris before responding to Hitler's offer. Paris waited for the decision of London. London was less concerned with the growing strength of Germany than with the possible Italian expansion in the Mediterranean region.

Events in Central Europe also began to turn Benes' attention away from the German non-aggression pact offer. The renewal of the Rome Protocols, the reintroduction of conscription in Austria, and the possibility of the same in Hungary revived his fear *vis à vis* these two countries. At the same time, the reappearance of rumors about the possibility of a Habsburg restoration activized the whole Little Entente. These events provided too much of a temptation for Benes to reassert his superiority among the small pro-status quo nations. The victory of the Popular Front government in France seemed to reinforce the Franco-Czechoslovak cooperation against Germany and created the impression that it was unnecessary to accept Hitler's peace offer. The outbreak of the Spanish Civil War, the passivity of France, and the activity of the Soviet Union seemed to prove that the Czechoslovak-Soviet treaty was the right step in the right direction. Therefore, Benes tried to delay the German-Czech negotiations with counterproposals.[88] This delaying tactic proved to be a mistake. By May 1936, Hitler changed his mind about Czechoslovakia and . . . "seeing that he could not win over the Republic, decided to destroy it."[89]

Benes continued negotiations with Austria and Hungary throughout 1936 and 1937, but without success since he was not willing to make territorial concessions and the Hungarian government was not willing to collaborate with Czechoslovakia without that. Public opinion in Czechoslovakia was divided: some supported Benes' policy; others advocated an understanding with Germany and were ready to sacrifice even the Soviet-Czech treaty to reach that goal.[90] But Benes' policy prevailed.

In the spring of 1938, the danger of *Anschluss* became real and with it the deterioration of Czechoslovakia's strategic position became a sad and unchangeable fact. Benes' foreign policy during 1936-1937 satisfied every requirement with the exception of the military one. The diplomats did not divide the enemies of Czechoslovakia nor neutralize any of them. The Czech statesmen now also had to confront a fast emerging new domestic crisis which was very closely connected with the foreign political situation. This new challenge was represented by the Sudeten-German problem.

Sudeten-German Problem

The difficulties with the different nationality groups in Czechoslovakia began to grow, and their relationship with the central government began to deteriorate, very fast in the winter of 1937-1938. The Sudeten-German Party became increasingly impatient. The elections of May 1935 gave the Party second place in the Parliament, but the government ignored this fact and was willing to cooperate only with the German Activists.[91] Due to popular dissatisfaction, the Activists submitted the grievances of the German minorities[92] to the Czechoslovak government on February 18, 1937; but the government delayed action, which only aggravated the situation.

By September, Hodza felt it necessary to hold a secret meeting with Konrad Henlein, leader of the Sudeten-German Party. Referring to Masaryk's credo of national self-determination, Henlein demanded not only the remedy of grievances, but also autonomy for the Sudeten-German population. Assuring Henlein of his goodwill, Hodza commented on the "enormous difficulties" he himself had to face from the Czechs. They agreed to keep in contact and work honestly for a *détente*.[93]

But by October it was clear that these *détente* plans had failed. During his visit in London on October 11-15, Henlein tried to enlist British support for an autonomy law for the Sudeten-Germans in Czechoslovakia.[94] Meanwhile, a propaganda war broke out between German and Czechoslovak newspapers over the minority rights of the Sudeten-Germans; and the Czech government considered the possibility of a Sudeten-German uprising, which would give Hitler an excuse for invading Czechoslovakia.[95] Krofta tried to extend the Franco-Czechoslovak mutual assistance treaty to cover such an occasion, but Delbos flatly refused to give French written assurances.[96] In light of the British and French attitude concerning the minority problems in Czechoslovakia, the Czech government was relieved when Goering ordered a halt to the press campaign against Czechoslovakia.[97] Henlein was seemingly deserted by Hitler, who wanted to neutralize Czechoslovakia.

The crisis was soon revived by the Czech National Defense Law, which authorized the expropriation of land for defense purposes. The Czech government used this law very effectively against the Sudeten-Germans whom they suspected were politically unreliable, and Germany naturally retaliated by expropriating the lands of Czechs living in Germany.[98] By the first week of February 1938, the Czech-German differences seemed to be in complete deadlock.

On February 16, 1938, Benes surprised the German ambassador by saying that he wanted to achieve a lasting, "manly and direct" relationship with Germany; he recognized "Germany had the right to demand that no power should use Czechoslovakia as an instrument against Germany," and he was willing to cooperate against communism.[99] Following this statement, Hitler demonstrated his goodwill *vis à vis* Czechoslovakia. He ordered the Sudeten-German Party to discontinue cooperation with the Slovak autonomists, rejected Hungary's proposals concerning the cooperation of the German and Hungarian minority groups in Czechoslovakia, and refused to resume negotiations with the Hungarian General

Staff aimed at coordinating strategic plans against Czechoslovakia.[100] On the day of the Austrian invasion, Hitler notified the Czechoslovak government that German troops would keep a distance of fifteen kilometers from the Czech frontier and expressed his desire to improve Czech-German relations.[101]

Czechoslovakia breathed freely. The Hodza government did not even alert the frontier guards. As usual, France recognized her loss too late.

ANSCHLUSS

The Lost Opportunity

The summer of 1937 found the Central European diplomats busily looking for a compromise solution which would secure for them a better position. On September 1, 1937, during the Sinaia conference of the Little Entente States, the Hungarian ambassador to Rumania presented his government's proposal for the conclusion of non-aggression pacts with the Little Entente states; all three states accepted the proposal as a good starting point for negotiations.[102] Britain regarded this new round of negotiations with sympathy; but France, afraid that a Hungarian-Little Entente agreement would deprive her of her allies and would push them into the German orbit, expressed dissatisfaction.[103] The Little Entente states, however, after the visits of Gamelin, were not too concerned about the French opinion. The topic of Gamelin's conversation was not what France would offer to her allies, but what the allies could offer France.

Delbos' visit to Poland and the Little Entente states in December 1937 "exposed the collapse of the Little Entente."[104] Even more, it brought home to Delbos the bitter reality that France's alliance system had collapsed. There was no more hope of reconciling Mussolini, who had joined the anti-Comintern pact on November 6. Therefore, France had only one ally (of questionable value as far as true French interests were concerned)—Britain. December 1937 produced two more events which completed France's isolation and her dependence on Britain. On December 11, Italy left the League of Nations; then, later in December, Litvinov announced that German-Soviet negotiations were in progress since the Soviet Union was disappointed with the French-English foreign policy.[105]

Yet France had unknown allies within Germany: the German General Staff and the Foreign Ministry under Neurath as well as some German economic and industrial leaders. From the economic point of view, 1937 was not a good year for Germany. The effects of the forced rearmament program began to appear in April in the form of shortages in raw materials.[106] The economic crisis first prevailed only in the area of small manufacturers, but it soon spread with great speed.

In November 1937, Hitler tried to turn attention away from the economic crisis by producing some spectacular foreign political success. The German action against Austria and Czechoslovakia was fixed for the 1943-45 period, but Hitler wanted to do it right away, and he revealed this decision to the foreign minister, the war minister, and the Chiefs of the three branches of the armed forces. The generals were shocked and opposed Hitler's plan, arguing that the German army was not ready. Neurath, recognizing the possible effects of such an action on the moral standing of Germany, openly asked the generals to prevent the move. They were not successful and soon bowed to Hitler's wishes. Hitler did not forgive them, though, and by February 1938 his opponents were removed from all key positions.[107]

During the same period, Hitler learned that no serious opposition could be expected to a military occupation of Austria. Britain opposed a possible Nazi *coup d'état* but was willing to accept a German military *fait à compli*.[108] France's ambassador to Austria reported in January that Hitler was preparing to annex Austria and urged immediate talks with Mussolini to avoid a catastrophe.[109] No contact was made; but it was too late anyway, for while not welcoming the *Anschluss*, Mussolini did not intend to do anything about it. France was again looking for an initiative from England and was more concerned about the future of Czechoslovakia, where Hitler very skillfully had also created a crisis mood, than Austria.[110] Poland already accepted the *fait à compli* and Beck was diligently working on the building of a Warsaw-Budapest-Belgrade block.[111] Hungary, while looking forward nervously to the *Anschluss* which would make Germany a neighbor, did not have any plans to oppose it or to help Austria militarily against Germany; nor was Yugoslavia willing to take part in military actions.[112] Rumania's King Carol told the German ambassador in March that "the Anschluss ought to come" and expressed his desire to cooperate more closely with Germany.[113] The stage was set for Hitler's next move.

Accepting an invitation from Hitler, Schuschnigg arrived at Berchtesgaden on March 12, 1938. On the same day, the last green light for the *Anschluss* was given by Krofta who informed the German ambassador that no one in Czechoslovakia "contemplated intervening in the Austrian affair."[114] Then, on March 13, Schuschnigg and other Austrian political leaders were placed under house arrest by the occupying German forces.[115] The Austrian drama had ended.

French Reaction

Hitler selected the most advantageous date to occupy Austria. The Chautemps government had resigned on March 10, and therefore France was vacillating. Chautemps and Delbos decided to act only in agreement with Britain, and Britain refused to take any energetic step.[116] On March 13, the day of the official proclamation of the *Anschluss*, Blum formed a new government; but he did not present it for a vote of confidence until March 18. Thus, during the crisis period, the old caretaker government of Chautemps as well as the new Blum government operated in a vacuum.

The German *fait à compli* demanded more reaction than a simple diplomatic note. France was confronted with the question of whether or not she was prepared to continue her diplomacy by the use of military means, and if so, the balance of forces had to be considered.

France was well protected against a German attack by the Maginot line. The only weak point was the Belgian frontier, should Germany attack through neutral Belgium. Though Italy could not be counted on as an ally, the probability of an Italian attack was very slim.[117] Czechoslovakia and Poland, both having a mutual assistance treaty with France, could be counted on in case of a Franco-German war. France had 50-60 divisions on the German frontier and 1500 combat-ready airplanes.[118] Czechoslovakia had 10 divisions on the German frontier,[119] while Poland had 32 divisions (with 15 additional reserve divisions).[120] Against this, Germany had 47 divisions, of which nine (three army corps) were already employed in Austria, plus an additional 29 reserve divisions and 1288 airplanes.[121] In case of war, then, 38 German divisions would have to stand, *on two fronts*, the concentrated attack of 100-110 French-Polish-Czech divisions.

The French army was well trained and well equipped. Any gap between the German and French tank and motorized forces was insignificant. The occupation of Austria revealed that the German army had great technical shortcomings and it was only "in a state of very much improvised combat-readiness."[122] The raw material shortages were still causing great problems for Germany, while the French economy was beginning to move again. But Hitler was so sure of the passivity of France that he did not order the mobilization of the troops on the French frontier.

It is true that France was in the middle of a government crisis, yet the President of the Republic was in control and the military leaders were not touched by the crisis. It is also true that the declaration of war is the business of the political leadership, but no political leader would do such a thing in a democracy without consulting his military advisors. Blum, did exactly that. Gamelin honestly described the tragic consequences for Czechoslovakia of the *Anschluss* and recommended a "strong reaction;" but he painted such a grim picture of the price France and Czechoslovakia might have to pay for victory, that the government shied away from the use of force.[123] Gamelin's only reaction was to ask for an additional credit of 171 million francs to strengthen the army.

The German generals opposed Hitler's gamble because they wanted to have at least a "51 percent chance of success."[124] The French generals, in light of the balance of forces, had a greater percent of chance for success, and they did nothing. The last opportunity to fight Germany with such superior forces was gone.

The French passivity from a statistical and selfish French point of view is understandable. Hitler expressed many times his conviction that, since the remilitarization of the Rhineland, he had no claims against France and wanted to live in peace with his Western neighbor. If these statements were taken at face value, why should a single French soldier shed a drop of blood for Austria? So Austria disappeared from the map. With the occupation of Austria, Czechoslovakia ceased to be a "dagger directed at the heart" of Germany. Instead, she was encircled completely by Germany. The great fortifications on the German frontier became worthless since the German forces, which grew stronger with the incorporation of the Austrian army,[125] outflanked them in the Danube valley. France's position was greatly weakened vis à vis Germany. Blum's government fell on April 9, 1938, and it was the duty of the new Daladier government to pick up the pieces and try to stop the deterioration of the situation.

CHAPTER XIII
DEFEAT AT MUNICH

France's Position After the Anschluss

From the point of view of France's security, her foreign policy alternatives after the *Anschluss* were very limited. She could have chosen from among the following: trust Hitler's promises concerning his peaceful intentions toward France and accept his *"Drang nach Osten"* policy without objection; organize international opposition to German aggression by appealing for help to the League of Nations; revitalize and *extend the* treaty commitments of France, Poland, and the Little Entente *vis à vis* Germany and try to reactivate Franco-Soviet cooperation; or continue passivity and follow Britain's lead in the upcoming events.

It was clear to the whole of Europe that Hitler's next target would be Czechoslovakia. If the sudden revival of Sudeten-German activities was not enough of a signal for France, then the intelligence reports and the flare up of revisionism in Hungary were additional warnings. Economically, there was very little at stake for France in Czechoslovakia,[1] militarily, there was very much. The liquidation of Czechoslovakia would free Hitler from the danger of a two front war since the poorly equipped Polish army, with no border fortifications to help them, would not represent much of a problem for Germany. Yet this aspect would be negligible if Hitler really kept his word. This was the only, but very great, risk involved in the first alternative. No French statesman could place the security and survival of his country on the honesty of Hitler's words.

The second alternative would require, according to the League's Charter, a concerted action of all the powers against an aggressor. The League's impotence in this area was proven many times: during the Manchurian crisis, the remilitarization of the Rhineland, the Ethiopian war, the Spanish Civil War, and lately the annexation of Austria. How could France convince the League of Nations to give up passivity, guarantee the integrity of Czechoslovakia and be ready to enforce, if necessary with the use of arms, the observation of its resolutions? Up to now not a single word was raised against the German aggression in Austria.

The small powers waited for the directions of the leaders, but directions never came. To have any success with the League, France had to enlist first the support of its most influential members, i.e., Britain and the Soviet Union.

British foreign policy, on the other hand, considered the cooperation of Italy essential in this matter, but Italy was no longer a member of the League. Therefore, they held direct negotiations with Mussolini and "On April 16, 1938, an Anglo-Italian agreement was signed giving Italy in effect a free hand in Abyssinia and Spain in return for the imponderable value of Italian goodwill in Central Europe."[2] As far as guarantees for Czechoslovakia were concerned, Chamberlain expressed the view that "It is impossible for the British government to give such guarantees, in one part because in this case her vital interests are less involved than in the case of France or of Belgium, and in the second part because the League of Nations Charter does not oblige her at all to do such a thing."[3] Privately, Chamberlain told Bonnet that "Neither the British people, nor above all the Dominions, would accept that Britain should go to war to prevent European populations from expressing their right to self-determination."[4]

The Soviet Union expressed her willingness to come to the aid of Czechoslovakia and honor the responsibilities of the Soviet-Czechoslovak treaty.[5] However, she emphasized that her actions would depend "on the practical measures taken by the other powers," and that it was France's duty to secure Polish and Rumanian permission for the crossing of Russian troops through their territories.[6] An appeal to the League of Nations thus promised very little hope that France could secure a collective guarantee for Czechoslovakia.

The third alternative required the restoration of harmony between the Little Entente, France, and Poland as well as between the individual members of the Little Entente. French efforts in this direction also proved futile. Beck repeatedly expressed his skepticism of the usefulness of the League of Nations and refused the idea of a Czech-Polish alliance because such an agreement would benefit only Czechoslovakia.[7] Instead of allowing Russian troops to hurry to the aid of Czechoslovakia through Poland, Beck promoted a Polish-Hungarian rapprochement in order to coordinate Polish-Hungarian military actions against Czechoslovakia.[8] Stoyadinovich assured Benes that Yugoslavia would give aid *vis à vis* Hungary, but refused to take up further obligations.[9] Rumania also was cool to the idea of a Russian troop crossing, and the Rumanian government was under heavy pressure from Poland to stay neutral in case of Hungarian action against Czechoslovakia.[10] Because of the refusal of cooperation by Poland, Rumania, and Yugoslavia, the revitalization of the old security system also failed.

Everything indicated to France that she was the only power willing to guarantee the integrity of Czechoslovakia. But the realization of this guarantee demanded that she also be willing to go to war against Germany *only* with the help of Czechoslovakia and Britain, which meant ten divisions from Czechoslovakia and two divisions from Britain.[11] French public opinion was opposed to the idea of war with Germany for the sake of Czechoslovakia.[12] Gamelin did not see any possibility of giving effective aid to Czechoslovakia since mounting an offensive would take a very long time.[13] In view of her strategic position and military capacity, France was not inclined to wage war against Germany almost completely alone. There remained only one alternative for France to follow: give up every initiative and yield the leadership to Britain. With this passivity, France abandoned Czechoslovakia and the Munich crisis became the crisis of Britain and not of France.

Britain and the Czechoslovak Crisis

Because Britain and France were trying so anxiously to avoid a sharp confrontation with Germany, Hitler considered the time right for the final destruction of Czechoslovakia. On April 22, 1938, he gave his "Operation Green" instructions to Keitel: first prepare world opinion by creating an incident which would put the blame on the Czechs for the German actions, then confront France and Britain with a *fait à compli* by speedily executing the military operation.[14] Everything started to roll according to this plan, especially since Hitler found an unexpected ally in the British ambassador to Berlin, Sir Neville Henderson.

Henderson was an admirer of Hitler's Germany and did not pass up any opportunity to advocate a policy of appeasement as the only right policy for Britain.[15] In light of Britain's military weakness,[16] the realistic interests of Britain also demanded a play for time, and the only way to do that seemed to be an appeasement policy.

In Czechoslovakia, the Sudeten-Germans presented their new demands at their April 24 meeting in Karlsbad.[17] They wanted full autonomy for the Sudeten-Germans areas, and threatened that the refusal of their demands would produce stronger demands, i.e., the right to national self-determination.[18] The same day, Britain and France sent *démarches* to Prague urging Benes to seek a settlement even at the price of great sacrifices.[19] Benes delayed a reply. Then, on May 21, the Czech government, reacting to German troop movements toward the Czech frontier, ordered partial mobilization of the Czech army. The same day, some German peasants were killed by a Czech sentry, which resulted in violent riots.[20] The situation was kept under control only by the intervention of Britain, who warned Germany about the consequences of a German military action.

Chamberlain blamed Czechoslovakia for the delaying tactics and felt it necessary to put pressure on Benes through France. The British ambassador in Paris notified Bonnet that "the British government had no present intention of undertaking joint action with the French Government to safeguard Czechoslovakia against German aggression;" and Bonnet, in turn, told the Czech ambassador that "Benes must profit from the present lull to settle the question at *whatever cost* in a friendly way and with *very large concessions.*"[21] (italics added)

On June 7, 1938, the Sudeten-German Party submitted a new memorandum to the Czech government.[22] It suggested a complete reorganization of the state on a federative basis with almost sovereign rights awarded to the individual states, thus paving the way for the complete dismemberment of Czechoslovakia. The Czech government prepared its own counter-proposals and a lengthy discussion began in Parliament. Britain grew impatient and sent a second *demarche* to Prague urging them to act promptly and grant great concessions.[23] The Czech reply was a legal and political masterpiece, but it did not satisfy the British government. News arriving from Germany was becoming serious. Hitler was really preparing for war.

Chamberlain still believed that the crisis could be settled by peaceful means without completely sacrificing Czechoslovakia. He did not know that Hitler had decided already in April to destroy Czechoslovakia and had given detailed military orders in May.[24] On July 25, the British announced that they intended to send Viscount Walter Runciman to Czechoslovakia to mediate in the Sudeten crisis.[25] On September 3, Hitler told his generals that the army had to be ready to start the attack any minute after September 27.[26] On September 12, in a speech to the Nazi Party Congress at Nuremberg, Hitler justified his support of the Sudeten-German demands by referring to the right of self-determination of every people and to the fact that this right was being denied by the Czechs; and he warned the supporters of Czechoslovakia: "If the democracies, however, should be convinced that they must in this case protect with all their means the oppressors of Germans, then this will have grave consequences."[27]

The democracies heeded his warning. Runciman condemned the Czech government for the conditions of the Sudeten-Germans and recommended a plebiscite. Benes refused. On September 14, the Czech army was mobilized, but the weakness of the army prevailed: national minority group members refused to serve and great numbers of them deserted. On September 22, Chamberlain met Hitler in Godesberg and Hitler openly stated that in a week, German troops would enter the Sudetenland. Meanwhile, Poland and Hungary also began to sound their demands concerning the Polish and Hungarian populated areas of Czechoslovakia.

Mussolini came to the rescue of world peace. At the simultaneous approches of Roosevelt and Chamberlain, he convinced Hitler to delay the invasion. Hitler accepted Mussolini's proposal and invited the leaders of the British, French, and Italian governments to meet him in Munich on September 28, 1938. World peace was saved, for a while.

Munich could be interpreted as the last diplomatic defeat of Britain and France before the outbreak of World War II. During and after the war, it became fashionable to criticize the statesmen who gave in to Hitler's aggressiveness at Munich. However, such critics forgot a very important circumstance: Hitler's demand concerning the right to self-determination for the German and later Polish, Hungarian, and Slovak minority groups created support for Germany among the anti-Nazi population. It created support for him in the revisionist states. It created support for him even in Britain, the United States, and France. Not because people who welcomed the revision of the Versailles and connected peace treaties were Nazis or Nazi-sympathizers, but simply because they realized that these documents were more dictates than treaties. They had to be guarded with arms in order to keep them in effect.

France will-nilly accepted the role of this armed guard after World War I. But her unilateral disarmament and the deterioration of her economic influence in Central Europe made her a very poor armed guard. Yet instead of facing realities, the French governments continued their uncompromising policy and torpedoed every plan (Tardieu, Laval-Mussolini, Hodza,) which could have created harmony in the Danube valley and Eastern Europe. Munich was only the terminal of the road which began at Versailles.

CHAPTER XIV
FINAL OBSERVATIONS

From 1920 to 1934, the French alliance system controlled Europe without challenge. However, in 1920, French leadership was accepted on the basis of superior strength—ideologically, economically, and militarily. The Versailles and other connected treaties were signed with the supposition that *France would always remain strong enough* to preserve the new status quo in Europe. Conditions destroyed this French superiority, however. French political leaders quarreled endlessly over the question of priority: whether French resources should be used to improve the domestic, economic and social situation, or whether they should be used to sustain France's military strength and thus her international position. The French leaders did not realize that posing this question in an either-or fashion was already a mistake. When economic and social conditions deteriorate, then, too, military capacity declines. Also, no nation, even with the most progressive economic and social system, can stand up if its military strength is not ready to defend that system against outside aggressions. The bitter either-or struggle hindered both socio-economic and military development and put France in an inferior position well before 1934. This was the first reason for the decline in French superiority.

The French leadership position in Europe also declined because of her abuse of democracy. Previously, democracy stood alone in Europe as the form of government of the strongest European country. Every nation respected it and more or less accepted it as the most workable political system. Up until 1933, the two existing totalitarian systems (the Soviet Union and Italy) did not command the admiration of other countries. Even the Yugoslavian royal dictatorship of King Alexander was regarded only as a temporary emergency measure. However, in 1934, the situation changed. The unrestricted number of political parties in France made the coalition governments unproductive, and the political arena of "free democracy" tragically performed a show that resembled anarchy more than democracy. The great masses, both within and outside of France, did not value or condemn a political system by the degree of political freedom alone. They also considered the number of unemployed, rising prices, and deteriorating wages. As a result, in the minds of millions, Fascist Italy, Nazi Germany, and the Soviet Union began to appear as better political systems.

Economics and foreign trade also contributed to the decline of French influence. French capitalists worked, naturally, for profit and if trade with the East-Central European countries returned less profit than they expected, they abandoned these business partners without hesitation. Of course, the same behavior pattern characterized the Central European tradesmen. The end result of this free enterprise mobility was an economic vacuum in Central Europe in the middle 1930's which Germany filled; and from then on, she had almost no competition for trade in Central and Eastern Europe. This almost unlimited source of food supplies and raw materials made it possible for Germany to become a great power again.

Another important reason for the disappearance of French leadership was created by the military. A communications gap existed between the General Staff and the political leadership; only in time of crisis was communication improved. The result was that the political leaders were shocked to learn the French army was of very doubtful value as an instrument of foreign policy. The military leaders, on the other hand, proved to be incapable of understanding the influence of changed technology on strategy. Relying strictly on their own experiences, they had only one thing in mind: avoid repetition of the bloody battles of World War I. The Maginot line was to them the greatest insurance for that. The theories of wars of attrition were so dominating at this time that they did not permit the development and employment of more dynamic theories and practices.

The last, but not least important reason for the disappearance of French leadership was the ignorance of the French leaders concerning the individual, nationalistic interests of their allies. Their simplistic approach was: since France was the protector of the small Central European states, the fulfillment of French political demands should be interpreted by these states as a service rendered also for their own interests. The Central European statesmen interpreted these French steps differently; and they were right, at least in their aim to serve their own national needs, if necessary even against the wishes of France.

Poland's two great neighbors, Germany and the Soviet Union, represented the greatest problem for the foreign policy of Poland. Through non-aggression pacts, Poland was able to normalize her relations with both powers. The two pacts guaranteed the peaceful, undisturbed evolution of Polish politics for a decade, at least on paper.

Since we know that neither Germany nor the Soviet Union honored these treaties in 1938, we are inclined to condemn the Polish leaders for not being willing to fall in line with Western political designs. Yet, the Polish leaders could only make decisions based on the facts of their contemporary setting. Pilsudski recognized that the leadership of Europe was slipping out of the hands of France, and therefore he could not blindly continue to trust France for protection against Germany. The continuation of the one-sided pro-French foreign policy would have been naive and at the same time unscrupulous on the part of any Polish patriot.

All of the circumstances at the time made it imperative for Poland to look for and find a better solution for Poland's international problems. The Polish leaders rightly evaluated the alternatives open to Poland. Perhaps they did not follow up the pursuit of these alternatives in the right order of importance. Perhaps Pilsudski's prejudices, coupled with Benes' distaste for the Polish political system, prevented them from exploring in depth all of the existing possibilities. But their aim, the service of their country, remained unchallengeable; and with the two non-aggression pacts, they served the interests of their country well.

If we mention only the changed relations with Danzig and the changed behavior of the German minorities in Poland from a position of open resistance and obstruction to an attitude of cooperation, the advantages to Poland of the German-Polish Pact would already be great. If we add the increased security of Poland and the improved economic and trade relations, then the balance sheet would be even more favorable.

The disadvantages, viewing the pact in its contemporary setting, were minimal. Thanks to the skillful maneuvering of Polish diplomacy, the pact did not create tension with the Soviet Union, and it did not worsen the existing relationship with Czechoslovakia and France. Even the French government's official announcements approved and sanctioned the Polish initiative.

Yet, the consequences of the Polish action were grave from the point of view of the status quo. Germany broke out of isolation and France could no longer say that she was willing to risk anything for the interests of her best allies. French passivity in the case of Poland's inquiries proved to all of Europe that Fichte's description really fit the policy of the French governments: "peace exists till her own frontiers are not invaded."

During the Rhineland crisis Poland again offered her cooperation to France, but to no avail. The year 1936 proved to Poland that Pilsudski was right when he sought and found a basis for the creation of a *modus vivendi* with Germany, independent of French approval or disapproval. The events of 1937 and 1938 confirmed for Poland that France was a very timid patron. It was natural that Beck dreamed about a Polish-Rumanian-Hungarian block, which promised more security against both of Poland's great neighbors than did the Czech or French alliances.

We may risk a speculation here. What would have happened if Poland had granted passage rights to Soviet troops? Knowing Stalin's realism and political conceptions, we still cannot suppose with all certainty that he would have declared war on Germany for the sake of the Western capitalist countries. Even if he would have done so, a Soviet-German war would have been fought on Polish territory. The only real loser in that case again would have been Poland. The only way out of this dilemma seemed to be to keep Poland in some kind of neutral position. Of course, this policy would have been unjustifiable if France would have kept her original military plans: attack on Berlin. But she did not.

Among the Central European states considered, Austria was the weakest, but yet she was seemingly at the center of political interest for every nation. Dollfuss and Schuschnigg both realized that their country was unable to withstand the pressure of the Great Powers. The opportunities of joining with Germany, and later Hungary or Czechoslovakia, were missed before 1934 due to the objections of France. It is a credit to the Austrian statesmen, especially to Schuschnigg, that they realized the situation and tried to do their best to secure Austrian independence through means other than subservient obedience.

In 1934 the situation was different. Britain, France, and even Czechoslovakia displayed a great understanding for Austria's domestic problems. The reoccurring obstacles for a better understanding with these countries were Schuschnigg's stubborn refusal to renounce the possibility of a Habsburg restoration and his unwillingness to participate in any combination of states directed against Nazi Germany. Both "questions of principle," as he put it, created great difficulties for Austria's foreign policy and finally left her no other alternative than the one she followed to the end.

The rejection of participation in anti-German combinations was based more on the Pan-German and pro-Nazi sympathies of a great number of Austrians than on the romantic, German nationalist and imperial sympathies of Schuschnigg. This Pan-German sentiment grew day by day and had no real opposition after the Socialists were driven underground. Though every statesman of Europe showed some understanding toward this problem, it probably hurt Austria's chances as much as the question of the Habsburg restoration.

Let us suppose that instead of the practiced policy, Schuschnigg, had accepted a pro-French policy in cooperation with the Little Entente. Knowing Benes' firm ideological convictions, the precondition of such cooperation would have been a change in Austrian domestic policy. Such a change would have exposed Austria to the concentrated attacks of Germany, Italy, and Hungary. Austria's economic dependence on these countries would have made it possible for them to crush her with an economic boycott since no French, Czech or other businessmen would have canceled their more beneficial business transactions with other countries just to save Austria from bankruptcy. In the case of no other country was it better demonstrated than in the case of Austria that the Central European states were only pawns in the chess game of the Great Powers.

Yugoslavia's problems came into the center of European diplomatic interest only with the assassination of King Alexander. Yet, the fear of Italy, and to a lesser degree Hungary and Bulgaria, existed well before that time. The pro-German Yugoslavian policy also had a well-founded basis. It was due to: economic interests, for Yugoslavia depended on German trade much more than on any other trade; political interests, because she found in Germany a more effective patron against Hungary than France ever was; and ideological interests, because her fear of Communism and the Eastern Pact would have forced her into closer cooperation with the Soviet Union.

After the assassination, Yugoslavia made an attempt to straighten up her relationship with France by agreeing not to accuse Italy in the affair. France did not realize the importance of this gesture, however, just as she did not realize the anxiety of Yugoslavia during the Danubian Pact negotiations. In response to the demanding voice of Laval, the Yugo-slavian statesmen answered with a selection of better opportunities. What is important to realize is that they saw these opportunities while France did not. Even if France had, Laval believed that Yugoslavia's loyalty and gratitude would force her to see the Nazi danger from the French side, forgetting the Yugoslavian side. If France had tried to understand the Yugoslavian interests, she could have reassured Yugoslavia that France would not abandon Yugoslavia and would restrain Mussolini from aggressive action. She could have used her tacit agreement with Mussolini over Abyssinia as a convincing argument to regain Yugoslavia's confidence. However, she did not.

After the alienation of Italy and France, after the bitter economic results of her participation in the sanctions, and after realizing that with the sanctions she had invited Mussolini's fury for the sake of France without receiving anything in exchange, the only possible way for the survival of Yugoslavia seemed to be to seek the patronage of another Great Power against revisionism. An alliance with the Soviet Union would have depended on the cooperation of Rumania. But Rumania was not willing to cooperate with the Soviet Union for the sake of France, much less for the sake of Yugoslavia. There was also the disapproval of such a policy by the Yugoslav domestic political forces. Economic interests tipped the balance in favor of Germany. What else could Yugoslavia do?

In regard to Hungary, the French policy was based on the assumption that Hungary was an anti-democratic state, but at the same time so weak that she would never play an important role in international politics. The complete neglect of geographic conditions allowed France to believe in the validity of this last assumption. Due to her geographic location, however, it was naive on the part of any power to believe that a strong Central European block could be created without the participation of Hungary. This geographic location made Hungary much more important than her military strength suggested. The Hungarian statesmen realized this and played skillfully to secure the most benefits for their nation.

It is true that the Hungarian politicians were short-sightedly revisionist. However, their revisionism was well-founded and justified even in the eyes of many prominent Little Entente statesmen. In the 1920's France would have been strong enough to lay down the solid basis for a Central European cooperation, using the League of Nations charter to prosecute a revision according to ethnographic borders. Yet, France did not feel it necessary to even analyze the consequences of such a move. Such a revision would have had a great effect on Hungary. By fulfilling this Hungarian demand, France would have been able to take away mass support from those very much resented authoritarian "Fascist" politicians. Pressing economic and social problems would have dominated Hungary's political life, and solutions to these problems would have created a basis for the closer cooperation of all the successor states in the Danube Basin.

After the rise of Hitler and the appointment of Gömbös, the French diplomacy made only one weak attempt to lure Hungary into the French camp. Such attempts might or might not have produced results. The pro-French groups in Hungary were so strong in the first half of 1934 that Gömbös openly complained against them and criticized their activity; at the same time, though, France was no longer in a position to force even the smallest concessions for revision. A deeper evaluation of Hungary's policy could have only produced the conclusion that the Gömbös government was not a servile and obedient ally of Italy; and while Gömbös praised German Nazism, he was not hesitant to react most aggressively toward German attempts to spread nazism in Hungary.

During the Danubian Pact negotiations, the French diplomacy looked upon Hungary as an Italian satellite and made no direct contacts with the Gömbös government. Yet, Mussolini's handling of Gömbös opened an opportunity for France not only to gain Hungary's confidence, but also to prevent her rapprochement with Germany. France, however, missed this opportunity.

Gömbös' foreign policy served Hungary's interests well. This foreign policy secured a unique position for Hungary among the small states of Central Europe. She remained uncommitted to a certain degree and could continue to attempt to change her policy as realistic interests demanded.

Gömbös' successors tried to continue this relatively independent policy. Naturally, for the sake of revisionism, they favored the Axis more than the French-Little Entente camp. The annexation of Austria partly frightened, partly reassured them. At the time of the Munich agreement, not a single sign in international politics indicated to the Hungarian politicians that Britain and France would ever stand up against the will of Hitler. Yet, they continued their cautious policy and, with the exception of Ruthenia (which was occupied by Hungarian troops against the will of Hitler), they did not pursue their revisionist policy with the use of arms.

Let us speculate again. Let us suppose that Hungary would have given up revisionism in 1937 and would have joined the Little Entente. Could she have played any role in international events which would have prevented the *Anschluss* or the dismemberment of Czechoslovakia? Because of her military weightlessness, probably not. Her stand on the side of the Axis did not represent help for the Axis, her possible stand with the Little Entente would not have changed French foreign policy. Though she tried an independent foreign policy, Hungary's fate was decided not by her, but again by the Great Powers.

Geographically, Rumania was maybe in the best position. Her foreign policy could freely follow French directions *vis à vis* Germany since she had no common frontier with Germany. On the other hand, the Little and Balkan Ententes gave her sufficient security against Bulgarian and Hungarian revisionism. Under Titulescu's direction, Rumanian relations with the Soviet Union steadily improved. The only factor which could have curtailed her independent foreign policy was her economic dependence on Germany.

But the underdeveloped conditions of the country, the lack of democratic political experiences, the growing gap between the rich and poor, and the dissatisfaction of the masses provided an opportunity for younger people to rise in political life to positions of influence and, enjoying popular support, to dominate Rumanian domestic and foreign policy. The fear of communism and of a revisionist Soviet Union prepared the way for the orientation of Rumania toward fascism and later nazism.

Independent from the turn to the right of Rumania's domestic policy, the Crown Council tried to serve Rumania's foreign political interests the best they could by accepting and following the idea of neutralism. This foreign policy, though it weakened the French alliance and the Little Entente, served Rumania well. Her economy did not suffer and her independence survived the longest among the French allies.

Rumania's resistance to granting passage rights to Soviet troops was condemned by the French. Yet even this action by Rumania's statesmen was justified and served her interests. The crossing of Russian troops would have undoubtedly made her a target of the German air force and would have risked her involvement in a war much sooner than it actually happened. Rumania's foreign policy can be condemned on the basis of ideological considerations and in knowledge of the events after 1938. But up to that time, the realistic interests of Rumania were served well by her foreign policy, and even the second Vienna award did not cripple completely her national life and ability to survive.

Czechoslovakia is generally praised the most as being the Central European country which remained faithful to the bitter end to the democratic form of government and to the democratic camp. Yet the continuous reelection of Masaryk and Benes concentrated as much power in their hands as any of the contemporary authoritarian leaders possessed. Accepting a strong nationalist line, the leaders of Czechoslovakia denied the possibility of their multinational country to work out any solid basis for a cooperative, unified action. Benes' ideological convictions made the creation of such an understanding even harder. He became the champion of democracy in the League of Nations, that is true. He believed firmly in the value of French and Soviet friendship and in the authority of the League. But only a prejudiced statesman could fail to see the realistic needs of Czechoslovakia. France was far away, less and less willing and able to help Czechoslovakia. Every consideration suggested that Czechoslovakia find a *modus vivendi* with her neighbors in order to survive. Ironically, when Hodza tried to satisfy these realistic demands and initiated negotiations, he was confronted not only by the tough negotiators of Hungary, Austria, and Poland, but also by his own president. Hodza was inclined to give concessions, Benes was not. Hodza felt the Habsburg restoration was a lesser evil than the *Anschluss*, Benes did not. Hodza preferred a settlement with Vienna and Budapest, Benes did not. Hodza wanted a Czech-German non-aggression pact, Benes did not. Even after he lost confidence in the Soviet Union, Benes was not willing to replace this lost patron by a conciliation with the Danubian states. When Benes finally realized the great deficiencies of his foreign political conceptions, he made peace with Hodza and tried to save as much as possible. But it was too late. It cannot be doubted that Benes was a champion of democracy. He was a faithful ally of France and a firm enemy of nazism. But are these idealistic qualities really the most important assets of a realistic statesman?

One cannot resist speculating about what might have happened in Central Europe if Czechoslovakia would have initiated a conciliatory policy when Germany was weak, Hungarian revisionism was unsupported, Poland was seeking a way out of the threatening situation with the Soviet Union and Germany, and Austria was still looking for more security outside of Italian friendship. Czechoslovakia would have lost the unconditional support of France, but the price she would have had to pay perhaps would have been lower than that which he paid in 1938.

Thus, France was not able to create a mood of reconciliation in Central Europe, nor was she able to enforce a loyal pro-French policy. She realized that she could not eliminate the revisionist forces, and yet she did not recognize that without solving the Danubian problem, she could not count on her allies' support against Nazi Germany. With this misunderstanding of the individual aims of the different Central European states, she left the door open for German penetration in the area. It was the short-sightedness and unfortunate steps of the French statesmen, military leaders, and deputies, not the political genius of Hitler nor Nazi diplomacy, that destroyed the spiritual unity of the Little Entente, prevented a possible reconciliation in Central Europe, and changed the status quo on the field of international relations well before the German armies began to march.

The French attitude prevailing during the Rhineland crisis further encouraged the Central European governments to adjust their individual foreign policies to the economic interests of their respective countries. Seeing the helplessness of France, realism demanded that they please Germany and neglect France. Thus, Hitler had no problem after the desertion of Central Europe by France and Italy. Without the economic resources of Central Europe, Hitler could not have so easily realized his rearmament program, could not have grown strong enough to challenge France and Britain openly, would not have dared to remilitarize the Rhineland, could not have annexed Austria, could not have destroyed Czechoslovakia without firing a shot, and could not have enslaved almost all of Europe in the first years of the war.

This study suggests one conclusion, a very pessimistic one indeed, concerning the freedom of diplomatic action of the smaller powers. They had this freedom of action only on those occasions when their free choice did not harm the interests of a Great Power, or when the statesmen of the Great Powers did not consider that free choice as a threat. These little states tried very different approaches to serve their own national interests and secure their own survival in the struggle of the Great Powers. None of the approaches was successful. The failures of these countries in the past may be worthy of evaluation not only by historians, but also by the statesmen of our own times.

NOTES

INTRODUCTION

1. C. A. Macartney and A. W. Palmer, *Independent Eastern Europe* (London: MacMillan, 1962), pp. 314-17.

2. During 1931-1932. Waclaw Jedrzejewicz, ed., *Diplomat in Berlin, 1933-1939* (New York: Columbia University Press, 1968), p. 50. (Hereinafter referred to as *Lipski Papers.)*

3. Central Europe was defined often with political considerations in mind. Poland, before her division in the seventeenth century, definitely belonged to Central Europe. The Great Powers regarded this territory as in their sphere of interest. Austria, Bohemia, and Hungary were considered Central European states until the Ottoman occupation of Hungary in the sixteenth century. From that time on, Hungary was looked upon as part of Eastern Europe. After the liberation of Hungary the different crowns of the Habsburg dynasty were again regarded as Central European countries. One may define Central Europe also according to geographic features. In this case the Brenner Pass, the Bohemian Forests and the Elbe River offer a "natural" separation line on the west, while the Carpathian Mountains represent a good dividing line in the east. North of the Carpathian Mountains, however, we cannot find "natural" frontiers unless we accept the arbitrary selection of the Pripjet marches as a separation point, ending the line in the north at the Gulf of Finland.

4. I.M. Oprea, "Nicolae Titulescu's Diplomatic Activity," in *Bibliotheca Historica Romaniae*, Vol. 22 (Bucharest: Publishing House of the Academy of the Socialist Republic of Rumania, 1968), p. 85.

5. Hungary even sent a strongly worded protest to Hitler: "Hungary does not consider herself as a Balkan state and regards it an offense to be treated alike." Magyar Tudományos Akadémia Történettudományi Intézete, *A Wilhelmstrasse és Magyarország: Német Diplomáciai Iratok, 1933-1944.* ("The Wilhelmstreet and Hungary: German Diplomatic Documents, 1933-1944") (Budapest: Kossuth Publ., 1968), Conversation of Mazirevich with Köpke, Berlin, March 9, 1934, Doc. No. 23 (Hereinafter referred to as *Wilhelmstrasse.)*

CHAPTER I

1. The Versailles Treaty regulated only the German question. Austria's future was decided by the St. Germain Treaty and Hungary's by the Trianon Treaty. The Treaty of Riga settled the peace between Poland and Lithuania and Poland and the Soviet Union.

2. These were the most commonly used terms in contemporary newspapers.

3. One of the reasons was the willingness of the Great Powers to accept as *fait a compli* the unauthorized occupations of Hungarian territories by Czech, Rumanian and Serbian troops. See: Francis Deák, *Hungary at the Paris Peace Conference,* (New York: Howard Fertig, 1972), (Reprint of the 1942 edition), p. 30.

4. Bruce F. Pauley, *The Habsburg Legacy, 1867-1939,* (New York: Holt, Rinehart and Winston, 1972), p. 85.

5. Felix Kreiszler, *Von der Revolution Zur Annexion,*(Vienna: Europa Verlag, 1970), p. 81, 12n and 13n.

6. Pauley, *Habsburg Legacy,* pp. 75, 85.

7. Czech-German and Czech-Polish frontiers were marked out in the Treaty of Versailles, Czech-Austrian frontiers in the Treaty of St. Germain, and Czech-Hungarian frontiers in the Treaty of Trianon.

8. *The Statesman's Yearbook 1927,* p. 777.

9. This number is misleading. The Czechs and Slovaks, though both Slavs, had different history, culture, religion, and territory. S. Harrison Thompson, *Czechoslovakia in European History,* (Princeton, N.J., Princeton University Press, 1953), p. 11.

10. This number is misleading again, because the majority of Jews assimilated with the Germans and Hungarians in the former Habsburg Empire. In the Czech census, the Jewish minority group was introduced artifically to reduce the number of Germans and Magyars.

11. *The Statesman's Yearbook 1943,* p. 817.

12. Könzponti Statisztikai Hivatal, *Magyar Statisztikai zsebkönyv, 1960,* ("Hungarian Statistical Almanac, 1960") (Budapest: Economic and Law Publications, 1960), pp. 7, 11.

13. Seton-Watson, *Eastern Europe Between the Wars, 1918-1941,* Harper Torchbooks (New York: Harper & Row, 1967), pp. 414-16. For further study of the minority question see C. A. Macartney, *National States and National Minorities* (Oxford: Oxford University Press, 1934); C.A. Macartney, *Problems of the Danube Basin* (Cambridge, England: Cambridge University Press, 1942); Robert Lee Wolff, *The Balkans in Our Times* (Cambridge, Mass.: Harvard University Press, 1956).

14. Seton-Watson, *Eastern Europe,* p. 343; also see Deák, *Hungary at Paris,* p. 16.

15. Ádám, Juhász, and Kerekes, eds., *Allianz Hitler-Horthy-Mussolini* (Budapest: Akadémia ed., 1966), p. 14 (hereinafter referred to as *Allianz)* states that the ruling classes kept revisionist propaganda alive to turn the population's attention from domestic problems. This statement suits the requirement of Marxist history but distorts the truth. Not only the government, but also opposing parties advocated revisionism in order not to lose popular support.

16. Prewar Hungary had a smaller bureaucracy than Trianon-Hungary, though the population of the former was 21 million, and the latter only 8 million.

17. *Statesman's Yearbook 1927,* p. 1191.

18. Seton-Watson, *Eastern Europe,* p. 413. The following explanation mirrors entirely his interpretation.

19. *Ibid.,* p. 278.

20. See *Publications of the Permanent Court of International Justice,* Nos. 9 and 10 in 1925; No. 2 in 1926; and No. 14 in 1928.

21. Colonel Jozef Beck, *Final Report,* (New York: Robert Speller & Sons, 1957), p. 6.

22. This and the following statistics are quoted from the census of December 29, 1930.

23. Max Beloff, *The Foreign Policy of Soviet Russia,* (2 vols; London: Oxford University Press, 1968), I., p. 22.

24. Seton-Watson, *Eastern Europe*, p. 416.

25. *Ibid.*

26. No statistics are available for Macedonians. The official government position was that "there was no such thing as a Macedonian, there were only Serbs." Wolff, *Balkans,* p. 145.

27. The epithet "absolute king" or "enlightened despot" would have fit him better.

28. Wolff, *Balkans,* pp. 87-88.

29. Stoyan Christowe, *Heroes and Assassins* (New York: Robert L. McBride and Co., 1935), p. 257.

30. *Ibid.*, p. 267.

31. L.S. Stavrianos, *The Balkans Since 1453,* (New York: Holt, Rinehart, and Winston, 1966), p. 638.

32. Pauley, *Habsburg Legacy*, p. 111.

33. Frederick Hertz, *The Economic Problem of the Danubian States* (New York: Howard Fertig, 1970), pp. 24-25, 207-17.

34. For examples of the survival of pro-Habsburg sentiments see: Magyar Tudományos Akadémia Történettudományi Intézete, *Diplomáciai Magyaroiszág Külpolitikájához, 1935-1945* ("Diplomatic Documents on the Foreign Policy of Hungary, 1935-1945") 4 Vols. (Budapest: Akadémia eds., 1962) (Hereinafter referred to as DHFP), I, Ullein-Reviczky to Kánya, Zagrab, February 19, 1936, Doc. No. 43; and Emil: Csonka, *Habsburg Otto* (Munich: Uj Europa Ed., 1972), p. 415.

35. The condensed word "Czechoslovak" came into use in 1923 to emphasize the unity of Czechs and Slovaks, although this unity and cooperation never worked satisfactorily because of the Slovak's ambitions to gain autonomy within the state.

36. Seton-Watson, *Eastern Europe,* p. 173.

37. Stephen D. Kertész, *Diplomacy in a Whirlpool,* (Notre Dame, Indiana: University of Notre Dame, 1953), p. 13. Károlyi lost popular support after being humiliated by the Entente Powers who authorized the occupation of Hungarian territories by Czech, Rumanian and Yugoslavian troops *before* the peace negotiations

38. The Habsburg restoration attempts failed according to Horthy (Nicolas Horthy, *Memoirs* (New York: Robert Speller & Sons, 1957), pp. 116-127 because of the threat of war on the part of the other successor states. According to Otto Habsburg, such a threat did not exist in reality, and Horthy blocked the restoration attempt because he wanted to keep the power for himself. Csonka, *Habsburg Otto,* pp. 33-43.

39. Seton-Watson, *Eastern Europe,*p. 191.

40. *The Cambridge Economic History of Europe* (6 vols; Cambridge, England: Cambridge University Press, 1965), VI, Part II, p. 609.

41. C. A. Macartney, *Hungary: A Short History* (Chicago: Aldine Publ. Co., 1962), p. 221.

42. Seton-Watson, *Eastern Europe*, p. 413.

43. Wolff, *Balkans,* p. 102.

44. No plebiscites were held to give the peoples of the former Austria-Hungary a free choice according to the principles of self-determination, with the exception of Sopron which voted to join Hungary.

45. Mutual assistance treaties were signed between Czechoslovakia and Yugoslavia on August 14, 1920, and between Czechoslovakia, Rumania, and Yugoslavia in April and July 1921. The formal creation of the Little Entente Pact was signed in May, 1929. The aims of the Little Entente and its problems are described in Felix Vondracek, *The Foreign Policy of Czechoslovakia 1918-1935,* (New York: Columbia University Press, 1937), pp. 151-204.

46. György Ránki, *Emlékiratok és valóság Magyarország második világháborus szerepéröl* ("Memoirs and Reality Concerning the Role of Hungary in the Second World War") (Budapest: Kossuth ed., 1964), p. 24.

47. Pál Auer, Fél Évszázad, *"Half a Century"* (Washington, D.C.: Occidential Press, 1971), pp. 126-139. Auer was the attorney for the French government during the trials held in Budapest.

48. Ránki, *Memoirs and Reality,* p. 24.

49. Macartney, *Hungary,* p. 216.

50. Piotr S. Wandycz, *France and Her Eastern Allies* (Minneapolis: University of Minnesota Press, 1962), p. 29.

51. Arnold Wolfers, *Britain and France Between Two Wars* (New York: Norton Co., 1966), pp. 265-66.

52. For the full texts of these two treaties see Wandycz, *Eastern Allies,* pp. 394-95.

53. Hans, Roos, *A History of Modern Poland* (London: Eyre & Spottiswoode, 1966), p. 126.

54. *Ibid.*

55. Wandycz, *Eastern Allies,* p. 395.

56. Roos, *Modern Poland,* p. 127.

57. *Ibid.*

58. *Lipski Papers,* p. 12.

59. *Ibid.,* pp. 15-19.

60. The name Yugoslavia was declared official only in October 1929.

61. Wolff, *Balkans,* pp. 120-26; Stavrianos, *Balkans Since 1453,* pp. 616-28.

62. A. J. P. Taylor, *A History of the First World War* (New York: Berkeley Publ. Co., 1966), pp. 55, 176-77; Maxwell Macartney and Paul Cremona, *Italy's Foreign and Colonial Policy, 1914-1937* (New York: Howard Fertig, 1972), pp. 96-111.

63. The French-Czechoslovak Friendship Treaty of January 25, 1924, was undoubtedly directed against Germany. However, Benes was not afraid of the Germans while, on the other hand, he believed that Czech-Hungarian problems could not be solved by peaceful means within the lifetime of his generation. Auer, *Half a Centrury,* pp. 109-112.

64. The French attempt to create a solid block of Central European states is described with great insight in Wandycz, *Eastern Allies,* pp. 186-207.

CHAPTER II

1. H. Stuart Hughes, *Contemporary Europe: A History* (Englewood Cliffs, N.J.: Prentice Hall, 1961), p. 207.

2. René Albrecht-Carrié, *A Diplomatic History of Europe Since the Congress of Vienna* (New York: Harper & Row, 1958), p. 449.

3. *Concise Statistical Year-Book of Poland, 1936* p. 106.

4. *Concise Statistical Year-Book of Poland, 1935* p. 102.

5. Jean Morini-Comby, *Les Échanges Commericieux entre la France et les États Successeurs de l'Empire Austro-Hongrois* (Paris: Centre d'Etudes de Politique d' Etrangère, No. 2, 1936), p. 91.

6. *Ibid.*, p. 13.

7. *Ibid.*, p. 94.

8. *Ibid.*, p. 92.

9. *Ibid.*, p. 62.

10. *Ibid.*, p. 101.

11. M. Vuglijenovic, *Die Stellung Englands und Frankreichs am Yugoslavishen Markte in Verhältniss zu der Italiens und des Deutschen Reiches* (Vienna: Holinek, 1940),p. 17.) Though the full amount of Yugoslavian trade declined only 9 million dinar, the trade balance became strongly unfavorable.

12. Morini-Comby, *Les Échanges Commerciaux*, p. 46.

13. *Ibid.*, p. 36.

14. Elisabeth Haag, *Die Französische Aushandelspolitik, 1931-1938* (Lachen: A. Kessler, 1942),p. 24.

15. *Revue de la Situation Economique Mondiale, 1934-1935* (Geneva: League of Nations, 1935), p. 9.

16. Haag, *Aushandelspolitik*, p. 25.

17. *Reports of the Austrian Ambassador Lothar Egger-Moellwald to Chancellor Dollfuss*, Jeanneney to Egger-Moellwald, Paris, Z1, 19/Pol. March 12, 1934,p. 480. (Hereinafter referred to as *RAA*).

18. Personal information of Dr. Stephen Kertész to the author.

19. *L'Action Française* (Paris), January 9, 1934.

20. William L. Shirer, *The Collapse of the Third Republic* (New York: Simon & Schuster, 1969), p. 214.

21 *RAA*, Jeanneney to Egger-Moellwald, Paris, Z1, 19/Pol., March 12, 1934.

22. For a description of "Doumergue's Plot Against the Republic" see: Alexander Werth, *The Twilight of France* (New York: Howard Fertig, 1966), pp. 26-31.

23. Treaty with Poland, February 19, 1920; with Czechoslovakia, January 25, 1924; with Rumania, June 10, 1926; and with Yugoslavia, November 11, 1927.

24. "The parliamentary commission, partly for political reasons, was hostile to the plan of a motorized army of Lt. Colonel Charles de Gaulle." Maurice Baumont, *Les Origins de la Deuxiéme Guerre Mondiale* (Paris: Payot, 1969), p. 67.

25. Speech of Colonel Jean Fábry on February 20, 1933, at the "*Conference on International Cooperation*" organized by the "Old Students" and the "Students of the Free School of the Political Sciences in Algir" (Paris: Edition of the Conference 1933), p. 131.

26. Maurice Gamelin, *Servir* (3 vols.: Paris: Plon, 1946), II, p. 20.

27. Paul-Marie de la Gorce, *The French Army* (New York: George Braziller, 1963), p. 254.

28. *Ibid.*, p. 254. The fact is that these divisions did not exist yet in reality, only on paper.

29. Herbert Tint, *The Decline of French Patriotism* (London: Weidenfeld and Nicolson, 1964), p. 156.

30. The exact figures were: 895,000 died in action; 245,000 died of wounds; 175,000 died of illness. 16.5% of the French soldiers died during the war; 27% of all the losses were 18-27 years old. See Jacques Chastenet, *Jours Sanglants* (Paris: Hachette, 1964), pp. 190-91.

31. Taylor, *First World War*, p. 178.

32. la Gorce (de), *French Army*, p. 181.

33. *Ibid.*, pp. 191-92.

34. Tint, *Decline*, p. 201.

35. Baumont, *Les Origins*, pp. 98-101.

36. Georges Bonnet, *Quai d'Orsay* (New York: Times Press, 1965), p. 112.

37. Francois-Poncet, *Fateful Years*, p. 112.

38. Bonnet, *Quai d'Orsay*, p. 112.

39. Gamelin, *Servir*, II, pp. 112-29, Pierre Cot, *Triumph of Treason* (Chicago Ziff-Davis, 1944), pp. 181-84. Cot's testimony is the more significant since he was an admirer of Leon Blum and also a Socialist.

40. la Gorce (de), *French Army*, p. 255.

41. For the text of the treaties see: Gamelin, *Servir*, II, pp. 465-75.

42. Alec de Montmorency, *The Enigma of Admiral Darlan* (New York: E.P. Dutton & Co., 1943), pp. 51-61.

43. Gamelin, *Servir*, II, pp. 465-75.

44. Interview with General Julien Flipo (chief of staff of the French Military Mission in Prague, 1931-1938), Paris, June 15, 1971.

45. Gamelin, *Servir*, II, pp. 465-75.

46. "Americans still believed that their encircling seas conferred a kind of mystic immunity. . . . As early as 1934 a spiteful Congress had passed the Johnson Debt Default Act, which prevented debt-dodging nations from borrowing further in the United States. If attacked again by aggressors, these deliquents could 'stew in their own juice.'" Thomas A. Bailey, *The American Pageant* (Lexington, 4 th ed., Mass.: D.C. Heath Co., 1969), p. 901.

CHAPTER III

1. M.K. Dziewanovski, *Joseph Pilsudski, A European Federalist, 1918-1922* (Stanford: Hoover Institution, 1969), p. 32.

2. The creation of a Polish state was declared by the Central Powers on November 5, 1916. The majority of Poles looked upon it as a hopeful development, but they judged the territory awarded to the state to be too small and, therefore, not entirely satisfactory.

3. Ministère des Affaires Étrangères, *Documents Relatifs aux Origines de la Guerre, 1939-1945,* Documents Diplomatic Français, 1932-1939 (Paris: Imprimerie Nationale, 1964), (Hereinafter referred to as *DDF*), I, 1, Chautemps to Herriot, Paris, September 28, 1932, Doc. No. 217; Francois-Poncet to Herriot, Berlin, October 25, 1932, Doc. No. 275.

4. Wandycz, *Eastern Allies,* p. 29.

5. Based on the 1929 census, there were only 15,890 Poles out of the total population of 407,500.

6. "East-Prussia is an extremely strong jumping board for a German offensive," wrote Wladyslaw Sikorski in a report to Pilsudski. Quoted in Hans Roos, *Polen und Europa,* Tübinger Studien zur Geschichte und Politik, No. 7, (Tübingen: J.C.B. Mohn, 1957), pp 62-63.

7. *Lipski Papers,* pp. 24-25.

8. Publications of the Permanent Court of International Justice, *Treatment of Polish Nationals and other Persons of Polish Origin or Speech at Danzig,* Series A/B, XXIII Session, (Lyden: Q.W. Sijthoff's Publ. Co., 1932), Publ. No. 56, Fascicule No. 44.

9. *Lipski Papers,* p. 24, Wysocki to Beck, Berlin, July 19, 1931, Doc. No. 6.

10. Clement Vollmer, "A New Polish Corridor," *Foreign Affairs,* (October, 1933), pp. 156-59.

11. *DDF,* I, I, de la Forest Devonne to Paul-Boncour, Berlin, August 22, 1932, Doc. No. 114.

12. Wandycz, *Eastern Allies,* pp. 180-85.

13. Due to the Czechoslovakian closing of the Hungarian frontiers, only fragments of the Hungarian aid reached Poland through Rumania under Polish supervision. Kertész, *Whirlpool,* pp. 22-23.

14. Germany and Czechoslovakia closed their borders to French armshipments directed to Poland. Wandycz, *Eastern Allies,* p. 151.

15. *Ibid.,* p. 152; Horthy, *Memoirs,* pp. 119-20.

16. Wandycz, *Eastern Allies.,* p. 395.

17. Waclaw Lypacewicz, *Polish-Czech Relations* (Warsaw: Polish Institute for Collaboration with Foreign Countries, 1936), p. 48.

18. Anna M. Cienciala, *Poland and the Western Powers, 1938-1939* (London: Routledge & Kegan Paul, 1968), p. 14.

19. U.S. Department of State, *Documents on German Foreign Policy, 1918-1945* (Washington, D.C.: Government Printing Office, 1957), C, I. Memorandum by Neurath, London, June 21, 1933, Doc. No. 328. (Hereinafter referred to as *DGFP*.)

20. *Concise Statistical Yearbook of Poland 1937;* R.H. Osborne, *East-Central Europe* (New York: Frederick A. Prager, 1967), p. 263.

21. Seton-Watson, *Eastern Europe,* p. 121.

22. *Cambridge Economic History,* VI, Part II, p. 656.

23. Roman Gorecki, *Poland and Her Economic Development* (London: George Allen & Unvin Ltd., 1935), p. 79.

24. Osborne, *East-Central Europe,* pp. 348-49.

25. Wandycz, *Eastern Allies,* pp. 44, 92.

26. Seton-Watson, *Eastern Europe*, p. 162.

27. Wandycz, *Eastern Allies*, p. 92.

28. This and the following trade statistics are calculated on the basis of: *Concise Statistical Yearbook of Poland, 1935*, p. 102.

29. August 27, 1928. The Pact generally condemned aggression and was a means to solve international differences.

30. S. Konovalov, ed., *Russo-Polish Relations* (Princeton, N.J.: Princeton University Press, 1945), p. 41.

31. William O. Scroggs, "Russia and World Trade", *Foreign Affairs*, XII (January, 1934), p. 332.

32. Roman Debicki, *Foreign Policy of Poland, 1919-1939* (New York: Frederick A. Praeger, 1962), p. 65.

33. Roos, *Modern Poland*, p. 128.

34. *DDF*, Dejean to Herriot, Moscow, July 25, 1932, Doc. No. 61.

35. Evans Scott Williams, *Alliance Against Hitler* (Durham, N.C.: Duke University Press, 1962), p. 33.

36. The preventive war plans of Pilsudski were doubted by many historians. Recent research, especially the contribution of Polish and Soviet historians, clarified the issue, and the existence of Pilsudski's preventive war plan is accepted today as an historical fact. The whole debate concerning the existence or nonexistence of such a plan is summarized in Waclaw Jedrzejewicz, "The Polish Plan for a 'Preventive War' Against Germany in 1933," *The Polish Review*, XI (Winter, 1966), pp. 62-91.

37. The reorganization of the German army was projected to start in 1935, according to the German military budget. Department of State, *Foreign Relations of the United States, 1934* (5 vols.; Washington, D.C.: U.S. Government Printing Office, 1951), I, pp. 56-57, the German Ambassador to the Secretary of State, Washington, April 21, 1934.

38. The incident is described in detail in the *Lipski Papers*, pp. 46-59; Debicki, *Foreign Policy*, p. 70; Beck, *Final Report*, pp. 14-15; Roos, *Poland und Europa*, pp. 61-71.

39. *Lipski Papers*, p. 53.

40. *Ibid.*, p. 57.

41. *Ibid.*, p. 63.

42. *DDF*, I, I, Laroche to Herriot, Warsaw, November 7, 1932, Doc. No. 306.

43. J. Paul-Boncour, *Entre Deux Guerre* 3 vols.; Paris: Librairie Plon, 1946), III, p. 1.

44. The French press condemned Poland in January 1932 for signing the Soviet Polish Non-Aggression Pact (Beck, *Final Report*, p. 19); but on November 29, France herself signed a similar pact with the Soviet Union.

45. Cot, *Triumph of Treason*, p. 35.

46. For the text of the treaty see *League of Nations Treaty Series*, Vol. 54 (1926-27), pp. 360-62.

47. Bismarck said that the country which possesses Bohemia controls Central Europe.

48. Beck, *Final Report*, p. 38.

49. *Ibid.*, p. 39.

50. Gordon A. Graig, ed., *The Diplomats* (Princeton, N.J.: Princeton University Press, 1953), p. 120.

51. Beck, *Final Report,* p. 37.

52. *DGFP*, C, I, Moltke to Neurath, Warsaw, April 23, 1933, Doc. No. 180.

53. *Ibid.*, Memorandum of Neurath, Geneva, September 25, 1933, Doc. No. 449.

54. Jedrzejewicz, *"The Polish Plan,"* pp. 88-89.

55. *Lipski Papers,* pp. 94-98; *Ibid.*, Lipski to Beck, Berlin, November 30, 1933, Doc. No. 15; *DGFP*, C, II, unsigned memorandum, (undated), Doc. No. 77.

56. *Le Temps* (Paris), December 2, 1933.

57. *RAA*, Egger-Moellwald to Dollfuss, Paris, February 28, 1934.

58. *Ibid.*

59. *Lipski Papers,* p. 104.

60. M. Baumont, *La Faillite de la Paix* (Paris: Presses Universitaires de France, 1967), I, pp. 480-82.

61. *DGFP*, C, II, Nadolny to Neurath, Moscow, November 18, 1933, Doc. No. 75; Bulow to Nadolny, Berlin, January 24, 1934, Doc. No. 211; also, p. 411, 4[n].

CHAPTER IV

1. Frederick L. Schuman, *Europe on the Eve: The Crisis of Diplomacy, 1933-1939* (New York: Alfred A. Knopf, 1942), p. 96.

2. The task was made harder by the fact that the French diplomats broke almost every friendly contact with their Polish colleagues. See Francois-Poncet, *Fateful Years,* pp. 113-14.

3. Albrecht-Carrié, *Diplomatic History,* p. 467. Carrié compares the Four Power Pact to the idea of the Concert of Europe.

4. la Gorce (de), *French Army,* p. 257.

5. *RAA*, Paris, Zl, 19/Pol., March 12, 1934, p. 480. Bouisson, president of the Chamber of Deputies, said to Egger-Moellwald on March 11, 1934 (speaking of the February 17, 1934, uprising in Vienna): "On the sixth of February, M. Léon Blum was informed through a phone call from Prague *what was in preparation for* the next days in Austria. If M. Léon Blum would have informed Mr. Daladier about that phone call, he could have warned, through the French ambassador, the Bundeschancellor not to *irritate* the Social Democratic Party." (italics added).

6. Hans Rogger and Eugen Weber, eds., *The European Right, A Historical Profile* (Berkeley: University of California Press, 1966), p. 118.

7. *Ibid.*, p. 106.

8. Phillip Gibbs, *European Journey* (Garden City, New York: Doubleday, Doran & Co., 1934), p. 28.

9. *RAA*, Moellwald to Dollfuss, Paris, Zl, 19/Pol., March 12, 1934, p. 480.

10. Rogger and Weber, *European Right,* p. 120.

11. *RAA*, Moellwald to Dollfuss, Paris, Zl, 11/Pol., February 3, 1934, p. 461.

12. Rogger and Weber, *European Right,* p. 122.

13. Gibbs, *Journey*, p. 24.

14. Baumont, *Les Origines*, P. 103.

15. Chambres des Députés, *Journal Officiel de la République Française*, "Débats Parlementaires" (Paris, 1934), pp. 1254-55.

16. Bonnet, *Quai d'Orsay*, p. 112.

17. *Le Temps* (Paris), February 18, 1934.

18. *Journal Officiel*, p. 4103.

19. *RAA*, Moellwald to Dollfuss, Paris, Zl, 13/Pol., February 12,1934, p. 467.

20. The Rome Protocols consisted of one political and two economic agreements. The political agreement stressed the importance of political cooperation. The states involved agreed that, in case of foreign political problems, they would consult each other if any of the three states should so desire. The first economic agreement projected the widening of Austrian-Hungarian-Italian trade relations, and the second agreement planned a new Austrian-Italian commercial exchange. The economic clauses of the protocols were realized in May 1934 when the three states signed new commercial treaties. In light of the economic crisis, the discriminating custom policy of the Little Entente states, and the deteriorating French foreign trade, it could be interpreted as a defensive economic policy which, if it hindered the commercial plans of any state, then it hindered the German economic penetration of Austria and Hungary.

21. *RAA*, Moellwald to Dollfuss, 26/Pol., April 2, 1934, p. 496.

22. *Ibid.*, 32/Pol., April 30, 1934, p. 513.

23. *Le Temps* (Paris), February 28, 1934.

24. *RAA*, Moellwald reported this to Dollfuss. He based this conclusion on the report of one of his informers from the French Foreign Ministry. Paris, Zl, 34/Pol., May 4, 1934, p. 524.

25. Vondracek, *Czechoslovakia*, p. 376.

26. Magda Ádám, *Magyarország és a Kisantant a Harmincas Években* ("Hungary and the Little Entente in the Thirties") (Budapest: Akadémia Publ., 1968), p. 62.

27. Interview with Gerneral Flippo.

28. *Le Temps* (Paris), February 23, 1934.

29. *Ibid.*, February 22, 1934.

30. la Gorce (de), *French Army*, pp. 233-34.

31. Quoted in Mária Ormos, *Franciaország és a Keleti Biztonság, 1931-1936* ("France and the Eastern Security, 1931-1936") (Budapest: Akadémia Publ., 1969), p. 297.

32. Gamelin, *Servir* II, pp. 132-33.

33. Ormos, *Eastern Security*, p. 305.

34. la Gorce (de), *French Army*, pp. 233-34.

35. Like the Ruhr Occupation in 1923.

36. *Lipski Papers*, Lipski to Beck, Berlin, June 22, 1934, Doc. No. 28.

37. The Anglo-American pledges in 1919 and the Locarno agreements based on the Briand-Stresemann cooperation.

38. Baumont, *Les Origins*, pp. 112, 114, 150.

39. Report of the Italian and (with similar wording) the Hungarian ambassadors from Paris. Quoted in Ormos, *Eastern Security*, pp. 506-507.

40. *RAA*, Moellwald to Waldenegg, Paris, Zl, 57/Pol., July 30, 1934, p. 581.

41. *Ibid.*, Moellwald to Dollfuss, Paris, Zl, 19/Pol., March 12, 1934, p. 480.

42. *Ibid;* Ormos, *Eastern Security*, p.300.

43. Gamelin, *Servir*, II, p. 131.

44. *RAA*, Moellwald to Dollfuss, Paris, Zl, 36/Pol., May 8, 1934, p. 526.

45. *Lipski Papers*, Lipski to Beck about the Hitler-Mussolini meeting, Berlin, June 22, 1934, p. 145.

46. *RAA*, Moellwald to Dollfuss, Paris, Zl, 50/Pol., July 5, 1934, p. 566.

47. *Ibid.*

48. *Ibid.*, 51/Pol., July 8, 1934,p, 568.

49. *Ibid.*

50. Gamelin, *Servir,* II, p. 129.

51. *Le Temps* (Paris), July 27, 1934.

52. Interview with General Flipo.

53. *RAA,* Moellwald to Waldenegg, Paris, Zl, 64/Pol., August 11, 1934, p. 609.

54. *Ibid.*; the Great Powers reference is to the Three Power Declaration of February 17, 1934.

55. *Ibid.*, p. 610.

56. *Ibid.*

57. An illustrated report of the *Excelsior* showed that the official German press service prepared the news release concerning the Nazi Putsch three days *before* it actually happened. *Excelsior* (Paris), August 11, 1934, p. 1.

58. *RAA*, Moellwald to Waldenegg, Paris, Zl, 62/Pol., August 8, 1934, p. 604.

59. *Ibid.*

CHAPTER V

1. In May 1933, the German government imposed a 1,000 mark "visa-fee" upon German tourists visiting Austria. This regulation brought German tourism to a standstill and increased the economic problems. *DGFP*, Doc. No. 262.

2. Horthy, the Regent of Hungary, saw the possible annexation of Austria by Germany as a "natural development" and expressed his views to the German ambassador in Hungary. *Wilhelmstrasse*, Doc., No. 21.

3. Gerhard L. Weinberg, *The Foreign Policy of Hitler's Germany* (Chicago: University of Chicago Press, 1970), p. 93.

4. Also, the Czech minister to Austria, Zdencky Fierlinger, "deemed it necessary to intervene," since certain members of the Czech minority in Vienna had been implicated in the Socialist movement. Vondracek, *Czechoslovakia*, p. 380.

5. Kurt von Schuschnigg, *Austrian Requiem* (London: Victor Gollanz Ltd., 1947), pp. 14-15.

6. *DGFP*, C, III, Hitler to Papen, Berlin, August 19, 1934, Doc. No. 165.

7. The expression tried to cover the real meaning: strong protectionist trade policy in imports and state-subsidized exports to prevent a loss of foreign markets. For example, Hungary sold sugar to Austria for half of the home consumer price.

8. Hertz, *Danubian States*, p. 93.

9. *Ibid.*, pp. 49, 98.

10. The trade statistics for the following discussion are taken from Ernst Haas, *Die Aussenhandelspolitik der Ehemaligen Republik Österreich Während der Welt Wirtshaftkrise bis zurn Anschluss* (Würzburg: Konrad Tiltsch Verlag, 1939).

11. He had only a slight majority if the Pan-Germans voted on his side. The Pan-Germans advocated a custom union and, if possible, a political union with Germany.

12. Macartney and Palmer, *Eastern Europe*, p. 310; *Chicago Daily News*, February 13, 1934, p. 2.

13. Pro-Habsburg sentiments grew in Austria in 1931-1935. By 1935 more than 700 Austrian villages awarded honorary citizenship to Otto Habsburg. Csonka, *Habsburg Otto*, p. 130. In the vew constitution of May 1934, the anti-Habsburg paragraphs were omitted; the laws of 1919, though, were retained, but not in the text of the new constitution.

14. Schuschnigg, *Austrian Requiem*, p. 88.

15. During his visit in Germany in June 1933. C. A. Macartney, *October Fifteenth* (2 vols.: Edinburgh: University Press, 1961), I, 312.

16. *Wilhelmstrasse*, Professor Bleyer's report to the German Embassy in Budapest, August 11, 1933, Doc. No. 13.

17. Schuschnigg, *Austrian Requiem*, p. 88.

18. Horthy, *Memoirs*, pp. 116-27.

19. Schuschnigg, *Austrian Requiem*, p. 88.

20. *Wilhelmstrasse*, MacKensen to Neurath, Budapest, May 10, 1934, Doc. No. 24.

21. Schuschnigg, *Austrian Requiem*, p. 90.

22. *Wilhelmstrasse*, Conversation of Kánya with Hitler, Berlin, August 6, 1934, Doc. No. 25.

23. In this study, "revision" refers to the peace treaties that followed World War I. Article XIX of the Covenant of the League of Nations allowed the revision of the peace treaties concerning the newly drawn orders (but only by the unanimous vote of the Assembly) to correct possible injustices. The revisionist states that demanded the application of that article were Germany, Hungary, Italy, Poland, and Bulgaria. "Revisionism" was the name of the movement pursuing the aim of revisions in each respective country.

24. Schuschnigg, *Austrian Requiem*, p. 99. Italian-Austrian antagonism existed in 1934 because of the Italian oppression of the Austrians in the former Austrian provinces awarded to Italy in the St. Germain Treaty.

25. *Ibid.*, p. 101.

26. *Ibid.*, p. 100.

27. Ádám, *Hungary and the Little Entente*, p. 62.

28. Interview with Dr. Francis Schwarzenberg (Official in the Czech Diplomatic Service, 1936-1939), Chicago, May 10, 1971.

29. Quoted in Ádám, *Hungary and the Little Entente*, p. 57.

30. Interview with Gustav Hennyey (Hungarian Military Attache in Belgrade, 1933-1934), Munich, July 17, 1969.

31. G. E. R. Gedye, *Betrayal in Central Europe* (New York: Harper, 1939), p. 146.

32. *Ibid.*, p. 153.

33. J. D. Gregory, *Dollfuss and His Times* (London: Hutchinson & Co., 1935), p. 181. The loan was recommended by a League of Nations Commission which was set up to deal with the economic problems of the Danube Basin.

34. For a strong pro-Social Democratic description of these events see: Charles A. Gulich, *Austria from Habsburg to Hitler* (Berkeley: University of California Press, 1948). More objective, but still pro-Socialist is Gedye, *Betrayal*.

35. *DGFP*, C, III, legation in Austria to Neurath, Vienna, July 26, 1934, Doc. No. 125 (unsigned document).

36. *Ibid.*, memorandum of Kordt, Berlin, July 27, 1934, Doc. No. 128.

37. *Ibid.*, Papen to Bülov, Berlin, August 19, 1934, Doc. No. 167.

38. *Ibid.*, Doc. No. 165.

39. *Ibid.*, Doc. No. 167.

40. Schuschnigg, *Austrian Requiem*, p. 100.

41. *Ibid.*

42. Gedye, *Betrayal*, p. 84.

43. *DGFP*, C, III, Lammers to Neurath, Berlin, August 7, 1934, Doc. No. 150.

44. *Ibid.*, Doc. No. 167.

45. Ulrich Eichstadt, *Von Dollfuss zu Hitler* (Wiesbaden: Franz Steiner Verlag, 1955), p. 82.

46. Her Majesty's Stationery Office, *Documents on British Foreign Policy, 1919-1939*, Second Series (Oxford, Her Majesty's Stationery Office, 1958), VI, Sir W. Selley to Sir J. Simon, Vienna, August 3, 1934, Doc. No. 563. (Hereinafter referred to as *DBFP*.)

47. Gedye, *Betrayal*, p. 167.

48. *DBFP*, Doc. No. 563.

49. Schuschnigg, *Austrian Requiem*, p. 143.

50. Magyar Tudományos Akadémia Történettudományi Intézete, *Diplomdciai Inatok Magyarorszdg Külpolitikájdhcz, 1936-1945 ("Diplomatic Documents on the Foreign Policy of Hungary, 1936-1945")*, (4 vols.: Budapest: Akadémia Publ., 1962), I, reports of the Hungarian ambassadors from Prague, Belgrade, and Vienna, January 16-25, 1936, Doc. Nos. 6, 7, 9, 13, 15. (Hereinafter referred to as *DHFP*.)

51. Schuschnigg, *Austrian Requiem*, p. 146.

52. *DHFP*, I, conversation of Kánya and Mackensen, Budapest, February 12, 1936, Doc. No. 31.

53. *Ibid.*, Kánya to Sztójay, February 27, 1936, Doc. No. 53. conversation of Kánya with Mackensen, Budapest, February 25, 1936, Doc. No. 49.

54. *Ibid.*, conversation of Kánya and Neustadter-Stürmer, Budapest, March 9, 1936, Doc. No. 61.

55. *Ibid.*, Wettstein to Kánya, Prague, March 16, 1935, Doc. No. 66.

56. Schuschnigg, *Austrian Requiem*, p. 131.

57. *RAA*, Moellwald to Waldenegg, Paris, Zl, 64/Pol., August 11, 1934, p. 610.

58. *Le Temps* (Paris), July 27, 1934.

59. Ormos, *Eastern Security*, p. 322-23.

60. *Ibid.*; John F. Montgomery, *Hungary, the Unwilling Satellite* (New York: Devin Adair Co., 1947), p. 66; *Le Temps* (Paris), July 27, 1934.

61. *RAA*, Moellwald's report to Waldenegg based on the evaluation of his informer, Paris, Zl, 64/Pol., August 1, 1934, p. 610.

62. *Ibid.*, 67/Pol., August 20, 1934, p. 621.

63. *Ibid.*; Ormos, *Eastern Security*, p. 326.

64. Quoted in Arnold Wolfers, *Britain and France* p. 229.

65. *RAA*, Moellwald to Waldenegg, Paris, Zl, 79/Pol., September 25, 1934, p. 646.

66. Ormos, *Eastern Security*, p. 329.

CHAPTER VI

1. F. B. Hoptner, *Yugoslavia in Crisis, 1934-1941* (New York: Columbia University Press, 1962), p. 10.

2. Schuschnigg, *Austrian Requiem*, p. 90.

3. The agreement guaranteed the Balkan frontiers against a non-Balkan country acting alone: Italy, Hungary, or the Soviet Union.

4. Stavrianos, *Balkans*, p. 638.

5. Hoptner, *Crisis*, p. 19; Montgomery, *Hungary*, pp. 245-61; Macartney and Cremona, *Italy's Foreign Policy*, Chapter V.

6. Hoptner, *Crisis*, p. 20.

7. *Ibid.*, p. 16.

8. Horthy, *Memoirs*, p. 141.

9. *Requète du Gouvernment Yugoslave: rélative aux résponsabilitiès encourés par les Autorites Hongroises dans l' action terroriste dirigée contre la Yugoslavie* (Beograd, 1935), p. 51.

10. Interview with Hennyey. Janka Puszta was a farmhouse complex near the Yugoslavian border, owned and operated by Gustav Percec as an USTASHE refugee camp.

11. Macartney, *October Fifteenth*, p. 146. Tibor Ekhardt, in his book *Regicide at Marseilles* (New York: The American-Hungarian Library and Historical Society, 1964), p. 30, says "at my request, the Hungarian Government had expelled the USTASHE's. . . from Hungary." Gustav Hennyey describes this expulsion as follows: "Gömbös and Kánya agreed that the Croatian refugees should be sent out of Hungary in one way or other. We looked for feasible solutions and finally we agreed that we should give Hungarian passports to about thirty politically prominent Croatian refugees in order to send them away. It was not a very good solution, but we could not find a better one. We gave Hungarian passports to two, three Croatian emigrants every month. They went to Lausanne. General Kvaternik then collected their passports upon their arrival and sent the passports back to us. We sent the first group in September 1933 and the system worked without flaws for a whole year." Interview with Hennyey.

12. Seton-Watson, *Eastern Europe*, p. 251.

13. Interview with Hennyey; Horthy, *Memoirs*, p. 141.

14. Macartney and Palmer, *Eastern Europe*, p. 308.

15. *Ibid.*, p. 276.

16. Stoyan Christowe, *Heroes and Assasins* (New York: Robert L. McBridge, 1935), p. 218; Eckhardt, *Regicide*, p. 29.

17. According to the Hungarian-Kvaternik agreement, the refugees were not supposed to register with the Hungarian passports. However, Kvaternik arrived late on this one occasion, and the two men became impatient. They registered in the hotel, left their baggage and went sightseeing, returning only in the evening when they finally met Kvaternik. A week later, they participated in a meeting which selected—by drawing lots—two emigrants for "an important assignment." Both of them drew the fatal card. They were selected as helpers of the assassin. Interview with Hennyey who learned this version of the story personally from Kvaternik in 1941.

18. Hoptner, *Crisis*, p. 29, 11[n].

19. Sir Anthony Eden, *Facing the Dictators, 1923-1938* (Boston: Houghton Mifflin, 1962), pp. 122-23,

20. la Gorce (de), *French Army*, pp. 256-57.

21. Eckhardt, *Regicide*, p. 120.

22. Interview with Hennyey.

23. *Ibid.*

24. League of Nations, *Official Journal*, December 1, 1934, pp. 1712-28.

25. Eden, *Facing Dictators*, p. 131.

26. Interview with Hennyey.

27. *Ibid.*

28. Hoptner, *Yugoslavia*, p. 25.

29. *Ibid.*

30. Montgomery, *Hungary*, p. 69.

31. Interview with Hennyey.

32. See the statement of the Little Entente ministers on October 19, 1934, in Belgrade, "we would insist with all possible force"—wording is clearly a threat of a possible military showdown. Quoted in Eden, *Facing Dictators*, p. 122.

33. The use of the word "sanctions" indicated that he was after guilty nations and not only after guilty persons. This expertise is interesting, because the trial of the criminals did not begin until November. Edkhardt, *Regicide*, p. 119.

34. *Journal Officiel*, 1934, p. 2201.

35. Montgomery, *Hungary*, p. 69.

36. Eden, *Facing Dictators*, p. 127.

37. *Le Temps* (Paris), October 13, 1934.

38. *RAA*, Moellwald to Waldenegg, Paris, Z1, 83/Pol., October 15, 1934.

39. *DGFP*, C, III, evaluation of Ermansdorff, Berlin, February 14, 1935, Doc. No. 491.

40. *RAA*, Moellwald to Waldenegg, Paris, 84/Pol., October 17, 1934, p. 659.

41. Laval attempted to enlist Benes' support for that. *Ibid.*

42. Hoptner, *Crisis,* p. 28.

43. Litvinov vigorously supported the Yugoslavian standpoint, though the Yugoslavian dislike of the Soviet regime did not disappear with the death of King Alexander. Beloff, *Soviet Foreign Policy* I., p. 138.

44. Seton-Watson, *Eastern Europe,* p. 231.

45. *Ibid.,* During the funeral of King Alexander, the German delegation "noticed the spiritual unity of the people." *DGFP,* C, III, Heeren to Neurath, Belgrade, October 22, 1934, Doc. Nos. 263-64.

46. Mussolini did not cease to demand the Dalmatian Coast promised to Italy during World War I but given to Yugoslavia in the Peace Treaty of 1919.

47. *DGFP,* C, III, p. 93, 5[n].

48. Hoptner, *Crisis,* p. 24.

49. *DGFP,* C, III, Heeren to Neurath, Belgrade, June 27, 1934, Doc. No. 39.

50. Interview with Hennyey.

51. *DGFP,* C, III, Heeren to Neurath, Belgrade, June 27, 1934, Doc. No. 459.

52. *Ibid.,* Doc. No. 263.

53. After the death of Dollfuss, the Austrian army rounded up the Austrian Nazi brownshirts and stormtroopers, with the exception of those who escaped to Yugoslavia. Yugoslavia accepted them as guests and later sent them by ship to Germany. They were feted as if they were friends and visitors. Montgomery, *Hungary,* p. 66.

54. Stavrianos, *Balkans,* p. 16.

55. *DGFP,* Doc. No. 264.

56. The terrorists planted time bombs in Austria in the wagons of the Intercontinental Express, and the bombs exploded after the train crossed over into Yugoslavian territory.

57. Hugh Seton-Watson, Robert Lee Wolff, L.S. Stavrianos.

58. The Radical Party was the party of the Serbian patriots with a "Great Serbian" conviction.

59. Stavrianos, *Balkans,* p. 630.

60. *Ibid.* According to the constitution, a simple majority won in the popular elections awarded the victorious party with two-thirds of the seats in the Skuptsina (parliament).

61. *DGFP,* Doc. Nos. 263, 264.

62. Seton-Watson, *Eastern Europe,* p. 232, Stavrianos, *Balkans,* p. 629.

CHAPTER VII

1. Edouard Bonnefous, *Histoire Politique de la Troisième République* (6 vols. Paris: Presses Universitaires de France, 1962), V, p. 304.

2. *Ibid.,* p. 308. *RAA,* Moellwald to Waldenegg, Paris, Zl, 96/Pol., December 2, 1934, p. 687.

3. *Ibid.,* 94/Pol., November 18, 1934, p. 683.

4. *Ibid.*, 96/Pol., December 2, 1934, p. 687.

5. Laval's attitude toward Germany is reflected in his statement: "Do you see this big red patch right in the middle of Europe? Do you *really* imagine that we can have peace and collective security in Europe so long as we haven't brought *this* into our peace system?" Werth, *Twilight of France*, p. 35.

6. *RAA*, Moellwald to Waldenegg, Paris, Zl, 96/Pol., 1934, Doc. No. 2, p. 690.

7. *Ibid.*

8. *DGFP*, C, III, unsigned memorandum, Berlin, without date (November?), Doc. No. 358.

9. *RAA*, Paris, Zl, 94/Pol., November 18, 1934, p. 684.

10. *Journal Officiel, 1934*, pp. 1396-98.

11. *DGFP*, C, III, memorandum by Köpke, Berlin, December 20, 1934, Doc. No. 399.

12. *RAA*, Moellwald to Waldenegg, Paris, Zl, 94/Pol., November 18, 1934, p. 699.

13. Interview with Theodore Hornbostel (Political Secretary-General of the Austrian Ministry of Foreign Affairs), Vienna, July 12, 1971.

14. *Ibid.*

15. la Gorce (de), *French Army*, p. 255.

16. Gamelin, *Servir*, II, p. 143.

17. *DGFP*, C, III, Memorandum of Neurath, Berlin, November 27, 1934, Doc. No. 356.

18. For a good bibliography of works written about Pierre Laval, see: Hubert Cole, *Laval: a Biography* (New York: G.P. Putnam's Sons, 1963), pp. 301-04.

19. *DGFP*, C, III, Hassel to Neurath, Rome, January 2, 1935, Doc. No. 405.

20. For the official French text see: *Le Temps* (Paris), January 13, 1935; also, *DGFP*, C, III, Hassel to Neurath, Rome, January 6, 1935, Doc. No. 406.

21. Gamelin, *Servir*, II, pp. 168-69.

22. *Ibid.*

23. la Gorce (de), *French Army*, p. 166-68.

24. Gamelin, *Servir*, II, p. 169, clearly stated the projected participation of the Czech army, while General Flipo, during his interview, denied the existence of any Czech offensive plans.

25. Cole, *Laval*, p. 60.

26. *Ibid.*; Gamelin, *Servir*, II, p. 172.

27. *Le Temps* (Paris), January 13-14, 1935.

28. *RAA*, Moellwald to Waldenegg, Paris, Zl, 18/Pol., February 6, 1935, p. 52.

29. *Budapesti Hirlap* (Budapest), January 1, 1935.

30. *Le Temps* (Paris), January 1, 1935.

31. *Ibid.*, January 3, 1935.

32. *Ibid.*, January 5, 1935.

33. *DGFP*, C, III, Hassel to Neurath, Rome, January 8, 1935, Doc. No. 417.

34. *Ibid.*, Doc. No. 405.

35. *Le Temps* (Paris), January 9, 1935.

36. *Ibid.*

37. *Le Temps* (Paris), January 13, 1935.

38. The Saar plebiscite was held in January 1935 according to the conditions of the Versailles Treaty. The result was a great victory for Germany: 2,124 votes were cast in favor of remaining with France and 477,000 in favor of rejoining Germany. Bonnet, *Quai d'Orsay,* p. 119.

39. *Budapesti Hirlap* (Budapest), January 14, 1935.

40. *RAA*, Moellwald to Waldenegg, Paris, Zl, 4/Pol., January 11, 1935.

41. Johann Wuescht, *Yugoslawean und das Dritte Reich* (Stuttgart: Seewald Verlag, 1969), p. 83.

42. Morini-Comby, *Les Échanges,* p. 54.

43. *Ibid.*, p. 25.

44. Gamelin, *Servir,* II, p. 165.

45. Quoted in full by Philippe Reorganization of the French army began in December 1934 with the vote of credits for armaments, an aviation program, a new phase of naval constructions, and further provisions for the Maginot line. See Flandin's speech in Lyon on March 6, 1935 in *Le Temps. Mussolini contre Hitler* (Paris: Fernand Sarlot, 1938), pp. 111-15.

46. *Lipski Papers,* p. 64.

47. Cole, *Laval,* p. 60. This is a question still contested today. Laval always denied it according to Werth (*Twilight of France,* p. 39). Laval probably only showed a lack of interest in Abyssinia and Mussolini interpreted this as consent.

48. *Lipski Papers,* Lipski to Beck, Berlin, March 16, 1935, Doc. No. 38.

49. *Ibid.*; Ádám, *Hungary and the Little Entente,* p. 70.

50. *DGFP*, C, III, memorandum by Bülow, Berlin, January 4, 1935, Doc. No. 410, enclosure.

51. *Lipski Papers,* Lipski to Beck, Berlin, February 5, 1935, No. 35.

52. *RAA*, Moellwald to Waldenegg, Paris, Zl, 6/Pol., January 15, 1935, p. 23.

53. Quoted in Desmond Donnelly, *Struggle for the World. The Cold War, 1917-1965* (New York: St. Martin's Press, 1965), pp. 49-50. For further details concerning the Soviet attitude see: Beloff, *Soviet Foreign Policy,* I, p. 158.

54. Ádám, *Hungary and the Little Entente,* p. 72.

55. *Ibid.* These demands quoted from Russian sources.

56. Quoted in Ormos, *Eastern Security,* p. 348.

57. *Ibid.*

58. Schuschnigg, *Austrian Requiem,* p. 124.

59. *Ibid.*, p. 133.

60. *Ibid.*, p. 140.

CHAPTER VIII

1. Macartney, *Hungary,* p. 218.

2. The government press frequently published abusive articles about Otto von Habsburg, the legal heir of the Hungarian throne. Csonka, *Habsburg Otto,* p.189.

3. Kónya, *Gömbös' Attempt,* pp. 47-63.

4. Since the time of Joseph II (1780-1790), the Habsburgs had made attempts to improve the conditions of the peasantry. Charles IV and his son Otto frequently urged the Hungarian landed estates to pass a land reform bill for the benefit of the peasantry. Csonka, *Habsburg Otto,* p. 186.

5. Gyula Szekfű, *Három nemzedék és ami utána következik.* ("Three Generations and after") (Budapest: Kiralyi Magyar Egyetemi Nyomda, 1934), p. 439.

6. Seton-Watson, *Eastern Europe,* p. 291.

7. Magyar Országos Levéltár, *Horthy Miklós Titkos Iratai* ("The Secret Documents of Nicholas Horthy"), (Budapest: Kossuth Publ. Co., 1965), Doc. No. 16. The latest arrests were made during the spring of 1931.

8. The interpretations differ on this point. C.A. Macartney accepts, on the basis of evidence, that the friendship treaty was directed more against Germany than against the Slavs (*October Fifteenth,* Part I, p. 136, footnote 3), while Ádám, Juhász, and Kerekes definitely state that "this alliance was directed first of all against the common opponent: Yugoslavia." *Allianz,* p. 15.

9. Macartney, *October Fifteenth,* Part I, p. 90, 5[n].

10. *Wilhelmstrasse,* Schnurte to Neurath, Budapest, February 12, 1935, Doc. No. 31.

11. Sandor Kónya, *Gömbös kisérlete, totalis fasiszte diktatura megteremtesere* "Gombos' Attempt, to create a Totalitarian Fascist Dictatorship") (Budapest: Akadémia Publ., 1968), p. 86.

12. Macartney, *October Fifteenth,* p. 112. The Hungarian Jews were divided into the modernized Neologs and the traditional Orthodox group. The Neologs were the more numerous.

13. Montgomery, *Hungary,* p. 47.

14. The regent was only a figurehead. He could not make any foreign political decisions. The real power was in the hands of the prime minister and foreign minister who acted upon the approval of the Crown Council. The regent's acts were not valid without the countersignature of a cabinet minister. Thus, Hungary had a parliamentary system of government.

15. Macartney, *October Fifteenth,* I, p. 108-10.

16. Seton-Watson, *Eastern Europe,* p. 373.

17. Kurt Schuschnigg, *Im Kampf gegen Hitler* (Vienna:) Fritz Molden Verlag, 1969), p. 142-43.

18. *Wilhelmstrasse.* Conversation of Köpke with Mazirevich, Berlin, July 14, 1933, Doc. No. 10, Doc. No. 9.

19. *Ibid.,* Doc. Nos. 4, 8, 13; *Allianz,* Gömbös' conversation with Hitler, Budapest, June 16, 1933, Doc. No. 3; Bleyer to Schoen, Budapest, August 11, 1933, Doc. No. 13; Schoen to Neurath, Budapest, June 21, 1933, Doc. No. 8.

20. A. F. Nandor, Dreisziger, *Hungary's Way to World War II* (Toronto: Hungarian Helicon Society, 1963), p. 34.

21. Macartney, *October Fifteenth,* pp. 141-145; Morini-Comby, *Les Exchanges,* p. 30. On July 22, 1933, Germany made a trade agreement with Hungary based on the quota system.

22. *Wilhelmstrasse,* Doc. No. 14.

23. The official historical interpretation of revisionism, accepted by every historian now *living in Hungary,* is reflected in the following statement: "The Hungarian ruling classes did not want the diminution of differences, but rather the continuation of them because by these means they could turn the bitterness of a great majority of the population against the dictates of Trianon and against the neighboring states. Their bitterness was actually caused by their misery." *Allianz,* p. 14.

24. Eckhardt, *Regicide,* p. 96.

25. Auer, *Half a Century,* p. 111.

26. *Wilhelmstrasse,* Koster to Neurath, Paris, September 18, 1933, Doc. No. 14.

27. Eckhardt, *Regicide,* pp. 58-59; Macartney, *October Fifteenth,* p. 143.

28. *DGFP,* C, I, Albert Dufour to the Foreign Ministry, Belgrade, June 1, 1933 Doc. No. 279.

29. *DBFP,* Second Series, V, Doc. No. 273; Interview with Auer; Auer, *Half a Century,* p. 100.

30. *DGFP,* Memorandum by Neurath, London, June 21, 1933, Doc. No. 328.

31. A. Basch, *The Danube Basin in the German Economic Sphere* (New York: Columbia University Press, 1943), p. 160.

32. Dreisziger, *Hungary's Way,* p. 61; Magda, *Hungary and the Little Entente,* p. 53.

33. *Wilhelmstrasse,* Negotiations of Kánya and Göring, Budapest, October 11, 1936, Doc. No. 14.

34. Interview with Hennyey.

35. 382,000 according to the census of 1921.

36. Horthy, *Memoirs,* p. 141.

37. *Wilhelmstrasse,* Schoen to Neurath, Budapest, May 9, 1933, Doc. No. 5.

38. Interview with Hennyey; Ádám, *Hungary and the Little Entente,* pp. 62-63.

39. Interview with Auer.

40. Quoted in Ádám, *Hungary and the Little Entente,* p. 58.

41. Seton-Watson, *Eastern Europe,* p. 344.

42. Macartney and Palmer, *Eastern Europe,* p. 308; Stavrianos, *Balkans,* pp. 738-39.

43. Ádám, *Hungary and the Little Entente,* pp. 58-59.

44. *Allianz,* negotiations of Gömbös with Hitler, Budapest, June 16, 1933, Doc. No. 3; Gömbös to Mussolini, Budapest, June 24, 1933, Doc. No. 4.

45. *Wilhelmstrasse,* Schoen to Neurath, Budapest, June 21, 1933, Doc. No. 8.

46. Quoted in Ormos, *Eastern Security,* p. 240.

47. Interview with Hennyey.

48. Seton-Watson, *Eastern Europe,* p. 347.

49. *DGFP,* C, II, memorandum by Köpke, Berlin, December 1, 1933, Doc. No. 95; memorandum by Bülow, Berlin, January 11, 1934, Doc. No. 175; memorandum by Neurath, Berlin, January 18, 1934, Doc. No. 192; memorandum by Bülow, Berlin, January 24, 1934, Doc. No. 216.; Gömbös to Hitler, Budapest, February 14, 1934, Doc. No. 252; Dr. Lammers to Neurath, Berlin, February 28, 1934, Doc. No. 288; Dr. Lammers to Neurath, Berlin, March 29, 1934, Doc. No. 371.

50. *Wilhelmstrasse,* Doc. Nos. 16, 18, 19, 20.

51. See Mussolini's letter to Gömbös on July 1, 1933, *Allianz,* Doc. No. 5.

52. The first interpretations may be found in Ádám, *Hungary and the Little Entente;* Ormos, *Eastern Security.*

53. Seton-Watson, *Eastern Europe;* Macartney and Palmer, *Eastern Europe.*

54. Andras Hóry, *A Kulisszák Mögött* ("Behind the Scenes" (Vienna: Author's Edition, 1965), p. 15.

55. *Ibid.,* The last active cooperation between Pilsudski and Horthy occurred during the Soviet-Polish War.

56. *Lipski Papers,* p. 64.

57. *Ibid.,* pp. 64-66.

58. *Ibid.,* Hory *(Behind the Scenes,* p. 15), mistakenly writes that the initiation for the revival of Polish-Hungarian friendship came on the part of Hungary.

59. Interview with General Flipo.

60. Hory, *Behind the Scenes,* p. 15. Poland had claimed the Czech territory of Teschen since the creation of the two states after World War I.

61. Macartney, *October Fifteenth,* I, p. 144.

62. *Wilhelmstrasse,* Doc. No. 19.

63. *Ibid.,* Mackensen to Neurath, Budapest, February 26, 1934, Doc. No. 20.

64. *Ibid.,* Doc. No. 21.

65. Regretably, the Hungarian-Italian documents were not available to me; but it can be safely concluded, by knowing the personal friendship of Mussolini and Gömbös, that Gömbös informed him of the negotiations just as he had informed Hitler about the state of affairs between Hungary and Italy. For the Italian view of these events see Macartney and Cremona, *Italian Foreign Policy,* pp. 203-204.

66. *Wilhelmstrasse,* p. 73, 5[n].

67. *Ibid.,* Doc. No. 20.

68. *Allianz,* p. 115, 8[n].

69. *Ibid.,* Gömbös' note for negotiations with Mussolini, Rome, March 13, 1934, Doc. No. 6.

70. *Ibid.* Gömbös stated that he had received this information from Theodore Hornbostel, political secretary-general of the federal chancellery of Austria. Hornbostel explained to me that "Austria was disappointed with the Rome Protocols because they did not include any statement of guarantee concerning the inviolability of Austria's territorial sovereignty. Dollfuss, keeping the door open to France, wanted to pressure Italy and Hungary to include such a statement in the Protocols, but could not succeed." Interview with Theodore Hornbostel (Political Secretary-General of the Austrian Ministry of Foreign Affairs, 1933-1938), Vienna, July 12, 1971.

71. Dollfuss, though he himself was not a monarchist, favored the Austrian Legitimists, because "they were for sure anti-Nazis." Interview with Hornbostel.

72. *Allianz,* Doc. No. 6; neogtiations of Kánya and Coloma, Budapest, February 21, 1933, Doc. No. 2.

73. *DGFP,* C, III, Hassel to Neurath, Rome, June 21, 1934, Doc. No. 26; circular of Neurath, Berlin, June 16, 1934, Doc. No. 10.

74. *Ibid.,* Doc. No. 17; Joseph Buttinger, *Am Beispiel Österreichs* (Cologne: Verlag für Politik und Wirtschaft, 1953), pp. 206-07.

75. *Ibid.*, memorandum of Ritter, Berlin, June 16, 1934, Doc. No. 9; E.R. Stahremberg, *Between Hitler and Mussolini* (London; Hodder & Stoughton, Ltd., 1942), pp. 114-15; Macartney, *October Fifteenth*, p. 146, 1[n].

76. *DGFP*, Hassel to Neurath, Berlin, October 25, 1934, Doc. No. 132. Between July 27 and August 1, 1934, the Hungarian press strongly hinted of German involvement in the putsch.

77. Ormos, *Eastern Security*, p. 242.

78. *Le Temps* (Paris), June 29, 1934.

79. Ormos, *Eastern Security*, p. 312.

80. Tibor Hetés and Tamás Morva, eds., *Csak Szolgálati Használatra. Iratok a Horthy Hadsereg Történetéhez, 1919-1938* ("Strictly confidential documents for the history of the Horthy Army, 1919-1938") (Budapest: Zriny: Military Books, 1968), No. 78.

81. Hennyey saw these plans. "They were prepared for only a coordinated action. None of the Little Entente states considered *alone* an attack on Hungary." (italics added) Interview with Hennyey.

82. Hetés and Morva, *Strictly Confidential*, No. 78. Burgenland, a Hungarian territory, was given to Austria by the Trianon Treaty. The diplomatic manuevering was to gain the consent only of the Little Entente since the General Staff did not expect any German objection.

83. *Ibid.*

84. Ormos, *Eastern Security*, p. 313.

85. Hetés and Morva, *Strictly Confidential*, p. 342.

86. *Wilhelmstrasse*, Doc. No. 25.

87. *DGFP*, Doc. No. 150.

88. Vladeta von Milicevic, *Der Königsmord von Marseilles* (Bad Godesberg: Hochwacht Verlag, 1959), pp. 24-26, 43-46; Ádám, *Hungary and the Little Entente*, p. 65.

89. Interview with Hennyey.

90. *DGFP*, C, III, Memorandum of Neurath, Berlin, October 25, 1934, Doc. No. 269.

91. *Ibid.*, Doc. Nos. 305, 284, 336.

92. *Ibid.*, Doc. No. 336.

93. *Wilhelmstrasse*, Mackensen to Stieve, Budapest, November 30, 1934, Doc. No. 29.

94. Quoted in Ádám, *Hungary and the Little Entente*, p. 68, 137[n].

95. Interview with Hennyey.

96. Mathias Rákosi was People's Commissar in Hungary during the 1919 Communist regime. After the regime fell, he escaped to the Soviet Union. In the fall of 1934, at Stalin's orders, he returned to Hungary to organize an underground Communist Party. He was promptly arrested for crimes committed in 1919, as well as for his illegal entry.

97. *Budapesti Hirlap*, (Budapest), March 7, 1935.

98. *Ibid.*, April 10, 1935. A revisionist program was promoted in spite of Mussolini's request to stop emphasizing the necessity of revision. Ádám, *Hungary and the Little Entente*, p. 71.

99. *Budapesti Hirlap* (Budapest), April 9, 1935.

100. Report of the Hungarian ambassador in Rome (Baron Frigyes Villáni) quotes in Ormos, *Eastern Security*, p. 351.

101. *Wilhelmstrasse*, Mackensen to Stieve, Budapest, April 6, 1935, Doc. No. 33. Knowing Gömbös' political conviction, we may safely say that Gömbös would not have chosen this alternative anyway.

102. *DGFP*, C, III, memorandum by Bülow, Berlin, January 4, 1935, Doc. No. 410.

103. *Wilhelmstrasse*, Doc. Nos. 33, 19, 30.

104. It started with Göring's visit to Belgrade for the funeral of King Alexander. Germany then began to play the role of Yugoslavia's protector against Hungarian revisionism. *DGFP*, Doc. Nos. 273, 305, 336.

105. The League of Nations' investigation ended with the December 1934 resolution, but the criminal procedure continued in the French courts until February 12, 1936. Milicevic, *Königsmord*, p. 81.

106. Quoted in Ormos, *Eastern Security*, p. 363.

107. *Budapesti Hirlap*, (Budapest), June 13, 1935 reported that according to Mussolini, nothing more could be expected from the Danubian Pact.

108. Macartney, *Hungary*, p. 224.

CHAPTER IX

1. Baumont, *Les Origins*, p. 140.

2. The negotiations were successfully concluded on June 18, 1935.

3. Albert Speer, *Au Coeur du Troisième Reich*, (Paris: Fayard, 1971), p. 104.

4. Baumont, *Les Origins*, p. 146.

5. Macartney and Cremona, *Italy's Foreign Policy*, p. 282.

6. Laval, in a December 22, 1935, letter to Mussolini, protested the use of force and stated that Mussolini received his consent only for a "pacific" action in Ethiopia. D. Franklin Laurens, *France and the Italo-Ethiopian Crisis, 1935-1936*, (The Hague: Mouton & Co., 1967), Appendix I, p. 404. England's "tacit approval" was obtained, according to the impression of Mussolini, Laval and Flandin, during the Stresa Conference. Pierre E. Flandin, *Politique Francaise 1919-1940*, (Paris: Edition Nouvelles, 1947), pp. 177-78.

7. Eden visited Rome on June 24-26, 1935, to try and talk Mussolini out of the Abyssinian war.

8. Debate in the British House of Commons, June 23, 1936, printed in Carnegie Endowment for International Peace, *International Conciliation, Documents for the Year 1936*. (New York: Publ. and Editorial Offices, 1936).

9. Macartney and Cremona, *Italy's Foreign Policy*, p. 317-19. The Little Entente states sought reimbursment from England for their losses because of the Italian counter-sanctions.

10. Bonnet, *Quai d'Orsay*, p. 127.

11. Julius Mader, *Hitlers Spionage Generale Sagen Aus*, (Berlin: Verlag der Nation, 1971), p. 305-308.

12. Gamelin, *Servir*, II, p. 194. The intelligences services included the Information Bureau, a government agency, and the Deuxieme Bureau, a department of the General Staff.

13. Francois-Poncet had sent warnings to the Quai D'Orsay since November 1935. Francois-Poncet, *Fateful Years*, pp. 189-92.

14. Bonnet, *Quai D'Orsay*, p. 132.

15. See: Baumont, *Les Origins*, p. 220; Raymond J. Sontag, *A Broken World, 1919-1939*, (The Rise of Modern Europe Series), (New York: Harper & Row, 1971), p. 292; A.H. Carr, *International Relations Between the Two World Wars, 1919-1939* (New York: Harper & Row, 1947), p. 220, Hughes, *Contemporary Europe*, p. 282; Taylor, *Second World War*, p. 101.

16. Beck, *Final Report*, p. 110; *Lipski Papers*, p. 254; *DDF*, I, I, Noel to Flandin, Doc. No. 303.

17. Wolfers, *Britain and France*, pp. 48-49.

18. Formed by Doumergue in February 1934 and continued under the prime ministership of Flandin (November 8, 1934-May 31, 1935), Bouisson (June 1-June 4, 1935), and Laval (June 7, 1935-January 22, 1936).

19. The elections were planned for April 7, 1936, and the Popular Front won the elections against the conservatives by a margin of 378 to 220. Bonnefous, *Histoire Politique*, V, pp. 375, 419. Though the idea of the Popular Front was originally Communist, in its revived new form in France, the Popular Front united all the political and social forces of the country in 1935 and led the fight to block the spread of Nazism.

20. *Ibid.*, p. 375.

21. *Ibid.*,

22. Tint, *French Patriotism*, p. 207.

23. Baumont, *Les Origines*, p. 140.

24. *Ibid.*, p. 219.

25. Already in May 1933, the French Army Council held the opinion that the French army could not face the German and Italian forces without grave risks. la Gorce (de), *French Army*, p. 255.

26. Gamelin, *Servir*, II, p. 201.

27. Report of the commission investigating the events in France, 1933-1945. Quoted in Bonnefous, *Troisième Republic*, V, p. 454.

28. *Ibid.*

29. Gamelin, *Servir*, II, p. 201.

30. *Ibid.*, p. 210.

31. Shepard B. Clough, Thomas Moodie, Carol Moodie, eds., *Economic History of Europe: Twentieth Century*, (New York: Harper & Row, 1968), p. 266.

32. Hughes, *Contemporary Europe*, p. 227.

33. *Foreign Relations*, 1935, II, Ambassador Dodd to the Secretary of State, Berlin, May 27, 1935, No. 2000.

34. Alan Bullock, *Hitler. A Study in Tyranny* (Rev. ed. New York: Harper & Row, 1962), p. 333.

35. Wheeler-Bennet, *Nemesis*, p. 344.

36. *Ibid.*, p. 349. Twenty-eight were to be completed for October 1936.

37. *Ibid.*, p. 350.

38. Speer, *Au Coeur de Troisième Reich*, p. 104.

39. Bullock, *Hitler*, p. 343; W.S. Churchill, *The Gathering Storm* (New York: Bantam Books, 1961), p. 173 estimated the number to be about 35,000 strong, still far below the estimate of the French General Staff (over 265,000 men). Gamelin, *Servir*, II, p. 201.

40. Paul Schmidt, *Statist auf Diplomatischer Bühne, 1923-1945* (Bonn: Athenaum Verl., 1949), p. 320.

41. Hugh Gibson, ed., *The Ciano Diaries* (Garden City, New York: Doubleday & Co., 1946), p. 19.

42. Wolfers, *Britain and France*, pp. 102-103.

43. *DHFP*, I, Conversation of Colonna with Kánya. Budapest, January 18, 1936, Doc. No. 8; Alth to Kánya, Belgrade, January 19, 1936, No. 9, Doc. Nos. 11, 12, 13, 14.

44. *Ibid.*, Rudnay to Papen, Wien, Jan. 3, 1936, Doc. No. 1.

45. *Wilhelmstrasse*, Stieve to the German embassy in Budapest, Berlin, January 30, 1936, Doc. No. 49.

46. Kreissler, *Von der Revolution zur Annexion*, p. 261; DHFP I, Rudnay to kánya, Vienna, January 24, 1936, Doc. No. 15.

47. *Ibid.*, Doc. No. 9; Sztojay to Kánya, Berlin, Jan. 27, 1936, Doc. No. 18.

48. *DGFP*, C, V, Neurath to the German Missions in Western Europe, Berlin, March 5, 1936, Doc. No. 3.

49. *Ibid.*, Hassel to Neurath, Rome, March 7, 1936, Doc. No. 18.

50. *Ibid.*, Forster to Neurath, Paris, March 13, 1936, Doc. No. 96.

51. *Ibid.*, Paul-Boncour, *Entre Deux Guerres*, III. p. 34 contradicts this report stating that he also approved a military action.

52. *Ibid.*, p. 33. Gamelin, *Servir* II, pp. 203-206, wholeheartedly supports this view.

53. Paul-Boncour, *Entre Deux Guerres*, III. p. 40.

54. *DGFP*, Doc. No. 18.

55. Beloff, *Foreign Policy of Soviet Russia*, II, p. 50.

56. Paul-Boncour, *Entre Deux Guerres*, III. p. 36.

57. *DGFP*, C, V, Kordt to Neurath, Athens, March 13, 1966, Doc. No. 97.

58. *Ibid.*, Heeren to Neurath, Belgrade, March 14, 1936, Doc. No. 114.

59. *Ibid.*, Eisenlohr to Neurath, Prague, March 14, 1936, Doc. No. 120.

60. *Ibid.*, Pochhammer to Neurath, Bucharest, March 9, Doc. No. 39.

61. Paul-Boncour, *Entre Deux Guerres*, III. p. 110.

62. *DGFP.*, Doc. No. 39.

CHAPTER X

1. *Foreign Relations of the U.S. 1935*, Vol. II, Doc. No. 204.

2. Morini-Comby, *Les Échanges*, p. 94.

3. Hertz, *Economic Problem* p. 80.

4. Morini-Comby, *Les Échanges*, p. 62.

5. Stavrianos, *Balkans*, p. 737.

6. Oprea, *Nicolae Titulescu*, pp. 96-97.

7. *Ibid.*, p. 61.

8. *Ibid.*, pp. 78,98.

9. The neglect displayed by each consecutive Rumanian government toward the economic needs of Bessarabia makes such a consideration possible. "The Rumanians. . .did nothing to improve communications–on the ground that it was a frontier province, and an enemy invasion would be assisted by good roads." Seton-Watson, *Eastern Europe*, p. 337.

10. Though the Little Entente Pact was designed only against Hungary, such an interpretation or revision of the text could be imagined in 1935.

11. Rumania had decided to build the first strategic railroad line in Bukovina only on June 15, 1936. *DDF*, 2, II, Doc. No. 304.

12. Litvinov himself rejected the idea of mutual assistance because the Soviet Union did not need the help of Rumania against anybody. Oprea, *Nicolae Titulescu*, pp. 98-99.

13. Hertz, *Danubian States*, p. 80.

14. Oprea, *Nicolae Titulescu*, pp. 83, 117.

15. *DGFP*, Doc. Nos. 53, 131, 142, Fabricius to Neurath, Bucharest, June 19, 1936, Doc. No. 385.

16. For the secret military clause of the treaty see Gamelin, *Servir*, II. pp.469-71.

17. Quoted in Debicki, *Foreign Policy of Poland*, p. 94.

18. Hóry, *Behind the Scenes*, p. 21. Ruthenia was the northeastern part of Hungary awarded to Czechoslovakia in the Trianon Treaty.

19. Oprea, *Nicolae Titulescu*, pp. 98-99; *DGFP.*, C, V, Fabricius to Neurath, Bucharest, Sept. 6, 1936, Doc. No. 528.

20. Oprea, *Nicolae Titulescu*, p. 97.

21. *Ibid.*, pp. 123, 129.

22. *RAA*, Egger-Moelwalld to Schuschnigg, Paris, June 9, 1935, Doc. No. 171; July 4, 1935, Doc. No. 197.

23. *Ibid.*, July 10, 1935, Doc. No. 209.

24. Titulescu pursued this hope with actual attempts. "On Nov. 1, 1935, he tried (with the help of his famous brandy) to convince the British Treasury Officials to award compensation to Rumania for the hardship created by her participation in the sanctions." His appeals were rejected on this occasion and also later not only in England but in France too. Eden describes this episode with great malice. Eden, *Facing Dictators*, pp. 321-22.

25. The Soviet Union demanded the application of economic sanctions also against those states (Albania, Austria and Hungary) which voted against the resolution. League of Nations, *Official Journal, 1935,* Special Supplement, No. 145, p. 40.

26. The League of Nations lost international respect during the Manchurian crisis in September 1931 and its authority declined further with the German renunciation of the Versailles Treaty and her withdrawal from the League on October 14, 1933.

27. See his comments on Oct. 19, 1935, at the Sixth Meeting of the Committee of Eighteen. League of Nations, *Official Journal, 1935.* Special Supplement, No. 145, pp. 73-74.

28. He put the blame on France for the ineffectiveness of the sanctions and called Laval "a pig" in his conversation with Eden. Eden, *Facing Dictators,* p. 423.

29. Massigli (Political Director of the French Foreign Ministry, assigned to Geneva) reported on April 11, 1936, that "Titulescu displays a more and more vivid anxiety concerning his own position" in Bucharest. *DDF,* 2, II, Doc. No. 58.

30. *Ibid.,* deLacroix to Flandin, Prague, April 19, 1936, Doc. No. 96, Dampierre to Flandin, Belgrade, April 27, 1936, Doc. No. 120.

31. *Ibid.,* Massigli to Flandin, Geneva, May 14, 1936, Doc. No. 209.

32. Quoted in Oprea, *Nicolae Titulescu,* p. 136. The puzzling question, which is not answered by the documents is: if the King and government were so dissatisfied with Titulescu's policy, why didn't they replace him?

33. Part III, Section 3, Articles 42, 43, 44. See: G.A. Kertész, ed., *Documents in the Political History of the European Continent 1815-1939,* (Oxford: Clarendon Press, 1968), p. 354.

34. Kertész, *Documents,* pp. 465-66.

35. Gorce (de la), *French Army,* p. 260.

36. The old Schlieffen plan, with slight modification.

37. Gorce (de la), *French Army,* p. 260.

38. *DDF,* 2, II, de Lacroix to Flandin, Prague, April 16, 1936, Doc. No. 84.

39. *DGFP,* Doc. No. 39.

40. *DDF,* 2, II, Flandin to the diplomatic representatives of France in Prague and Vienna, Paris, April 9, 1936, Doc. No. 42. Also see Churchill, *Gathering Storm,* pp. 176-77.

41. *DGFP,* C, V, Memorandum by Bülow, Berlin, March 21, 1936, Doc. No. 174.

42. Based on Article 2 of the Franco-Soviet Pact. See: Beloff, *Foreign Policy of Soviet Russia,* II. p. 153 and Oprea, *Nicolae Titulescu,* p. 137.

43. *Ibid.*

44. *DGFP,* C, V, Pochhammer to Neurath, Bucharest, March 10, 1936, Doc. No. 53.

45. Quoted in Oprea, *Nicolae Titulescu,* p. 138.

46. *DGFP,* C, V, Memorandum by Fink, Berlin, March 16, 1936, Doc. No. 130.

47. Paul-Boncour, *Entre Deux Guerres,* III, p. 62.

48. *DDF,* 2, II, de Dampierre a Flandin, Belgrade, April 27, 1936, Doc. No. 120; Belgrade, May 6, 1936, Doc. No. 168.

49. *Ibid.,* d'Ormesson to Flandin, Bucharest, May 4, 1936, Doc. No. 158.

50. *Ibid.,* Doc. No. 159.

51. Stavrianos, *Balkans,* p. 697.

52. Andreas Hillgruber, *Hitler, König Carol und Marschall Antonescu,* (Wiesbaden: Franz Steimer Verlag, 1954), p. 1.

53. Iron Guard was the popular name of the "League of the Archangel Michael," a Fascist organization founded by C. Zelea Codreanu in 1927 after he broke away from the "League of National Christian Defense," an early anti-Semitic organization founded in 1923. For the history of the Iron Guard seen through the eyes of its founder; see: Corneliu Zelea Codreanu, *Eiserne Garde,* (Berlin: Brunnen Verlag, 1939).

54. Stavrianos, *Balkans,* pp. 697-98.

55. *Ibid.* Hillgruber, *Hitler, König Carol,* p. 13, states that Rumanian anti-Semitism was based on religious and not racist convictions. The end result was the same from the Jewish viewpoint.

56. Hannah Arendt, *The Origins of Totalitarianism,* (New York: The World Publishing Co., 1958), p. 29.

57. Nagy-Talavera, *Green Shirts,* p. 287. The corporatist ideas of Italian fascism were adjusted to the special Rumanian conditions by economist Mihail Manoilescu. Rogger-Weber, *European Right,* p. 546.

58. *Ibid.,* pp. 548-50.

59. The first news concerning these German subsidies was published in June and July 1936 and produced the exchange of several diplomatic notes between the German and Rumanian Foreign Ministries. See: *DGFP,* C, V, Doc. Nos. 397, 432, 440 492. Also see Hillgruber, *Hitler, König Carol,* p. 13.

60. Nagy-Talavera, *Green Shirts,* pp. 283-84. Since the National Peasant government had dissolved the Legion, the candidates in the 1931 election ran as members of "C.Z. Codreanu Group." The dissolution decree was pronounced illegal by the friendly courts. Rogger-Weber, *European Right,* pp. 544-45.

61. Codreanu, *Eiserne Garde,* p. 436.

62. Nagy-Talavera, *Green Shirts,* p. 291.

63. Oprea, *Nicolae Titulescu,* p. 101.

64. The Communist Party was outlawed in Rumania during the interwar period. It never had more than about one thousand members. Nagy-Talavera, *Green Shirts,* p. 351[n].

65. *DDF,* 2, II, de Lacroix to Flandin, Prague, April 1, 1936, Doc. No. 1., d' Ormesson to Flandin, Bucharest, April 2, 1936, Doc. No. 7; de Dampierre to Flandin, Belgrade, April 2, 1936, Doc. No. 8; de Montbas, Charge d'Affaires in Vienna to Flandin, Vienna, April 7, 1936, Doc. No. 34.

66. *Ibid.,* Doc. No. 1.

67. Ádám, *Hungary and the Little Entente,* p. 113. Rumania had already alerted three divisions in Transylvania in March, during the Rhineland crisis. *DGFP,* Doc. No. 53.

68. Quoted in Ádám, *Hungary and the Little Entente,* p. 113.

69. *DDF,* 2, II, de Lacroix to Flandin, Prague, April 7, 1936, Doc. No. 32.

70. Paul-Boncour, *Entre Deux Guerres,* p. 62.

71. *DDF,* 2, II, de Dampier reproduces in his report the full text of the official communique. Belgrade, May 8, 1936, Doc. No. 184.

72. *Ibid.,* Doc. No. 275.

73. *Ibid.,* Clauzel, ambassador of France in Bern to Delbos, Bern, June 6, 1936, Doc. No. 277. These troops were removed in 1935 according to the Laval-Mussolini agreement.

74. *Ibid.,* d'Ormesson to Delbos, Bucharest, June 12, 1936, Doc. No. 291; Doc. No. 304.

75. Quoted in Oprea, *Nicolae Titulescu,* pp. 138-39.

76. The full text of the "French Declaration on Foreign Policy" was printed in *The New York Times,* New York, June 24, 1936.

77. Lefranc, *Front Populaire*, p, 390.

78. Codreanu, *Eiserne Garde*, p. 440.

79. *DDF*, 2, II, Francois-Poncet to Delbos, Berlin, June 15, 1936, Doc. No. 300.

80. *Ibid.*, Nöel to Delbos, Warsaw, July 7, 1936, Doc. No. 404.

81. Hugh Thomas, *The Spanish Civil War*, (New York: Harper & Row, 1963) p. 211.

82. Macartney and Cremona, *Italy's Foreign Policy*, p. 184.

83. Eden, *Facing Dictators*, p. 461; Taylor, *Origins of the Second World War*, p. 120.

84. Churchill, *Gathering Storm*, pp. 191-92.

85. In France no one could avoid remembering the Hohenzollern candidacy affair. Baumont, *Les Origins*, p. 260.

86. German aid amounted to 43 million pounds, but after the war Franco was not willing to pay it back. Thomas, *Spanish Civil War*, p. 634.

87. *DDF*, Doc. No. 275; Macartney and Cremona, *Italy's Foreign Policy*, p. 331.

88. Thomas, *Spanish Civil War*, p. 215.

89. *DGFP*, C, V, Circular of the German Foreign Ministry, Berlin, May 19, 1936, Doc. No. 334; Thomas, *Spanish Civil War*, p. 216.

90. *Ibid.*, p. 214; Paul-Boncour, *Entre Deux Guerres*, p. 89; Lefranc, *Front Populaire*, p. 418.

91. Churchill, *Gathering Storm*, p. 193; Thomas, *Spanish Civil War*, p. 219.

92. Eden, *Facing Dictators*, p. 587.

93. *DHFP*, 1936-1945, I, Vörnle (temporary charge d'affaires of Hungary in Prague) to Kanya, July 15, 1936, Doc. No. 131. Alth to Kánya, Bled, July 21, 1936, Doc. No. 139; *DGFP*, C, V, Eisenlohr to Neurath, Prague, July 15, 1936, Doc. No. 450; Fabricius to Neurath, Sept. 6, 1936, Doc. No. 528.

94. Conversation of King Carol with Paul-Boncour, Paris, 1936. Quoted in Paul-Boncour, *Entre Deux Guerres*, pp. 60-62.

95. Oprea, *Nicolae Titulescu*, p. 99.

96. Germany was very anxious about the possibility that Rumania would grant permission for Soviet troops to cross her territory. *DGFP*, Doc. Nos, 392, 396, 397, 432.

97. *DDF*, 2, II, Ltd. Col. Delmas to Daladier, Bucharest, June 28, 1936, Doc. No. 365.

98. Negotiations between the French and Rumanian General Staffs were never held. Gamelin, *Servir*, II, p. 468.

99. Nagy-Talavera, *Green Shirts*, pp. 292-93; *DGFP*, Doc. Nos. 397, 492.

100. *Ibid.*, C, V, Pochhammer to Neurath, Bucharest, March 10, 1936, Doc. No. 53 reports the preparations made for the transportation of Soviet arm shipments.

101. *DHFP*, I, Hóry to Kánya, Warsaw, June 30, 1936, Doc. No. 113.

102. *Allianz*, Sztojay to Kánya, Berlin, Aug. 1, 1936, Doc. No. 13; Macartney and Palmer, *Eastern Europe*, p. 337, 2[n].

103. On Aug. 7, 1936, "Léon Blum proposed that the various powers should declare themselves neutral and follow a policy of non-intervention. Britain approved the suggestion as did Germany and Italy." Bonnet, *Quai D'Orsay*, p. 147.

104. Oprea, *Nicolae Titulescu*, p. 60.

105. During the Soviet-Rumanian negotiations, Litvinov "appeared to be better informed on conditions in Rumania than Mr. Titulescu himself." *Foreign Relations of the United States 1936*, Vol. I, Memorandum by the Chief of the Division of Near Eastern Affairs (Wallace Murray), Washington, Nov. 13, 1936. p. 370.

106. *DDF*, Doc. No. 58.

107. Codreanu revealed that some Rumanian politicians received large "loans" of public funds for their personal purposes. Titulescu led the list with 19 million lei. Codreanu, *Eiserne Garde*, p. 374.

108. Oprea, *Nicolae Titulescu*, p. 139.

109. *Ibid.*, p. 41.

110. Macartney and Palmer, *Eastern Europe*, p. 355, 4[n]; Oprea, *Nicolae Titulescu*, p. 140.

111. Paul-Boncour, *Entre Deux Guerres*, pp. 64-65.

112. *DHFP*, I, Alth to Kánya, Belgrade, Feb. 16, 1936, Doc. No. 40.

113. Lefranc, *Front Populaire*, p. 390.

114. Cot, *Triumph of Treason*, p. 49.

115. *Foreign Relations, 1936*, I, The Minister in Czechoslovakia, (F. Butler Wright) to the Secretary of State, Prague, Sept. 5, 1936, p. 340.

116. *DDF*, 2, II, Payart (Charge d'Affaires in Moscow) to Delbos, Moscow, Sept. 2, 1936, Doc. No. 228.

117. Hillgruber, *Hitler, König Carol*, p. 12.

118. *DGFP*, Doc. No. 528.

119. *DDF*, 2, II, Thierry to Delbos, Bucharest, Doc. No. 372.

120. Baumont, *Les Origines*, p. 385.

CHAPTER XI

1. On June 7, 1936, during a meeting at the Matignon Hotel, representatives of the labor unions (Confédération Générale du Travail) and the Popular Front government reached an agreement which ended the strikes and factory occupations and restored normalcy in France. The main points of the agreement were: right to collective bargaining; freedom of the labor unions; general wage raises; elected union delegates; no punishment for strikes and workers will respect the laws. See for more details: Lefranc, *Front Populaire*, p. 162.

2. *Ibid.*, p. 378.

3. *Ibid.*, Gamelin, *Servir*, II. P. 243 describes the army reforms necessary to keep the balance of force *vis à vis* the German army.

4. Chautemps was President of the Radical Socialist Group in the Chamber of Deputies, Minister of State in the first Blum cabinet, and then prime minister.

5. *DDF*, Doc. No. 275.

6. Bonnet, *Quai d'Orsay*, pp. 155-56.

7. Quoted in Lefranc, *Front Populaire*, p. 403; Bonnet, *Quai d'Orsay*, p. 156 Giacomo Matteotti, a Socialist Deputy who spoke out against Fascist terrorism during the Spring 1924 sessions of the Italian parliament, disappeared in June and later Mussolini accepted responsibility for his murder.

8. *DDF*, 2, II, Chambrun to Delbos, Rome, June 24, 1936, Doc. No. 346.

9. Gamelin, *Servir*, II. pp. 240-43.

10. *DDF*, 2, II, Minutes of the Meeting of the Defense Council, Paris, June 29, 1936, Doc. No. 369.

11. How he wanted to support the material needs of the Czechoslovak army with 16 heavy transport planes against the German Air Force possessing near 3,000 planes is a mystery.

12. Paul-Boncour, *Entre Deux Guerres*, p. 52.

13. *DDF*, 2, II, Chambrun to Delbos, Rome, October 7, 1936, Doc. No. 318.

14. *Ibid.*, October 9, 1936, Doc. No. 329.

15. *Ibid.*, October 9, 1936, Doc. No. 330; October 31, 1936, Doc. No. 426.

16. *Ibid.*, Daladier to Delbos, Paris, October 13, 1936, Doc. No. 343. Annex.

17. *Ibid.*, Laroche to Delbos, Brussels, October 14, 1936, Doc. No. 346.

18. *Ibid.*, Doc. No. 217.

19. The frontier had not been manned since January 1935.

20. *Ibid.*, Doc. No. 369, Gorce (de la), *French Army*, p. 266.

21. This information turned out to be the fabrication of the German Intelligence Service, but Benes did not know it. *Ibid.*, p. 265.

22. Eden, *Facing Dictators*, pp. 483-84; Bonnet, *Quai d'Orsay*, p. 156.

23. *DDF*, Doc. No. 275.

24. Cot, *Triumph of Treason*, pp. 22-23. Is it possible that the use of little *d* in democracy and the use of capital *C* in communism is a subconscious judgment of Cot?

25. Blum to Maurice Thorez on Aug. 25, 1936. Quoted in Lefranc, *Front Populaire*, p. 194.

26. Schuschnigg, *Im Kampf gegen Hitler,*, p. 185.

27. *DHFP*, I, Rudnay to Kánya, Vienna, June 17, 1936, Doc. No. 106.

28. *DDF*, 2, III, Chambrun to Delbos, Rome, July 21, 1936, Doc. No. 6.

29. *Ibid.*, Charles Roux to Delbos, Rome, July 29, 1936, Doc. No. 43.

30. *Ibid.*, Chambrun to Delbos, Rome, October 26, 1936, Doc. No. 410.

31. Quoted in Lefranc, *Front Populaire*, p. 405. Goering's visit was unproductive since Mussolini still hesitated to abandon Austria.

32. Macartney and Cremona, *Italy's Foreign and Colonial Policy*, p. 167.

33. John E. Dreifort, *Yvonne Delbos at the Quai D'Orsay*, (Lawrence, Kansas: University Press of Kansas, 1973), pp. 125-50.

34. France still believed that she could act from a position of power and made French aid to Poland conditional: Blum, Delbos, and Nöel agreed that this condition should be the dismissal of Beck. *Ibid.*, pp. 127-28.

35. *DDF*, 2, II, Nöel to Flandin, Warsaw, April 15, 1936, Doc. No. 75, Minutes of the meeting of the Chiefs of Staffs, Paris, April 30, 1936, Doc. No. 138.

36. *Ibid.*, Doc. Nos. 320, 326, 352. According to the report of General Pujo, "Germany's entire air force was prepared against France and Czechoslovakia, but not against Poland." *Ibid.*, Doc. No. 138.

37. *Ibid.*, Nöel to Delbos, Warsaw, November 16, 1936, Doc. No. 494.

38. *Ibid.*, de Lacroix to Delbos, Prague, November 2, 1936, Doc. No. 434; Thierry to Delbos, Bucharest, October 16, 1936, Doc. No. 362; de Dampierre to Delbos, Belgrade, November 10, 1936, Doc. No. 464.

39. Interview with General Flipo. Flipo remarked that the Czech General Staff did not believe in the sincerity of Schuschniggs' rapprochement attempts, nor Rydz Smygli's friendly gestures in the spring of 1936.

40. *DDF*, 2, III, de Lacroix to Delbos, Prague, August 26, 1936, Doc. No. 207; Delbos to de Lacroix, Paris, October, 22, 1936, Doc. No. 391.

41. *Ibid.*, de Lacroix to Delbos, Prague, November 14, 1936, Doc. No. 483.

42. *Ibid.*, Lt. Col. Salland to Daladier, Vienna, Aug. 14, 1936, Doc. No. 148.

43. *Ibid.*, de Montbas to Delbos, Vienna, Aug. 20, 1936, Doc. No. 178.

44. *Ibid.*, Lt. Col. Salland to Daladier, Vienna, Aug. 25, 1936, Doc. No. 202.

45. Bonnet, *Quai d'Orsay*, p. 159.

46. Gamelin, *Servir*, II. p. 312.

CHAPTER XII

1. Baumont, *Les Origins*, p. 234.

2. *Ibid.*, p. 237.

3. Eden, *Facing Dictators*, p. 675.

4. To what degree Eden neglected East-Central Europe can be sensed from his quoted book. He wrote *two hundred forty-four pages* describing the events in 1936-37 with *less than six pages* devoted to the affairs of East-Central Europe.

5. Vondracek, *Czechoslovakia*, pp. 77-78.

6. Seton-Watson, *Eastern Europe*, p. 121.

7. Wiskemann, *Czechs and Germans*, pp. 147-60.

8. Mikus, *La Slovaquie*, p. 10; Seton-Watson, *Eastern Europe*, p. 178.

9. Statistics for the following discussion are taken from: *Statistischen Staatsamt der Cechoslovakie, Statistisches Jahrbuch der Cechoslovakischen Republik*, 1936 (Prague: Orbis, 1936), pp. 124, 127, 135; *Ibid.*, 1937, p. 135.

10. Craig, *Diplomats*, p. 104.

11. Interview with General Flippo.

12. Interview with Schwarzenberg.

13. It is interesting to note that in the case of Yugoslavia and Rumania, Benes did not object to the authoritarian, royal dictatorships. It is very likely that in his later years Benes tried to pursue a more realistic than idealistic policy and was ready to compromise his political convictions.

14. Hodza, a member of the Agrarian Party, was from the small Lutheran minority of Slovakia. He advocated a reconciliation of all the states of the Danube valley in order to combine their forces against the German menace.

15. Mikus, *La Slovaquie*, pp. 89-93.

16. Interview with Schwarzenberg; Benes, *Munich*, p. 13.

17. Seton-Watson, *Eastern Europe*, p. 183. For the role of the Sudeten-Germans also see Vondracek, *Czechoslovakia*, pp. 407-11.

18. Out of 800,000 unemployed, 500,000 were Sudeten-Germans. *DGFP*, Doc. No. 284.

19. Benes, *Munich*, p. 11.

20. Seton-Watson, *Eastern Europe*, pp. 176-81 gives an excellent short description of the Czech-Slovak relations, pointing out the reasons for friction.

21. *DGFP*, D, II, Report on the conversation of the two parties' representatives, Feb. 8, 1938, Doc. No. 54; Eisenlohr to Ribbentrop, Prague, Feb. 17, 1938, Doc. No. 57.

22. Seton-Watson, *Eastern Europe*, p. 180.

23. They did not understand the fancy words of the politicians. In 1938, during a campaign speech, Volosin was interrupted when he asserted the needs of the Ruthenes for *auto*nomy. "We do not want *auto* all we need is more draught-animals." Written information of a close friend of Mr. Volosin's wife. Feb. 22, 1972.

24. Seton-Watson, *Eastern Europe*, p. 396.

25. Interview with Hennyey.

26. Ádám, *Hungary and the Little Entente*, pp. 199-202.

27. *Czechoslovak Statistics 1935*, p. 271. Tables XV. 7-8.

28. Interview with General Flippo.

29. *Ibid.* According to General Flippo, the airports were built up for the use of the Czech air force, but the Czech air force did not have such large planes.

30. In 1935 the French and Czechoslovak armies held their yearly maneuvers on the German borders, while the Soviet army held its own in Ukraine. Though they mutually sent observers to these manuevers, no positive cooperative plans were worked out. Vondracek, *Czechoslovakia*, pp. 414-15.

31. Interview with General Flippo.

32. Interview with Schwarzenberg.

33. *DHFP*, I, Rudnay to Kánya, Vienna, Feb. 1, 1936, Doc. No. 22; Hungarian chargé d'affair in London to Kánya, Feb. 10, 1936, Doc. No. 29.

34. Eichstadt, *Von Dollfuss zu Hitler*, p. 87.

35. *DHFP*, I, Alth to Kánya, Belgrade, Feb. 16, 1936, Doc. No. 40.

36. *DDF*, Doc. No. 96.

37. *Ibid.*, Doc. No. 84. Krfota replaced Hodza, who resigned from the post of foreign minister in February 1936 after the failure of his plan to organize a Central European block against German domination of their territories. Krofta was considered a puppet of Benes who, indeed, directed Czechoslovakian foreign policy, sometimes even bypassing his own foreign minister, *DGFP*, Doc. No. 284.

38. *DHFP*, I, Rudnay to Kànya, Vienna, Jan 15, 1936, Doc. No. 5; Doc. Nos. 9, 10, 11.

39. *Ibid.*, Doc. No. 9.

40. *Ibid.*, Doc. Nos. 10, 18.

41. *Ibid.*, Sztójay to Apor, Berlin, Feb. 1, 1936, Doc. No. 21; Sztójay to Kánya, Berlin, Feb. 21, 1936, Doc. No. 47.

42. *Ibid.*, Villáni to Kánya, Rome, Jan. 24, 1936, Doc. No. 17; Rome, Feb. 29, 1936, Doc. No. 55.

43. *Ibid.*, Negotiations of Berger-Valdenegg and Kánya, Vienna, Feb. 4, 1936 Doc. No. 23; Villami to Kánya, Rome, Feb. 5, 1936, Doc. No. 25.

44. *Ibid.* Conversation of Mackensen with Kánya, Budapest, Feb. 25, 1936, Doc. No. 49.

45. *Ibid.*, Doc. No. 13; Wettstein to Kánya, Prague, Feb. 13, 1936, Doc. No.34.

46. *Ibid.*, Ullein-Revitzky to Kánya, Zagreb, Feb. 19, 1936, Doc. No. 43; Bárdossy to Kánya, Bucharest, Feb. 21, 1936, Doc. No. 46.

47. *Ibid.*, Doc. No. 131; The official text of the agreement is incorporated in *Ibid.*, Doc. No. 143.

48. *Ibid.*, Masirevich to Kánya, London, July 14, 1936, Doc. No. 130. *DDF*, 2, II, François-Poncet to Delbos, Berlin, July 13, 1936, Doc. No. 437.

49. *DHFP,* Doc. No. 139.

50. *Ibid.*, I, Jungerth to Kánya, Moscow, July 11, 1936, Doc. No. 120; Hóry to Kánya, Warsaw, July 18, 1936, Doc. No. 137.

51. *DDF*, 2, II, de Lacroix to Delbos, Prague, July 14, 1936, Doc. No. 446; *DHFP*, I, Vormle to Kánya, Prague, July 29, 1936, Doc. No. 145.

52. *Ibid.*, Wodianer' letter to Baron Apor, Geneva, July 28, 1936, Doc. No. 144.

53. Interview with Hornbostel.

54. Interviews with Schwarzenberg and Hennyey.

55. After his return from Berchtesgaden, Ciano permitted the Hungarian ambassador to read the secret text of the Hitler-Ciano negotiations. The sentence which caused suspicion in Hungary was: "The two governments will handle the political and economic problems of the Danube basin in the spirit of friendly cooperation." *DHFP*, I, Villani to Kánya, Rome, Oct. 27, 1936, Doc. Nos. 164, 174.

56. Ádám, *Hungary and the Little Entente,* p. 134.

57. *Ibid.*

58. *DHFP*, II, Nagy (secretary of the Hungarian embassy in Bucharest) to Kánya, Bucharest, Sept. 22, 1936, Doc. No. 36. Stoyadinovich opposed it while Antonescu expressed his agreement.

59. *Ibid.*, Note of the Hungarian Foreign Ministry, Budapest, Jan. 1936, [No date given], Doc. No. 53.

60. *Ibid.*, Conversation of Milos Kobr (Czechoslovak ambassador to Budapest) with Kánya, Budapest, Jan. 19, 1937, Doc. No. 54.

61. *Ibid.*, Conversation of Vukcevic with Kánya, Budapest, Jan. 21, 1937, Doc. No. 56.

62. *Ibid.*, Conversation of Bossy withKánya, Budapest, Jan. 23, 1937, Doc. No. 57.

63. *Ibid.*, Conversation of Mackensen with Kánya, Budapest, Jan. 23, 1937, Doc. No. 59. The Federation circulated fake postage stamps portraying the picture of Basch, the Nazi leader of the Federation.

64. *Ibid.*, Sztojay to Kánya, Berlin, Feb. 6, 1937, Doc. No. 61.

65. *Ibid.*, Villani to Kánya, Rome, Feb. 2, 1937, Doc. No. 60.

66. *Ibid.*, I, Conversation of Lt. Gen. Alberto Pariani, Chief of Staff of the Italian army with Lt. Col. László Szabó, military attache of Hungary, Rome, Nov. 13, 1936, Doc. No. 177.

67. *Ibid.*, Doc. No. 60; Ádám, *Hungary and the Little Entente*, p. 145.

68. *DHFP*, II, Villani to Kánya, Rome, March 30, 1937, Doc. No. 69.

69. *Ibid.*, Wettstein to Kánya, Prague, April 8, 1937, Doc. No. 71.

70. *Ibid.*, Sztójay to Kánya, Berlin, April 27, 1937, Doc. No. 74.

71. *Ibid.*, László Velics's (Leader of the Hungarian delegation to the League of Nations) conversation with Eden, Geneva, May 27, 1937, Doc. No. 78.

72. In May 1937, the Italian royal couple visited Hungary. *At the request of the Italian ambassador* in Vienna, the Hungarian government included in the list of celebrities an Austrian army-officer delegation. *Wilhelmstrasse*, Werkmeister to Neurath, Budapest, May 25, 1937, Doc. No. 90.

73. *DHFP*, I, Khuen-Héderváry to Kánya, Paris, May 26, 1937, Doc. No. 259.

74. *DDF*, Doc. No. 84.

75. *Ibid.*, Doc. No. 75.

76. *DHFP*,I, Wettstein to Kánya, Prague, April 4, 1936, Doc. No. 81.

77. Krofta had expressed his desire to cooperate more closely with Italy already in the middle of February. *Ibid.*, Doc. No. 34. The rapprochement with Austria began with Schuschnigg's visit in Prague in January 1936.

78. Eden, *Facing Dictators*, pp. 191-94.; Interview with Schwarzenberg.

79. *DHFP*, I, Wettstein to Kánya, Prague, April 27, 1936, Doc. No. 93.

80. Quoted in Wolfers, *Britain and France*, pp. 213-14.

81. *DHFP*, Doc. No. 34.

82. Interview with Schwarzenberg.

83. *DDF*, Doc. No. 84.

84. *DHFP*, I, Neustadter-Stürmer (Austrian ambassador in Budapest) to Kánya Budapest, April 2, 1937, Doc. No. 227.

85. Seton-Watson, *Eastern Europe*, p. 391.

86. *DGFP*, Doc. No. 3.

87. *Ibid.*, C, V, Eisenlohr to Neurath, Prague, March 26, 1936, Doc. No. 220.

88. Benes wanted to negotiate the non-aggression pact with Germany as part of a broader security pact within the League of Nations. Germany rejected this proposal. *DGFP*, Doc. No. 258.

89. Seton-Watson, *Eastern Europe*, p. 392.; *DHFP*, II, Wettstein to Kánya, Prague, May 7, 1936, Doc. No. 20.

90. *Ibid.*, Feb. 12, 1937, Doc. No. 63.

91. The Activists were the German Christian Socialist, German Social Democrats, and German Agrarians.

92. For the full text of the demands of Activists see Benes, *Munich*, Documents, p. 245, Doc. No. 1.

93. *DGFP*, D, II, Conversation of Hodza with Konrad Heinlein, Prague, Sept. 16, 1937, Doc. No. 1.

94. *Ibid.*, Doc. No. 8.

95. *Ibid.*, Doc. No. 10.

96. Ádám, *Hungary and the Little Entente*, p. 173.

97. *DGFP*, D, II, Minutes of Mackensen, Berlin, Nov. 3, 1937, Doc. No. 11.

98. *Ibid.,* Eisenlohr to Neurath, Prague, Dec. 17, 1937, Doc. No. 31; Doc. Nos. 35, 36, 40, 41, 42, 43, 51, 52, 55.

99. *Ibid.,* Doc. No. 56.

100. *Ibid.,* Eisenlohr to Ribbentrop, Prague, Feb. 17, 1938, Doc. No. 57; Report by a Deputy (Kunzel) of the Sudeten-German Party, Feb. 19, 1938, Doc. No. 60; Keitel to Ribbentrop, Berlin, March 7, 1938, Doc. No. 66.

101. *Ibid.,* Eisenlohr to Ribbentrop, Prague, March 12, 1938, Doc. No. 72.

102. *DHFP,* II, Doc. Nos. 85, 85a; Bárdossy to Kánya, Bucharest, Sept. 2, 1937, Doc. No. 87.

103. *Ibid.,* Conversation of Kánya with Vansittart, Geneve, Sept. 16, 1937, Doc. No. 88; Conversation of Ivan Subotich, leader of the Yugoslavian delegation at the League of Nations, with Kánya, Geneve, Sept. 18, 1937, Doc. No. 89.

104. Bonnet, *Quai d'Orsay,* p. 158; *DHFP,* Doc. No. 51.

105. Lefranc, *Front Populaire,* p. 412.

106. *DHFP,* I, Szabó (Hungarian consul in Müchen) to Kánya, Munich, April 23, 1937, Doc. No. 237.

107. Wheeler-Bennett, *Nemesis of Power,* pp. 360-82; Bullock, *Hitler,* pp. 411-20.

108. *DGFP,* D, II, Woerman (chargé d'affaires in Britain) to Neurath, London, Nov. 9, 1937, Doc. No. 14.

109. Bonnet, *Quai d'Orsay,* p. 160.

110. Schuschnigg, *Im Kampf gegen Hitler,* p. 285; *DGFP,* D, II, Forster (chargé d'affaires in France) to Neurath, Paris, Nov. 16, 1937, Doc. No. 21.

111. *Lipski papers,* Conversations of Beck and Goering, Warsaw, Feb. 23, 1938, pp. 345-51; *DHFP,* I, Hory to Kánya, Warsaw, Jan 19, 1938, Doc. No. 342.

112. *Wilhelmstrasse,* Circular of Neurath, Berlin, Nov. 26, 1937, Doc. No. 105; *DGFP,* D, II, Hassel to Neurath, Rome, Dec. 20, 1937, Doc. No. 37.

113. Hillgruber, *Hitler, König Carol,* p. 17.

114. *DGFP,* D, II, Eisenlohr to Ribentroop, Prague, March 12, 1938, Doc. No. 70.

115. *DHFP,* I, Vienna, March 13, 1938, Doc. No. 414.

116. Gamelin, *Servir,* II. p. 316; Bonnet, *Quai d'Orsay,* p. 161.

117. Hitler was not sure about Mussolini's intentions and his excited words after receiving the news about Italy's neutral position reveal that he gambled on the neutrality of Italy. Bullock, *Hitler,* pp. 431-32; Speer, *Au Coeur du Troisième Reich,* pp. 156-57.

118. Gamelin, *Servir,* II, p. 345; Gorce (de la), *French Army,* pp. 260-69.

119. The strength of the Czech army differs greatly according to the sources. The number of divisions shown here was given by General Faucher, Head of the French Military Mission, who testified that Czechoslovakia had 17 divisions (doubled in case of war). Six in Bohemia, four in Moravia, seven in Slovakia. Quoted in Henri Nogueres, *Münich* (New York: McGraw-Hill, 1965), p. 37.

120. Kennedy, *German Campaign,* pp. 51-52.

121. *Ibid.,* p. 23; Gorce (de la), *French Army,* p. 260.

122. Klaus Hildebrand, *Deutsche Aussenpolitik 1933-1945,* (Stuttgart: Kohlhamer, 1971), p. 66.

123. Gamelin, *Servir*, II. pp. 315, 322-28.

124. Wheeler-Bennett, *Nemesis of Power*, p. 351.

125. The Austrian army was reorganized and contributed 6 divisions to the *Wehrmacht*. Kennedy, *German Campaign*, p. 24.

CHAPTER XIII

1. France was the fourth best trading partner of Czechoslovakia, but Czechoslovakia was only the twentieth partner of France. Morini-Comby, *Les Échanges*, p. 99.

2. Churchill, *Gathering Storm*, p. 253.

3. Quoted in Benes, *Munich*, p. 36.

4. Bonnet, *Quai d'Orsay*, p. 36.

5. Benes, *Munich*, p. 169.

6. *DGFP*, Doc. No. 96.

7. Benes, *Munich*, p. 39.

8. *DHFP*, II, March 1938, Doc. Nos. 135, 137, 139, 140, 141.

9. Benes, *Munich*, pp. 37-38.

10. *DGFP*, D, II, Report of Fabricius, Berlin, April 21, 1938, Doc. No. 131. *DHFP*, II, Bárdossy to Kánya, Bucharest, April 16, 1938, Doc. No. 155.

11. Churchill, *Gathering Storm*, p. 266.

12. *DGFP*, Doc. No. 120.

13. Gamelin, *Servir*, p. 324.

14. *DGFP*, D, II, Conversation of Hitler with Keitel, Berlin, April 22, 1938, Doc. No. 133.

15. Schlabrendorff, *Secret War*, pp. 93-96.

16. Britain was defenseless against air attacks. B.H. Liddel-Hart, *The Liddel Hart Memories*, (2 vols.: New York: G.P. Putnam's Sons, 1966), II, pp. 152-56.

17. For the full text of the demands see International Conciliation, *Documents for the Year 1938*, p. 401.

18. *DGFP*, D, II, Memorandum by Weizsacher, Berlin, May 12, 1938, Doc. No. 155.

19. *Ibid.*, Eisenlohr to Ribbentrop, Prague, May 12, 1938, Doc. No. 157.

20. Bonnet, *Quai d'Orsay*, p. 171.

21. *Ibid.*, pp. 171, 173.

22. International Conciliation, *Documents for the Year 1938*, pp. 403-06.

23. Benes, *Munich*, p. 85.

24. *DGFP*, Doc. Nos. 133, 175.

25. *Ibid.*, Kordt to Ribbentrop, London, July 25, 1938, Doc. No. 314.

26. *Ibid.*, Conference on "Operation Green," Berghof, Sept. 4, 1938, Doc. No. 424.

27. For the text of the speech see International Conciliation, *Documents for the Year 1938*, pp. 411-16.

BIBLIOGRAPHY
Documents

Adám, Magda; Juhász, Gyula; and Kerekes, Lajos; eds. *Allianz Hitler-Horthy-Mussolini, Documents zur Ungarischen Aussenpolitik, 1933-1944.* ("Hitler-Horthy-Mussolini Alliance. Documents of Hungarian Foreign Policy, 1933-1944.") Budapest: Akadémia Publisher, 1966. (Referred to in footnotes as *Allianz*).

Board of Governors of the Federal Reserve System. *Banking and Monetary Statistics.* Washington, D.C.: Federal Reserve System, 1943.

Carnegie Endowment for International Peace. *International Conciliations, Documents for the Year.* New York: Publ. and Editorial Offices, 1936-1938.

Chief Bureau of Statistics of the Republic of Poland. *Concise Statistical Year-Book of Poland. 1935, 1936, 1937.* 3 vols. Warsaw: Chief Bureau of Statistics, 1935, 1937.

Department of State. *Foreign Relations of the United States, 1934, 1935.* Washington, D.C.: U.S. Government Printing Office, 1951.

Her Majesty's Stationery Office. *Documents on British Foreign Policy, 1919-1939.* Second Series. Oxford: Her Majesty's Stationery Office; 1958. (Referred to in footnotes as *DBFP*).

Hetés, Tibor and Morvai, Tamás eds. *Csak Szolgálati Használatra. Iratok a Horthy Hadsereg Történetéhez, 1919-1938.* ("Strictly Confidential. Documents for the History of the Horthy Army, 1919-1938.") Budapest: Zrinyi Military Books 1968.

Jedrzejewicz, Waclav, ed. *Diplomat in Berlin, 1933-1939.* New York: Columbia University Press, 1968. (Referred to in footnotes as *Lipski Papers).*

Journal Officiel de la République Française. Chambre des Députés. *Debats Parlementaires, 1934.* Paris: 1919-1939.

League of Nations. *Official Journal.* Geneva: 1934-1936.

League of Nations. *Revue de la Situation Economique Mondiale, 1934-1935.* Geneva: 1935.

League of Nations. *Treaty Series 1926-1927.* Vol. 54. Geneva: 1928.

Magyar Országos Levéltár. *Horthy Miklós Titkos l ratai.* ("The Secret Documents of Nicholas Horthy.") Budapest: Kossuth Publ., 1965.

Magyar Tudományos Akadémia Történettudományi Intézete. *Diplomáciai Iratok Magyarország Külpolitikájához, 1936-1945.* ("Diplomatic Documents on the Foreign Policy of Hungary, 1936-1945.") 4 vols. Budapest: Akadémia ed., 1962. (Referred to in footnotes as *DHFP*).

Magyar Tudományos Akadémia Történettudományi Intézete. *A Wilhelmstrasse és Magyarország. Német Diplomácial Iratok, 1933-1944.* ("The Wilhelmstreet and Hungary. German Diplomatic Documents Concerning Hungary, 1933-1944.") Budapest: Kossuth Publ., 1968. (Referred to in footnotes as Wilhelmstrasse).

Ministère des Affaires Étrangères. *Documents Relatifs aux Origines de la Guerre 1939-1945. Documents Diplomatic Français 1932-1939.* Series I. Volumes I and II. Paris: Imprimerie Nationale, 1964. (Referred to in footnotes as *DDF*)

Morini-Comby, Jean. *Les Échanges Commerciaux Entre la France et les États Successeurs de l'Empire Austro-Hongrois.* Paris: Centre d'Études de Politique Étrangère, 1936.

Publications of the Permanent Court of International Justice. *Treatment of Polish Nationals and Other Persons of Polish Origin or Speech at Danzig.* Series A/B. Volume Nos. 9 and 10 in 1925; No. 2 in 1926; No. 14 in 1928; No. 56 in 1932. Lyden: A.W. Sijthoff's Publ. Co., 1932.

Reports of Austrian Ambassador Lothar Egger-Moellwald from Paris during the years 1934-1936. Typewritten unpublished documents. (Referred to in footnotes as *RAA*).

Requète de Gouvernement Yugoslave Relative aux Résponsabilitées Encourés par les Autorites Hongroises dans l'Actions Terroriste Dirigée Contre la Yugoslavie. Belgrade: Yugoslava Govt. ed., 1935.

Statistischen Staatsamt der Čechoslovakischen Republic. *Statistisches Jahrbuch der Čechoslovakischen Republic.* Prague: Orbis, 1935-1937.

United States Department of State. *Documents on German Foreign Policy, 1918-1945.* Series C, D. Washington, D.C.: U.S. Government Printing Office, 1957. (Referred to in footnotes as *DGFP*)

United States Department of State. *Foreign Relations of the United States.* Washington: U.S. Government Printing Office, 1935-1938.

Interviews

Auer, Dr. Pál. Attorney of the French Embassy in Budapest, 1926-1930; President of the Committee to Promote Economic Cooperation of the Danubian States, 1932-1933. Interviewed in Paris, June 25, 1971.

Flipo, General Julien. Chief of Staff of the French Military Mission in Prague, 1931-1938. Interviewed in Paris, June 15, 1971.

Hennyey, General Gustave. Hungarian Military Attache in Athens and Belgrade, 1933-1934; Chief of the Intelligence Department of the Hungarian General Staff, 1934-1935. Interviewed in Munich, July 17, 1969.

Hornbostel, Dr. Theodore. Political Secretary-General of the Austrian Ministry of Foreign Affairs, 1933-1938. Interviewed in Vienna, July 12, 1971.

Radvánsky, Baron Anton. First Secretary of Hungarian Foreign Minister Kálmán Kánya, 1933-1934. Interviewed in Paris, July 15, 1971.

Schwarzenberg, Prince Dr. Francis. Official in the Czech Diplomatic Service, 1936-1939; Diplomatic Representative of Czechoslovakia, 1945-1948. Interviewed in Chicago, May 10, 1971.

Memoirs, Diaries, and Eyewitness Reports

Auer, Dr. Pál. *Fél Évszázad.* ("Half a Century.") Washington, D.C.: Occidental Press, 1971.

Beck, Colonel Jozef. *Final Report.* New York: Robert Speller & Sons, 1957.

Benes, Edouard. *Munich.* Paris: Stock, 1969.

Bonnet, Georges. *Quai d'Orsay.* New York: Time Press, 1965.

Churchill, W.S. *The Gathering Storm.* New York: Bantam Books, 1961.

Codreanu, Corneliu Zelea. *Eiserne Garde.* Berlin. Brunnen. Verlag, 1939.

Cot, Pierre. *Triumph of Treason.* Chicago: Ziff-Davis, 1944.

Eckhardt, Dr. Tibor. *Regicide at Marseilles.* New York: The American-Hungarian Library and Historical Society, 1964.

Eden, Sir Anthony. *Facing the Dictators,* 1923-1938. Boston: Houghton Mifflin Co., 1962.

Gamelin, General Maurice. *Servir.* 2 vols. Paris: Plon, 1946.

Gibson, Hugh, ed. *The Ciano Diaries.* Garden City, N.Y.: Doubleday & Co., 1946.

Horthy, Admiral Nicholas. *Memoirs.* New York: Robert Speller and Sons, 1957.

Milicevic, von Vladeta. *Der Königsmord von Marseille.* Bad Godesberg: Hochwacht Verlag, 1959.

Paul-Boncour, I. *Entre Deux Guerres.* 3 vols. Paris: Librarie Plon, 1946.

Schmidt, Paul. *Statist auf Diplomatischer Bühne, 1923-1945.* Bonn: Atheneum Verl., 1949.

Schuschnigg, Kurt von. *Austrian Requiem.* London: Victor Gollanz Ltd., 1947.

Shirer, William L. *The Collapse of the Third Republic.* New York: Simon & Schuster, 1969.

Speer, Albert. *Au Coeur de Troisième Reich.* Paris: Fayard, 1971.

Secondary Sources

General

Albrecht-Carrié, René. *A Diplomatic History of Europe Since the Congress of Vienna.* New York: Harper & Row, 1958.

Arendt, Hannah. *The Origins of Totalitarianism.* New York: The World Publishing Co., 1958.

Basch, A. *The Danube Basin in the German Economic Sphere.* New York: Columbia University Press, 1943.

Baumont, Maurice. *La Faillite de la Paix.* Peoples et Civilisations Series, 2 vols. Paris: Presses Universitaires de France, 1967.

Baumont, Maurice. *Les Origins de la Deuxième Guerre Mondiale.* Paris: Payot, 1969.

Bailey, Thomas A. *The American Pageant.* 4th ed. Lexington, Mass.: D.C. Heath Co., 1971.

Beloff, Max. *The Foreign Policy of Soviet Russia.* 2 vols. London: Oxford University Press, 1968.

Bonnefous, Edouard. *Histoire Politique de la Troisième République.* 6 vols. Paris: Presses Universitaires de France, 1962.

Bullock, Alan. *Hitler, A Study in Tyranny.* Rev. Ed. New York: Harper & Row, 1962.

The Cambridge Economic History of Europe. 6 vols. Cambridge, England: Cambridge University Press, 1965.

Carr, E.H. *International Relations Between the Two World Wars, 1919-1939.* New York: Harper & Row, 1947.

Chastenet, Jacques. *Jours Sanglants.* Paris: Hachette, 1964.

Clausewitz, Carl (von). *On War.* Baltimore: Penguin Book Ltd., 1968.

Clough, Shepard B.; Moodie, Thomas; and Moodie, Carol; eds. *Economic History of Europe; Twentieth Century.* New York: Harper & Row, 1968.

Cole, Hubert. *Laval, a Biography.* New York: G.P. Putnam's Sons, 1963.

Craig, Gordon A., ed. *The Diplomats.* Princeton, N.J.: Princeton University Press, 1953.

Csonka, Emil. *Habsburg Otto.* Munich: Uj Europa Ed., 1972.

Donnelly, Desmond. *Struggle for the World. The Cold War, 1917-1965.* New York: St. Martin's Press, 1965.

Dreifort, John E. *Yvon Delbos at the Quai d'Orsay.* Lawrence, Kansas: University Press of Kansas, 1973.

Flandin, Pierre E. *Politique Française, 1919-1940.* Paris: Edition Nouvelles, 1947.

Francois-Poncet, Andre. *The Fateful Years.* New York: Howard Fertig, 1972. (Reprint of the 1949 edition).

Gibbs, Phillip. *European Journey.* Garden City, New York: Doubleday, Doran & Co., 1934.

Gorce, Paul-Marie de la. *The French Army.* New York: George Braziller, 1963.

Haag, Elisabeth. *Die Französische Aussenhandels Politik, 1931-1938.* Lachen: A. Kesler Ausl., 1942.

Hertz, Frederick. *The Economic Problem of the Danubian States.* New York: Howard Fertig, 1970.

Hildebrand, Klaus. *Deutsche Aussenpolitik, 1933-1945.* Stuttgart: W. W. Kohlhammer Veil, 1971.

Hughes, H. Stuart. *Contemporary Europe, a History.* Englewood, New Jersey: Prentice-Hall, 1961.

Kertész, G.A., ed. *Documents in the Political History of the European Continent, 1815-1939.* Oxford: Clarendon Press, 1968.

Laurens, D. Franklin. *France and the Italo-Ethiopian Crisis, 1935-1936.* The Hague: Mouton & Co., 1967.

Lefranc, Georges. *Histore du Front Populaire.* Paris: Payot, 1965.

Liddel-Hart, B.H. *The Liddel-Hart Memoires.* 2 vols. New York: G.P. Purnam's Sons, 1966.

Macartney, C.A. *National States and National Minorities.* Oxford: Oxford University Press, 1934.

Macartney, C.A. *Problems of the Danube Basin.* Cambridge, England: Cambridge University Press, 1942.

Macartney, C.A., and Palmer, A.W. *Independent Eastern Europe.* London: Macmillan, 1962.

Macartney, Maxwell H.H., and Cremona, Paul. *Italy's Foreign and Colonial Policy, 1914-1937.* New York: Howard Fertig, 1972.

Mader, Julius. *Hitlers Spionage Generale Sagen Aus.* Berlin: Verlag der Nation, 1971.

Montmorency, Ale. (de). *The Enigma of Admiral Darlan.* New York: E.P. Dutton & Co., 1943.

Noguères, Henri. *Munich.* New York: McGraw Hill, 1965.

Ormos, Mária. *Franciaország és a Keleti Biztonság, 1931-1936.* ("France and the Eastern Security.") Budapest: Akadémia Kiadó, 1969.

Osborne, R.H. *East-Central Europe.* New York: Frederick A. Praeger, 1967.

Pauley, Bruce F. *The Habsburg Legacy, 1867-1939.* New York: Holt, Rinehart and Winston, 1972.

Rogger, Hans, and Weber, Eugen, eds. *The European Right, a Historical Profile.* Berkeley: University of California Press, 1966.

Schlabrendorff, Fabian (von). *The Secret War Against Hitler.* New York: Pitman Publ. Corp., 1965.

Schuman, L. Frederick. *Europe on the Eve: The Crisis of Diplomacy, 1933-1939.* New York: Alfred A. Knopf, 1942.

Scott, William Evans. *Aliance Against Hitler.* Durham, N.C.: Duke University Press, 1962.

Seton-Watson, Hugh, *Eastern Europe Between the Wars, 1918-1941.* Harper Torchbooks. New York: Harper and Row, 1967.

Shirer, William L. *The Rise and Fall of the Third Reich.* New York: Simon and Schuster, 1960.

Societé des anciens élèves et élèves de l'école libre de sciences politiques. *Conference du Colonel Fábry, 20 Février 1933 in Algir.* Paris: 1933.

Stavrianos, L.S. *The Balkans Since 1453.* New York: Holt, Rinehard & Winston, 1966.

Taylor, A. J. P. *A History of the First World War.* New York: Berkeley Publ. Corp., 1966.

Taylor, A. J. P. *The Origins of the Second World War.* Greenwich: Fawcet, 1966.

Thomas, Hugh. *The Spanish Civil War.* New York: Harper & Row, 1963.

Tint, Herbert. *The Decline of French Patriotism.* London: Weidenfeld and Nicolson, 1964.

Wandycz, Piotr S. *France and Her Eastern Allies, 1919-1925.* Minneapolis: University of Minnesota Press, 1962.

Warner, Geoffrey. *Pierre Laval and the Eclipse of France.* New York: MacMillan, 1968.

Weinberg, Gerhard L. *The Foreign Policy of Hitler's Germany.* Chicago: University of Chicago Press, 1970.

Werth, Alexander. *The Twilight of France, 1933-1940.* New York: Howard Fertig, 1966. (Reprint of the 1942 Harper-Row edition).

Wheeler-Benet, J.W. *The Nemesis of Power.* London: Macmillan & Co., 1964.

Wolfers, Arnold, *Britain and France Between Two Wars.* New York: Norton & Co. 1966.

Wolff, Robert Lee. *The Balkans in Our Time.* Cambridge, Mass.: Harvard University, 1956.

Zara, Philippe de, ed. *Mussolini Contre Hitler.* Paris: Fernand Sorlot, 1938.

Austria

Brook-Shepherd, Gordon. *The Anschluss.* Philadelphia: F.B. Lippincot, 1963.

Buttinger, Joseph. *Am Beispiel Österreichs.* Cologne: Verlag für Politik und Wirtshaft, 1953.

Eichstadt, Ulrich. *Von Dollfuss zu Hitler.* Wiesbaden: Franz Steiner Verlag, 1955.

Gedye, G.E.R. *Betrayal in Central Europe.* New York: Harper, 1939.

Gregory, J.D. *Dollfuss and His Times.* London: Hutchinson & Co., 1935.

Gullich, Charles A. *Austria from Habsburg to Hitler.* Berkeley: University of California Press, 1948.

Haas, Dr. Ernst. *Die Aussenhandelspolitik der Ehemaligen Republik Österreich Während der Welt Wirtschaftkrise bis zum Anschluss.* Würzburg: Konrad Tiltsch Verlag, 1939.

Kreiszler, Felix. *Von der Revolution zur Annexion.* Vienna Europa Verlag, 1970.

Schuschnigg, Kurt von. *In Kampf Gegen Hitler.* Vienna: Verlag Fritz Molden,1969.

Stahremberg, E.R. *Between Hitler and Mussolini.* London. Hidder & Stoughton Ltd., London, 1942.

Czechoslovakia

Benes, Eduard. *Democracy Today and Tomorrow.* New York: Macmillan, 1939.

Hoch, E. *The Political Parties in Czechoslovakia.* Prague: Orbis Publ. Co., 1936.

Krofta, K. *Les nouveaux états dans l'Europe centrale.* Prague: Orbis Publ. Co., 1930.

Mikus, Joseph A. *La Slovaquie dans le drame de l'Europe.* Paris: Les Iles D'Or., 1955.

Namier, L. B. *Europe in Decay.* London: Macmillan & Co., 1950.

Strauss, E. *Tschechoslovakische Aussenpolitik.* Prague: Orbis Publ. Co., 1936.

Thompson, S. Harrison. *Czechoslovakia in European History.* Princeton, N.J.: Princeton University Press, 1953.

Vondracek, J. Felix. *The Foreign Policy of Czechoslovakia, 1918-1935.* New York: Columbia University Press, 1937.

Wiskeman, Elisabeth. *Czechs & Germans.* London: Oxford University Press, 1938.

Hungary

Ádám, Magda. *Magyarország és a Kisantant a Harmincas Években.* ("Hungary and the Little Entente in the Thirties.") Budapest: Akadémia Kiadó, 1968.

Dálnoki-Veress, Lajos. *Magyarország Honvédelme a II Vilaghábor& Előtt és Alatt.* ("Hungary's Defense Organization Before and During World War II") Munich: Danubia Druckerei, 1972.

Deák, Francis. *Hungary at the Paris Peace Conference.* New York: Howard Fertig, 1972. (Reprint of 1942 edition.)

Dreisziger, A. F. Nándor. *Hungary's Way to World War II.* Toronto: Hungarian Helicon Society, 1963.

Hóry, András. *A Kulisszák Mögött.* ("Behind the Scenes.") Vienna: Author's Ed., 1965.

Jászi, Oscar. *Revolution and Counter-Revolution in Hungary.* New York: Howard Fertig, 1969.

Kertész, Stephen D. *Diplomacy in a Whirlpool.* Notre Dame, Indiana: Notre Dame University Press, 1953.

Kónya, Sándor. *Gömbös Kisérlete totális fasiszta diktatura megteremtésére.* ("Gömbös' Attempt to Create a Totalitarian Fascist Dictatorship.") Budapest: Akadémia Publ., 1968.

Kónzponti Statisztikai Hivatal. *Magyar Statisztikai Zsebkönyv 1960.* ("Hungarian Statistical Almanac 1960.") Budapest: Economic and Law Publications, 1960.

Macartney, C. A. *Hungary, a Short History.* Chicago: Aldine Publ. Co., 1962.

Macartney, C. A. *October Fifteenth.* 2 vols. Edinburgh: University Press, 1961.

Montgomery, John F. *Hungary, the Unwilling Satellite.* New York: Devin Adair Co., 1947.

Ránki, György. *Emlékiratok és valóság Magyarország második vilagháborús szerepéről.* ("Memoirs and Reality Concerning the Role of Hungary in World War II.") Budapest: Kossuth Publ., 1964.

Szekfű, Gyula. *Három nemzedék és ami utána Következik.* ("Three Generations and After.") Budapest: Királyi Magyar Egyetemi Nyomda, 1934.

Windisch-Graetz, Ludwig. *Helden und Halunken.* 2nd. Rev. Ed. Vienna: Wilhelm Frick Verlag, 1967.

Poland

Cienciala, Anna M. *Poland and the Western Powers, 1938-1939.* London: Routledge & Kegan Paul, 1968.

Debicki, Roman. *Foreign Policy of Poland, 1919-1939.* New York: Frederick A. Praeger, 1962.

Dziewanovski, M. K. *Joseph Pilsudski, A European Federalist, 1918-1922.* Stanford: Hoover Institution, 1969.

Gorecki, Dr. Roman. *Poland and Her Economic Development.* London: George Allen & Unvin Ltd., 1935.

Kennedy, Robert M. *The German Campaign in Poland.* Washington, D.C. Department of the Army, 1956.

Konovalov, S. ed., *Russo-Polish Relations.* Princeton, N.J.: Princeton University Press, 1945.

Lypacewicz, Waclaw. *Polish-Czech Relations.* Warsaw: Polish Institute for Collaboration with Foreign Countries, 1936.

Roos, Hans. *A History of Modern Poland.* London: Eyre & Spottiswoode, 1966.

Roos, Hans. *Polen und Europa.* Tübinger Studien zur Geschichte und Politik, No. 7. Tübingen: J. C. B. Mohr, 1957.

Rumania

Fischer-Galati, Stephen, ed. *Romania.* New York: Frederick A. Praeger, 1957.

Gafencu, Grigore. *Last Days of Europe: A Diplomatic Journey in 1939.* New Haven: Yale University Press, 1948.

Hillgruber, Andreas. *Hitler, König Carol und Marschall Antonescu: Die Deutsch-Rumänische Beziehungen 1938-1944.* Wiesbaden: Franz Steiner Vetlag, 1954.

Kerner, R. J., and Howard, H. N. *The Balkan Conferences and the Balkan Entente, 1930-1935.* Berkeley: University of California Press, 1936.

Matley, Ian. *Romania: A Profile.* New York: Frederick A. Praeger, 1970.

Nagy-Talavera, Nicholas. *The Green Shirts and the Others.* Stanford: Hoover Institution, 1970.

Oprea, I. M. "Nicolae Titulescu's Diplomatic Activity." *Bibliotheca Historica Romaniae:* Vol. 22. Bucharest: Publishing House of the Academy of the Socialist Republic of Rumania, 1968.

Roberts, H. L. *Rumania: Political Problems of an Agrarian State.* New Haven: Yale University Press, 1951.

Roucek, J. S. *Contemporary Rumania and Her Problems.* Palo Alto: Stanford University Press, 1932.

Yugoslavia

Christowe, Stoyan. *Heroes and Assassins.* New York: Robert L. McBridge & Co., 1935.

Hoptner, F. B. *Yugoslavia in Crisis, 1934-1941.* New York: Columbia University Press, 1962.

Vuglijenovic, M. *Die Stellung Englands und Frankreichs am Yugoslawishen Markte im Verhältnis zu der Italiens und des Deutschen Reiches.* Vienna: Hollinek Verlag, 1940.

Wuescht, Johan. *Yugoslawien und das Dritte Reich.* Stuttgart: Seewald Verlag, 1969.

Articles

Jedrezejewicz, Waclaw. "The Polish Plan for a "Preventive War" Against Germany in 1933." *The Polish Review,* Vol. XI, No. 1 (Winter, 1966), pp. 62-91.

Scroggs, William O. "Russia and the World Trade" *Foreign Affairs* Vol. XII, (January, 1934), p. 332.

Vollmer, Clement. "A New Polish Corridor." *Foreign Affairs* Vol. XII, (October, 1933), pp. 156-59.

Newspapers

Budapesti Hirlap. (Budapest) 1934-1935.

Chicago Daily News. (Chicago) 1934-1935.

Excelsior. (Paris) 1934.

Humanité. (Paris) 1934.

L'Action Francaise. (Paris) 1934.

Le Temps. (Paris) 1934-1935.

EAST EUROPEAN MONOGRAPHS

The *East European Monographs* comprise scholarly books on the history and civilization of Eastern Europe. They are published by the *East European Quarterly* in the belief that these studies contribute substantially to the knowledge of the area and serve to stimulate scholarship and research.

13. *Tolerance and Movements of Religious Dissent in Eastern Europe.* Edited by Bela K. Kiraly. 1975.

14. *The Parish Republic: Hlinka's Slovak People's Party, 1939-1945.* By Yeshayahu Jelinek. 1976.

15. *The Russian Annexation of Bessarabia, 1774-1828.* By George F. Jewsbury. 1976.

16. *Modern Hungarian Historiography.* By Steven Bela Vardy. 1976.

17. *Values and Community in Multi-National Yugoslavia.* By Gary K. Bertsch. 1976.

18. *The Greek Socialist Movement and the First World War: The Road to Unity.* By George B. Leon. 1976.

19. *The Radical Left in the Hungarian Revolution of 1848.* By Laslo Deme. 1976.

20. *Hungary Between Wilson and Lenin: The Hungarian Revolution of 1918-1919 and the Big Three.* By Peter Pastor. 1976.

21. *The Crises of France's East Central European Diplomacy 1933-1938.* By Anthony Tihamer Komjathy. 1976.